I0817580

Everyday Genius

To those becoming
who they're meant to be

Everyday Genius

Hacks to Boost Your Memory, Focus, Problem-Solving, and Much More

Nelson Dellis

Illustrations by Adam Hayes

Foreword by Barbara Oakley

Abrams Press, New York

CONTENTS

FOREWORD

I've spent decades studying how the mind learns, and I can tell you this: The gap between ordinary thinking and extraordinary thinking is much smaller than most people believe. What separates a "genius" from everyone else isn't some mysterious gift bestowed at birth—it's the willingness to change your brain.

Nelson Dellis understands this truth better than almost anyone I know.

When Nelson and I first met, he was already a multiple-time memory champion. But what struck me wasn't his ability to memorize thousands of digits or entire decks of cards; it was his genuine curiosity about the mechanisms behind these feats and his passion for teaching others that *anyone* can develop extraordinary mental abilities.

In *Everyday Genius*, Nelson has created something remarkable: a practical road map for unlocking capabilities you didn't know you had. This isn't about becoming a savant or developing supernatural powers (although you may sometimes feel you are!); it's about discovering that your brain is far more powerful and adaptable than you've been led to believe.

As someone who has written and taught millions of students about learning and the brain, I can say that what truly impresses me about Nelson is something you'll virtually never see from a professor or professional academic: He's actually on the front lines, testing his mental prowess in real competition. He doesn't just theorize about memory and learning; he puts himself to the test, again and again, in high-stakes memory championships where there's nowhere to hide. The techniques he teaches are battle-tested methods forged in the crucible of the world's most brutal mental competitions, not dry academic theories or laboratory constructs. When Nelson shows you how to memorize or focus, you know these techniques work, because he's used them to win championships under the most stressful conditions imaginable.

The memory techniques alone are worth the price of admission to this great book. But Nelson goes much deeper; for example, showing how to focus in a distraction-filled world and how to think through problems like the great minds of history. He also reveals insane tricks with mental math that even the most math-phobic mind can acquire. (Think Marie Curie was a natural genius? Perhaps. But she had help: Her father taught her mental math, much as Nelson teaches mental math here.) When you can rapidly calculate in your head, you develop an intuitive sense for numbers and relationships that no calculator can provide. It's this kind of internal knowledge structure that makes true insight possible.

What I love most about this book is its honesty. Nelson doesn't claim these techniques are effortless. They require practice and persistence. But he proves, through his own journey from average student to world-class mental athlete, that the rewards are extraordinary.

Whether you're a student looking to ace your exams, a professional seeking a mental edge, or simply someone curious about the untapped potential of your own mind, this book offers tools that can genuinely transform how you think, learn, and perceive the world around you.

The ancient Greeks believed that excellence was not an act but a habit. Nelson Dellis shows us how to make genius a habit we can all cultivate.

BARBARA OAKLEY

Author of *Learning How to Learn* and *A Mind for Numbers*
Distinguished Professor of Engineering, Oakland University

INTRODUCTION

UNLOCKING YOUR INNER GENIUS

"WITHIN YOU ARE ALL THE ANSWERS YOU SEEK."
—MEISTER ECKHART

LONG AGO, ON THE SUNLIT ISLE OF CYPRUS, THERE LIVED A SCULPTOR NAMED PYGMALION, A KING DISILLUSIONED BY HIS OWN UNREALISTIC EXPECTATIONS OF MORTAL WOMEN.

TURNING FROM SOCIETY, HE POURED HIS SOUL INTO CARVING A STATUE OF IVORY SO FLAWLESS, IT ECLIPSED THE BEAUTY OF ALL HUMAN FLESH. EACH DAY HE ADORED IT, LAYING FLOWERS AT ITS FEET, WHISPERING WORDS OF AFFECTION, UNTIL HE FELL DEEPLY IN LOVE WITH HIS OWN CREATION. SO GREAT WAS HIS DEVOTION THAT, IN HIS SILENT PRAYERS TO APHRODITE—GODDESS OF LOVE—HE PLEADED FOR SUCH PERFECTION TO EXIST.

THE GODDESS, MOVED BY HIS FAITH, ANSWERED.

ONE EVENING, AS HE KISSED THE STATUE'S LIPS, HE FOUND THEM SUDDENLY WARM. THE STATUE HAD COME TO LIFE. HIS IMAGINED TRUTH HAD BECOME REALITY.

THIS MYTH ENDURES NOT FOR ITS MIRACLE BUT FOR ITS MESSAGE: THAT UNWAVERING BELIEF CAN SHAPE REALITY, THAT WITHIN EACH OF US LIES A FIGURE YET UNCARVED, WAITING TO AWAKEN . . .

What if I told you that genius *isn't what you think it is?*

We've all been sold this idea that geniuses are born, not made. That they pop out of the womb solving equations, composing symphonies, or inventing the next great product. That they're special, different, untouchable. But what if most of what we call "genius" is just a set of skills that are learnable, trainable, and repeatable?

This book isn't going to turn you into Einstein overnight. Sorry. If there were a book that could do that, we'd all be walking around with Nobel Prizes. But what this book *will* do is offer you the skills, tricks, and techniques that make people *seem* like geniuses—and these skills don't just make you *look* smarter; they actually *make* you smarter as well.

Genius is subjective. The definition itself is fuzzy. It's one of those words that we *think* we understand until we try to define it. For some, it's used to describe Einstein, Mozart, da Vinci . . . but also the kid in your class who could do math in their head, or the stand-up comic who can nail those perfect one-liners. For others, it's more clear-cut: A genius is simply someone with an enviably high IQ. But it could just as easily be the artist who paints a masterpiece with ease, or the entrepreneur who sees what no one else does and who always seems to be one step ahead. The list goes on.

So what *is* genius?

A commonly accepted formal definition is *a person who is exceptionally intelligent or creative, either generally or in some particular respect*. That sounds neat on paper, but in real life, it's hardly that clean.

Take Leonardo da Vinci, for example—often called a genius, but without any official record of his IQ or cognitive testing. His brilliance was obvious but hard to quantify. And maybe that's the point. We don't usually call someone a genius because of some strict, measurable criteria; we do it because they *feel* like one. Sometimes it's a personal feeling, a *sense*. In other cases, it can be a collective agreement that has just been assumed by many as fact.

Da Vinci is universally regarded as one of history's greatest minds. He was a polymath who dabbled in everything from painting to anatomy to engineering. But there's no actual evidence that he had an unusually high IQ, was a prodigy, or even received any formal education beyond basic reading, writing, and arithmetic. Yet we unequivocally—without hesitation—consider him a genius.

And why wouldn't we? Much of what makes Leonardo *seem* like a genius is a mix of his curiosity, his notebooks full of ideas, and the mystique that history has built around him. He was undeniably talented. His paintings are masterpieces (*Mona Lisa, The Last Supper, Virgin of the Rocks*—too many to list!), but he was known as a master procrastinator, and there are many works he never even finished. His scientific sketches were ahead of his time, but believe it or not, most of his inventions never actually worked or were

GENIUS PROFILE:
LEONARDO DA VINCI

Leonardo da Vinci was once caught staring at a simple swirling eddy in a stream. He watched it for hours, completely transfixed. He believed that by understanding the motion of water, he could understand the movement of blood through the human heart. This wasn't just a passing thought, though. He filled page after page with fluid dynamics sketches, long before modern science caught up. In fact, hundreds of years later, researchers confirmed that the spiral motion of blood Leonardo described plays a key role in how heart valves function. Da Vinci didn't have a degree. He didn't even have a microscope! He just had a relentless ability to observe and the audacity to believe that nature's patterns, whether in rivers or in veins, were all connected.

ever realized.* And even his anatomical discoveries, while they turned out to be incredibly accurate, weren't widely published or influential in his lifetime. Many of his ideas were just that: ideas.

And yet, we label him as a genius. Why?

Because he *looked* like one. His insatiable curiosity, his endless pursuit of knowledge, his prolificness, his ability to *think differently*—those were

* It has been speculated, though, that some of his designs purposefully had flaws in them to prevent others from copying his work.

his true superpowers. He wasn't necessarily the smartest man of his era, but he sure acted as if he was, and history filled in the rest.

And that's exactly what this book is about. We're living in the age of AI, where every convenience comes at a cost: our brain capital. Technology encourages us to outsource our thinking, to use our brains less and less. But our intellect, creativity, and genius are worth fighting for. You don't need an off-the-charts IQ—just learn to think and act like a genius. In doing so, you'll unlock your own untapped abilities. Because the truth is, we all have it. It's just a matter of learning how to wield it.

More than a decade ago, my loving grandmother passed away from Alzheimer's disease. At the time, I had never experienced such a devastating loss. As I tried my best to carry on with my life, one thought kept replaying over and over in my mind: Was the same thing going to happen to me when I got older? Was I destined to lose my memory as well?

That turned out to be the catalyst that changed my life. Before then, I was just your average Joe. Sure, I had varied interests and was relatively smart. But I don't think anyone would have ever labeled me a genius. Not even close.

But then, after my grandmother's passing, something changed. I was driven to explore the fascinating world of memory techniques and mnemonics. And in a relatively short amount of time, I was able to master those techniques and flip the competitive memory space on its head. Over the next decade, I went on to win the USA Memory Championships six times, break numerous memorization records (including two Guinness World Records, mind you!), become a Grandmaster of Memory, and create a whole career out of teaching others how to unlock their own amazing memory abilities.

When I first started dabbling in the art of memory, I noticed very quickly that just because I had learned a memory trick or two, and had competed in (and won) some memory competitions, most people assumed I was a "genius." And then, when I would perform some very simple memory techniques (simple to those "in the know"), it would blow their minds! I *must* be a genius, right?

My point is, there are certain tricks and skills you can learn in this book that are really easy (and, dare I say, fun) that can make you seem like a genius to anyone, even yourself!

Being labeled a genius feels great, but what I've discovered is more valuable: As you develop your mental abilities, your intelligence evolves. You gain intuitive skills you never had. Your problem-solving amplifies. Your confidence soars. The outside world's perception doesn't matter—what matters is how you see your *own* potential. Unlocking *your* inner genius is an incredibly empowering feeling that transforms all areas of your life.

In the 1960s, the American psychologist Robert Rosenthal told a group of elementary school teachers that certain students had been identified (randomly) as "intellectual bloomers" and would show significant academic improvement that year.* In truth, these students were chosen at random. The results were fascinating. By the end of the year, those randomly selected students *did* outperform their peers. The teachers' expectations (even if unknowingly) shaped how they treated the students. This led to better student confidence, engagement, and ultimately performance. This phenomenon is now called the Pygmalion effect: *high expectations can elevate performance, while low expectations can hold it back*. The same effect can be applied inward. What we believe about our own potential can shape what we become.

When you're a memory champion, being casually labeled a genius happens quite often. The first time someone labeled me as a genius, I hated it. I felt completely misread and feared being exposed as a fraud. But over time, I began to realize that people's perception of genius isn't really grounded in any consistent or rigorous criteria—it's actually quite subjective. Are you quick to process information? *Genius.* Can you solve puzzles and problems quickly? *Sure, why not . . . genius.* Can you work a room and remember everyone's name? *Yup, a genius!*

You, me, the person sitting next to you as you read this book are all capable of being that genius. Sure, maybe not those famous geniuses like Thomas Edison, Albert Einstein, or Nikola Tesla (there are some people who *are* naturally gifted), but rather, a person who can, at times, exhibit genius-seeming traits, and who can *oftentimes* exhibit high levels of cognitive ability.

So, what *are* those traits and abilities you'll learn in this book? I'm glad you asked . . .

The first part of the book is devoted to building the foundation for genius skills. We'll tackle memory mastery—my bread and butter, and what started my journey. I truly believe that to be smart, you need to have a strong memory. If you've ever wished you could remember things better, this book has all the strategies you'll need and makes them easy to digest. With a bit of practice (and my guidance), you'll be rapidly (and confidently) memorizing information in no time.

Then, we'll speed up your reading game. Who doesn't want to blaze through a book and still remember all the good stuff? I have all the secrets to supercharge your reading skills. Once we've covered memory and reading, we'll transition into applying those two fundamental abilities to focusing, studying, and learning more effectively.

In the second part of the book, we'll take everything you've learned and put it into action. You'll learn how to navigate social situations with ease, sharpen your ability to read people, and tackle problem-solving with a more

* Robert Rosenthal and Lenore Jacobson, *Pygmalion in the Classroom: Teacher Expectation and Pupils' Intellectual Development* (Holt, Rinehart and Winston, 1968).

strategic, analytical mindset. We'll dive into mental math tricks, hacks for winning popular games and solving puzzles (Rubik's Cubes, for one), and work on fine-tuning your intuition—even to the point where you might be able to *sense* things before they happen. Sounds crazy, I know. But stick with me. You'll see.

By the time you're through, you'll have not only a portfolio of mind-blowing abilities but also the confidence to rock your newfound genius status!

Now, you might be thinking that it'd be tough to reach the same level of genius as someone like Einstein, Tesla, or Edison (trust me, I'm not claiming to be anywhere in the same universe as these three either!), but there's a lot we can learn from each of them. Throughout the book you'll find memorable anecdotes about some famous geniuses for a bit of inspiration (some you may already know, and others you may be surprised to learn about).

GENIUS PROFILE:
ALBERT EINSTEIN

In 1905, while still working as a patent clerk in Bern, Einstein published four groundbreaking papers in a single year—any one of which would have made a distinguished career. He explained the photoelectric effect (which would later win him the Nobel Prize), proved that atoms actually exist, introduced special relativity, and derived the most famous equation in physics: $E=mc^2$. He was just twenty-six years old, had no academic position, and was doing this work in his spare time between reviewing patent applications. It remains one of the most astonishingly productive years in the history of science. Talk about true genius!

Let's start with the one person whose name is basically synonymous with genius. One whom almost everyone might immediately blurt out as *the* most iconic and well-known genius of all time: Albert Einstein.

Einstein was an incredible physicist who revolutionized our understanding of the universe with his groundbreaking theories in physics. What set Einstein apart was not just his remarkable intellect but his unique approach to scientific inquiry.

Einstein had an uncanny ability to think outside the established norms of his time. He questioned fundamental assumptions about the nature of reality and sought to understand the underlying principles governing the universe. This led to his development of the theory of relativity, which transformed our understanding of space, time, and gravity.

Einstein's capacity for thought experiments is a great example of a simple genius trait. With these "gedankens," as he called them,* he would imagine hypothetical scenarios—like chasing light beams, riding elevators in space, or floating in free fall—and use them to derive profound insights into the universe's inner workings. Sounds simple enough, but these mental exercises allowed him to explore concepts that were beyond the reach of traditional experiments.

One of Einstein's most well-known gedankens (and one I love to show people, usually right on the back of a napkin) involved a moving train and a beam of light. He imagined an observer on the train shining a light straight up at a mirror on the ceiling and watching it reflect back down. He then compared this to how the same event would appear to a stationary observer standing *outside* the train as it passed by.

He realized that to the person riding on the train, the beam of light would appear to travel straight up and down. But to the observer standing outside the train, that same beam would follow a diagonal path, because the train itself is moving forward (see the illustration in chapter 6, page 164). Using this simple thought experiment and a bit of algebra, Einstein derived an equation for time dilation, showing that time doesn't tick at the same rate for everyone—it depends on how fast you're moving. This idea shook the foundations of physics and eventually paved the way for even deeper breakthroughs, like general relativity and the development of quantum field theory.

I'll walk you through this simple proof in chapter 6 (see page 163). But don't worry, it's not nearly as hard as it sounds! In fact, it's the kind of thing you don't even need to memorize. Just by sketching out the thought experiment, logically, step-by-step, you can always derive the same equations Einstein came up with. It's surprisingly intuitive—and honestly, really cool.

---

* Literally translates from German to "thoughts."

A GENIUS MINDSET

What Einstein shows us is that genius is about how you *think*, not necessarily about filling your brain with facts. His true brilliance was his mindset: thinking creatively and chasing ideas with relentless curiosity.

Before we dive deeper into this book, let's get clear on what that mindset looks like. The following are the key ingredients. They'll serve as your foundation for everything else you'll learn in the pages ahead:

1. BE CURIOUS, PLAYFUL, AND A LITTLE WEIRD.

Ask why. Ask how. Ask "What if?" Let your brain wander. Genius often begins with the tiniest question and a willingness to follow it down a deep rabbit hole. And don't be afraid to look silly in the process; playfulness is where the magic happens. Doodle your ideas. Build strange models. Talk to yourself if it helps! The more fun you're having, the more likely you are to stumble on something brilliant.

And don't worry about where it leads. Just engaging in creative activities, without any pressure to produce something "useful," keeps your childlike curiosity alive. You'll often find those meaningful breakthroughs when you're truly exploring for the fun of it, not just for the finish line.

2. BELIEVE IN YOURSELF.

Self-belief isn't about pretending to be a genius; it's about realizing that you *can* think in genius ways. Remember the Pygmalion effect. Trust that your ideas matter, that your brain is capable of growth. That you, too, can understand "hard stuff." This doesn't mean you'll get everything right on the first try (you won't). It means showing up with the quiet confidence that you'll figure it out eventually and that your perspective is worth exploring. That belief in yourself is what gives you the guts to take bold creative leaps.

3. PUT IN THE WORK.

There's no substitute for practice. The people we call geniuses typically have spent *hours* (and hours . . . and, yep, even more hours) honing their craft. Look at any proclaimed genius and you'll be sure to find that they didn't just rely on talent.

They continuously showed up, messed up, tweaked things over and over again, and kept going. Whether you're training your memory, solving puzzles, or learning a new language, repetition is your best friend. Repetition doesn't just build skill, it builds identity. Every time you practice, you're casting a vote for the kind of thinker you want to become.

4. SHOW UP CONSISTENTLY.

This one is huge. I truly believe consistency is the bedrock of genius. Inspiration is great, but it's inconsistent. Discipline, on the other hand, gets results. Make it a habit. Show up when it's exciting *and* when it's boring. Genius doesn't come in a single flash; it's a slow burn. A series of small steps that eventually add up to something powerful.

5. HAVE FUN AND ENJOY THE RIDE.

If you're not having fun, you're probably doing it wrong. Seriously. Learning, creating, exploring—these things are meant to feel good. They might be hard sometimes, but they should also be rewarding. Find what excites you. Follow your interests. Let your passion drive your practice. Trust the process. And when you start to master a skill, use it. Show it off. Apply it in the real world. That's how you lock it in and start to think, *Hey . . . maybe I am a bit of a genius after all!*

Remember, the path to genius is nonlinear, each journey unique. Embrace the process, celebrate small victories, and remain open to unexpected insights that may arise. With dedication, curiosity, and belief in your own potential, you have the power to unlock your inner genius.

Whether you're a student looking to ace your exams, an entrepreneur trying to develop the next big idea, or simply someone who wants to unlock their full potential, this book is for you.

Are you ready to take the first step to becoming an everyday genius? Let's get started.

PART 1

CORE GENIUS SKILLS

(THE BASICS)

1 4 7
3
5 9
0
0:01'00"

Being a genius isn't about having a high IQ but about having the right tools. Anyone can train their brain to think, learn, and remember at a level that seems almost superhuman, because we all have a little bit of genius within us that isn't born but *built*.

Over the years, I've met people with incredible minds—memory champions, speed readers, deep thinkers, visionary artists, brilliant scientists, and world-class problem-solvers. And none of them (save a very select few) were born with some magical, gifted brain. They just learned how to use their brain more efficiently. And that's what Part 1 of this book is about: giving you the tools to unlock the full potential of your mind.

In these next few chapters, we'll dive into the *core genius skills*—the foundational abilities that, once mastered, will make everything else easier. Memory, reading, focus, learning—it's all here. These are the superpowers that allow you to absorb information faster, retain it longer, and apply it more effectively.

If you knew how to memorize anything effortlessly, how would that change your life? If you could read twice as fast while understanding more, what doors would that open? If you had rock-solid focus, how much more could you accomplish? This section is all about sharpening your mental tools so that when we get to the second half of the book (where I show you all the tricks and strategies to apply these skills) you'll be fully equipped to use them.

Most people assume that things like memory and focus are fixed, but that's not true. These skills can be trained, hacked, and optimized. The best thinkers in history weren't necessarily smarter than everyone else; they just knew how to learn better. And in an age where AI can answer questions instantly, what sets you apart isn't what you can look up—it's how deeply you can think, how well you can learn, and how effectively you can apply knowledge in novel situations.

The best part is that once you develop these core genius skills, they stack. If you improve your focus, your ability to read faster improves. If you improve your memory, your ability to learn improves. If you improve your learning ability, everything improves. It's a feedback loop of genius.

So, as you dive into the upcoming chapters, think of this as your training ground. These next sections are the *foundational skills* you'll need to start thinking, learning, and remembering like a genius. You're about to build a mental tool kit, piece by piece, that will change how you approach everything. And once you have that, you'll be unstoppable.

CHAPTER 1

MEMORY MASTERY

"MEMORY IS THE SCRIBE OF THE SOUL."
—ARISTOTLE

I REMEMBER THE EXACT MOMENT I BECAME TERRIFIED OF ALZHEIMER'S DISEASE. IT WAS THE SUMMER OF 2007, AND I WAS VISITING MY GRANDPARENTS IN THEIR TINY APARTMENT IN THE MIDDLE OF REIMS—A GORGEOUS FRENCH CITY RIGHT IN THE HEART OF CHAMPAGNE COUNTRY.

MY GRANDMOTHER WAS THE DEFINITION OF A SWEET OLD WOMAN. SHE KEPT THEIR COUNTRY HOUSE COZY, WHIPPED UP MEALS THAT TASTED LIKE PURE LOVE, AND WAS ALWAYS DOTING ON MY GRANDFATHER. SPEAKING OF MY GRANDFATHER, HE WAS YOUR CLASSIC FARMER—WORKING THE FIELDS, TENDING TO CROPS LIKE POTATOES, CARROTS, AND TOBACCO ON THEIR SPRAWLING FARM, LA VICOMTÉ. THAT PLACE WAS STRAIGHT OUT OF A MOVIE SET—THINK FRENCH COUNTRYSIDE MEETS ROMANTIC COMEDY VIBES. BUT AS MY GRANDPARENTS GOT OLDER, LIFE ON A BIG FARM BECAME TOO MUCH, SO THEY DOWNSIZED TO A LITTLE APARTMENT IN THE CITY.

My grandma and I were close. I'd hover around her in the kitchen, watching her knead dough for her country bread or whip up her famous gâteau rose. So, imagine this: I'm sitting at the dinner table, right across from my grandpa and next to her, when she leans over to my grandfather and asks, "Who's the young man sitting next to me?" Spoiler: She was talking about me.

At first, I thought, *Okay, people forget stuff. It happens.* But forgetting a person? Me, her grandson? That moment lodged itself in my brain like a splinter. Sure, there were other signs that her memory was slipping, but that was the one that made it feel real.

She passed away a few years later, which absolutely wrecked me. But it also lit a fire under me. I started devouring every book I could find on the brain and memory. I needed answers. Could I prevent this from happening to me? Was there a way to fight back?

That's when I stumbled across something called the USA Memory Championship. At first, I thought it was for geniuses with freakishly good memories, but no—the competitors were all just "regular" people who had apparently learned a few ancient memory techniques and practiced them like crazy.

That idea alone—the idea that you could *practice* memory—blew my mind. Before then, I thought memory was something fixed—that you were either born with a good memory, or not.

From then on, I was hooked. And fifteen years later, here I am. I've mastered memory techniques, trained obsessively, won multiple memory championships, and broken records, and now I teach people how to unlock their own memory superpowers.

In this chapter I'm going to share the same process I've used to build a memory that'll make people's jaws drop. These are the same techniques I've used to memorize some incredible things such as multiple decks of playing cards, thousands of digits, and hundreds of names from a roomful of people.

Genius *starts* with memory.

Think about it—yes, you can look up anything with AI or search engines in seconds. But without memory, how do you retain knowledge, connect ideas in real time, or have genuine insights? Technology might store information for us, but it's eroding our natural human ability to remember—and, with it, our capacity to think deeply. You *need* a strong memory to juggle ideas and demonstrate mastery at a high level. Master the techniques, and everything else gets easier. Memory is *the* cornerstone of becoming an everyday genius. Do NOT underestimate its importance!

HOW TO MEMORIZE ANYTHING

The process for memorizing anything can be mastered in three simple and straightforward steps:

Visualization—Storage—Review.

That's it.

Let's say you've got some piece of information you want to memorize. There's the information itself (the stuff out in the world), your brain taking it in and processing it, and then the ultimate goal: locking it away in your mind so you can access it whenever you need it.

Simple enough, but it's important to acknowledge.

The processing part and ensuring you can reliably access the information later are the keys to understanding how and why memory techniques work.

Step one: *Visualize* the information. Turn it into a mental picture. Something that makes sense to your brain, something meaningful, something that'll stick.

Step two: Give that mental picture some organizational structure. Think of it as putting the image in a specific "mental folder" so you know exactly where to find it later.

Step three: Review, review, review. That's how you keep the information locked in for good for the long term.

VISUALIZATION

By "visualization," I mean: Picture the thing you're trying to memorize in your mind. Literally, *see* it. It's that simple!

Much of the information we process is abstract: a foreign word, a random number, someone's name . . . our brains weren't exactly built to handle that kind of data. Back in the day (I'm talking caveman days), our brains were wired to remember pictures and images that helped us survive—like the pattern on a plant that meant it was safe to eat, or the path back to shelter (and not into a lion's den). But today, we're constantly bombarded with information our brains weren't naturally designed to retain. Names, foreign languages, modern tech concepts—the list is long and always evolving. So what can we do? We can translate that information into a format our brain *does* like. We can make it brain-friendly. And that starts with one simple step: Turn whatever you're trying to memorize into a mental image. See it. Picture it. Lock it in.

Hold on, though . . . What does it *actually* mean to "see it" in your mind?

Well, take the information you want to memorize and think of something it sounds like, looks like, or reminds you of. It doesn't matter what that representative thing is. As long as it's meaningful to you, it's likely to stick.

But don't stop there. You need to make these mental images truly *unforgettable*. How? By bringing in all your senses. Visualization isn't just about what you see with your mind's eye, it's about what you can hear, smell, taste, or even touch in your mind as well. What does that image feel like? Smell like? Feel like to the touch? The more sensory data you can add, the more vivid and alive the image will become.

Next, pump it full of emotion and exaggeration. Our brains are really good at remembering anything with emotional weight. So make it funny, weird, gross, gruesome, over-the-top, or even a little (or a lot) sexual. The crazier, the better. Think of how easy it is to recall some of the more emotional moments from your life. We're trying to mentally emulate *that*.

And finally, give it action. Make your image move! A static mental image is okay, but adding even a little movement can make it unforgettable. Picture your image doing something wild. The more dynamic, the more memorable it will be.

Here's an example.

I'll never forget the visual I came up with when I memorized the definition of "syzygy." It's an astronomy term for when three celestial bodies align—like the Earth, moon, and sun during an eclipse. Pretty abstract, right?

But here's what I did: I pictured myself staring up at a clear night sky where above me, the Earth, moon, and sun were in perfect alignment—but instead of these astronomical celestial bodies, they were . . . well, *actual* bodies and they were having a "sizzling orgy" up in the sky ("syz-orgy" is a pretty close reminder for "syzygy"). I'll let your imagination take care of the rest . . . But, hey, that's the kind of vivid, multisensory image that *sticks*.*

STORAGE

So, you've created a mental image—awesome. Now what?

Sometimes, if the image is memorable enough, that might be all you need to lock it in for a good while. But usually, you'll need a little more, especially if you're trying to remember multiple things (even more so if in order). Say it's not just a single fact but a long list of stuff—like a grocery list. That's when you need a more concrete strategy for organizing and storing all those mental images you just created.

Here's the problem, though: Most of us don't have a system for storing information. We're basically winging it—reading or hearing something a few times and hoping it sticks. It's as if we're tossing information onto a big,

---

* Keep in mind, if you want to dive even deeper into memory techniques than what's found in this chapter (and trust me, it *does* get deeper) make sure to check out my other book on memory: *Remember It!*

messy pile in some imaginary "brain storage closet." Sure, sometimes it's right there on the top of the pile, easy to find. But usually, it's buried under a mountain of other random facts, making it a nightmare to find when you need it. You know that all-too-common feeling—*I KNOW this, it's on the tip of my tongue!* That's not a memory issue; that's a *retrieval issue*. It's all about how you've organized the information (or rather, how you didn't organize it in the first place).

This is where the Memory Palace technique comes in.

The Memory Palace is an ancient technique that's been around for thousands of years. Back in the day, people didn't have smartphones, notepads, or even easy access to writing materials. If you wanted to remember something—a story, a speech, a hymn, the names of a hundred people—your brain had to do all the heavy lifting. So people came up with methods to make it easier, and the Memory Palace was born.

What is it, exactly? A Memory Palace is a mental space you create in your mind. Usually, it's a place or route you already know well, such as your house, your office, your daily commute, your favorite park, or . . . I don't know, an actual palace (if you're lucky enough to own one). In your imagination, you walk through this space in a specific order and place the images you've created at specific anchor points or locations along the way.* The route preserves the order of all the information, and the palace itself acts like a mental filing cabinet. Cool concept, right?

As cool as it may sound, it really is *easier done than said*. So let's walk through an example together.

Here's a random list of incredibly random facts that will blow your mind (all true, by the way!):

1. **The heart of a blue whale weighs as much as a car.**
2. **Bananas are berries, but strawberries aren't.**
3. **Wombat poop is cube-shaped.**
4. **Octopuses have three hearts.†**
5. **Sharks existed before trees.**
6. **Sloths can hold their breath longer than dolphins.**
7. **A bolt of lightning is five times hotter than the sun.**
8. **A group of flamingos is called a "flamboyance."**

---

* The proper term for these locations is "loci"—the plural of "locus," a Latin word meaning "place."

† Genius fact: The correct plural of "octopus" is "octopuses" (not "octopi," as many incorrectly presume)! A plural *-i* ending comes from Latin, but "octopus" is actually Greek.

PLUTO
KLIK
KLIK
KLIK

9. There's enough DNA in your body to stretch to Pluto and back.
10. Butterflies taste with their feet.

Now, we've got ten pieces of information, so we're going to need a Memory Palace with ten locations (one image per location). Then we're going to create a mental image to represent each fact, and then imagine it interacting with the locations of our Memory Palace—the first image on the first location, the second on the second, and so on. Don't forget that we're going to need to make our mental visuals as wild as possible, so they stick better.

Imagine using the house in the illustration opposite as your first Memory Palace. Here's how I'd store the facts—follow my lead:

- ***LOCATION 1: FRONT DOOR***—A blue whale's giant heart wedged in your doorway, making it impossible to get inside. Make that heart rev like the engine of a car (so we know the size of the heart has to do with a car).
- ***LOCATION 2: LIVING ROOM***—A banana wearing a berry crown, smugly kicking a strawberry out of the "berry club."
- ***LOCATION 3: KITCHEN COUNTER***—A wombat rolling cube-shaped poop like dice across the counter.
- ***LOCATION 4: DINING TABLE***—An octopus with three hearts on each tentacle, serving them up like a fancy meal.
- ***LOCATION 5: STAIRS***—A shark lounging on the stairs, biting into a very old tree.
- ***LOCATION 6: BATHROOM***—A sloth soaking in your bathtub, holding its breath as if it's competing in the Olympics, while making dolphin sounds.
- ***LOCATION 7: BEDROOM***—A lightning bolt sizzling through your bed, with a thermometer reading "5× hotter than the sun."
- ***LOCATION 8: CLOSET***—Flamingos dressed in sequins, having a *flamboyant* dance party inside.
- ***LOCATION 9: HOME OFFICE***—A strand of DNA stretching out of your desk drawer and through the window, labeled "Pluto or bust."
- ***LOCATION 10: BACKYARD***—Butterflies tap-dancing on a picnic table, tasting everything with their feet.

Pretty memorable, right? By visualizing these wild scenes along a specific pathway through your house, you'll have no trouble recalling the list.

The beauty of this technique is how difficult it makes the information to forget. And the list works out of sequence, too! Just reverse the direction of traversal through your palace if you want to say it backwards.

Before we move on, without peeking back, try recalling the list for yourself and see how effective the technique is. I also encourage you to try to test yourself later today, or even tomorrow. See if the information lasts the night, and if not, practice, practice, practice. It's powerful stuff.

Having one Memory Palace is cool. But you know what's cooler? Having dozens upon dozens of Memory Palaces, like me. I am constantly using my catalogue of Memory Palaces to store the information I need throughout my day. I never have to write anything down or keep track of anything on my phone or device. It's all up here (I'm pointing to my head). And it can be the same for you, too. At the end of the chapter (page 48), I'll share some more tips and suggestions, exercises, and resources to help you hone this technique further.

One more quick tidbit about Memory Palaces. You may have noticed I placed just one item per location. Could I have placed more? Sure . . . but only to a point. Personally, I'll often use two items per location to be more efficient with the space in my Memory Palace. Even three or four can work. But there's an eventual trade-off. The more you cram onto a single location, the more challenging it will be to recall all the items clearly for that location. You get diminishing returns. So yes, you *can* stack more—just keep in mind it comes at a cost.

REVIEW

Unfortunately, our brains are absolute champs at forgetting things. Seriously, they're world-class forgetting machines. But that's not necessarily a bad thing. Imagine if you remembered every single piece of information that crossed your path—it'd be absolute chaos!* Forgetting is actually a survival mechanism, a way for our brains to clear out the clutter and save space for what really matters.

But here's the good news: If you consciously decide to revisit and recall certain information regularly, your brain takes notice and starts to prioritize it. That's why review is so powerful. The more you review something, the longer it sticks and the easier it is to access.

* Some people actually have this mind-blowing ability and can recall almost every detail of their lives. It's a condition called highly superior autobiographical memory (HSAM) and those who have it can remember what they were doing, wearing, eating, or even the weather on nearly any given day of their lives. It's an incredibly rare condition, but what's fascinating about it is that it doesn't rely on memory techniques or training. Instead, it seems to be an innate ability, tied to unique wiring in the brain.

Now, I know that might sound tedious, but there is an upside. If you've used the visualization techniques and storage strategies we've talked about so far in this chapter, the review process becomes way easier, and way more fun. Jumping into your Memory Palace and revisiting all those wild, ridiculous images you placed there is like watching your own personal comedy-action movie, except it's actually helping you retain important info. It's a win-win.

We'll go deeper into how to build your long-term memory and the science of review in chapter 4 (see page 82), where I'll show you how to learn more efficiently. But for now, just remember this:

Review is the glue that holds your memory together in the long run.

GENIUS PROFILE: KEN JENNINGS

Ken Jennings has one of the best memories in history. With a seventy-four-game *Jeopardy!* winning streak and total earnings of more than $4 million, he was unstoppable. But Jennings wasn't born with a photographic memory—he built his knowledge through obsessive childhood reading. Growing up in South Korea, young Ken became what he calls "a weird information sponge," frustrated that libraries wouldn't let him check out the books he wanted most: encyclopedias, atlases, and *The Guinness Book of World Records*. That childhood habit of absorbing random facts, combined with mnemonic techniques connecting new information to things he already knew, turned him into the greatest *Jeopardy!* champion of all time.

MEMORIZING NAMES

Memorizing a list is cool and all, but what about something trickier (and arguably more useful) like names? Names aren't as straightforward as grocery items or fun facts, but the good news is, the same basic principle applies: Create a picture and link it to a location. The only real difference here is the "location" is now a feature on the person's face.

Think about it: When you meet someone in person, their face is always there, right? So why not use it as a sort of makeshift portable Memory Palace to store their name? Whenever you see them again, their face will trigger the visual you created to help remember their name, and BOOM, you've got their name ready to go. No more awkward moments asking someone to remind you of their name.

Here's how it works:

- **Pick a unique feature on the person's face—it could be their nose, eyebrows, hair, or even something they're wearing.**
- **Then create a mental image that reminds you of their name.**
- **Link the image to their feature. The weirder and more exaggerated the image, the better it will stick.**

Let's break it down with a few examples:

EXAMPLE: BILL

You meet Bill, and you choose his big nose as his notable feature. Imagine his nose turning into a dollar bill, fluttering in the wind every time he talks. You'll never forget it! Bill's nose equals dollar bill.

EXAMPLE: LUCY

Lucy has bright red hair. Picture her hair transforming into a glowing red light bulb, shining like a diamond, so brightly it lights up the whole room. That bright light bulb should make you think of the Beatles song "Lucy in the Sky with Diamonds." Once that association is made, her name will be locked in your memory.

EXAMPLE: TOM

Tom has a thick beard. Imagine his beard turning into a giant tomato plant, with tomatoes dangling off it. "Tomato" here has the alliteration to remind you of the name, "Tom." Tomato plant beard. Simple and effective.

By linking the person's name to a standout feature, you're anchoring the memory to something you're guaranteed to notice every time. It's like turning their face into a walking, talking sticky note for their name.

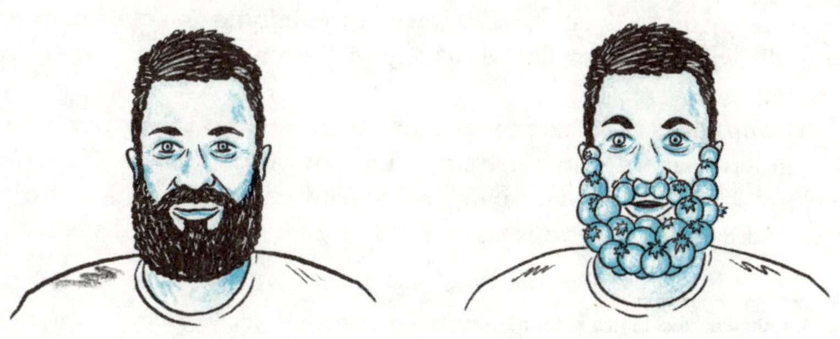

EXAMPLE: SANDY STEVENS

Here's an example where we need to memorize a first *and* last name. How do we go about that? We approach the first name just the same. Then, we can create a *second* image for the last name and incorporate it into our original image. It's a bit like creating a sequence or story, rather than just a singular image.

Let's say Sandy has beautiful blue eyes. Imagine throwing sand into her eyes (Sandy → Sand)—that's the first name. After she gets sand thrown in her eyes, she presses her face down on a stove to melt out the sand (Stevens → Stove*). A completely nonsensical sequence of events (and a bit gritty, I admit), but that's the kind of image we never forget!

In principle, you can add as much information as you want about a person if you just continue adding to that sequence—their hobbies, what they do for work, their kids' names, even their phone number. Just start by linking their first name to *them* (their facial feature) and then you can adjust the image accordingly.

It takes practice to be able to do this quickly and effortlessly. But practice this technique a few times, and you'll be amazed at how quickly and reliably you'll be able to remember names. It may feel a bit silly, but all you're really doing is taking advantage of the information our brains are naturally wired to remember (absolutely wildly bonkers things that are out of the norm!).

The upside is that there are *so* many opportunities to practice in real life. Practice at work in meetings, with new acquaintances at parties; heck, practice with movie characters whenever you watch a new film! Just find a way to get your reps in, and I guarantee you'll have many,

* It's not a perfect match in terms of sounds, but we really only need some word or image that will be close enough to cue the actual full name. Most of the time, your memory will fill in the rest if you just give it a little nudge or cue like that.

many fewer (if any) awkward name-fumbling encounters—just pure memory wizardry!

MEMORIZING NUMBERS

What about memorizing something more abstract, like the number 324,177? Oof! Coming up with a mental image for a number like that isn't at all intuitive, right? Numbers are pretty much as abstract as information gets. Unlike a word like "broccoli," numbers don't naturally spark images in our minds. That's why we need a system to make them memorable.

Thankfully, such a system exists, and it's called the Major System (there are many mnemonic systems for numbers, but the Major System is one of the most well known). Using it will let you turn numbers into words, which we can then memorize with ease (since words are way easier to visualize).

The Major System is a phonetic code that assigns each digit to specific sounds.* By combining these sounds, and filling in the gaps with vowels, you create words that are easy to visualize. Let's break it down (along with a quick mnemonic for each one):

0	s, z	"zero" starts with a z sound
1	t, d	*t* and *d* both have 1 downstroke when written
2	n	*n* has 2 downstrokes
3	m	*m* has 3 downstrokes and looks like an *m* on its side
4	r	think "fourrrrr" ends in *r*
5	L	hold up your left hand: an *L* shape is made with your thumb and index finger
6	j, sh, soft g	a 6 is an upside-down fancy *g* or *j* shape
7	k, hard g or c	a *k* is two 7s stacked back to back on their sides
8	f, v	a cursive *f* looks like an 8
9	p, b	a 9 looks like a *p* and *b* flipped and/or mirrored

* We'll discuss how to use a variation of this phonetic number system for memorizing playing cards in chapter 8. Stay tuned for that!

Notice anything? These are all consonants. That's intentional. Two consonant sounds on their own don't usually form meaningful words, so we toss in vowels (*a*, *e*, *i*, *o*, *u*, and *y* if you want) as glue to make real words. Once you convert the number, all you have to do is memorize the words (and we already know that words are easy to picture in your mind).

Here's how to use it: Take numbers in pairs, translate them into their corresponding consonant sounds, and then sprinkle in vowels to create a word. Once you've got a word, visualize it using the techniques we covered earlier—add senses, exaggeration, emotion, and action. Voilà! You've just turned a random number into something unforgettable. If you're trying to memorize a long sequence of numbers, store each two-digit image in a Memory Palace to keep it all in order.

A few things to keep in mind . . . First, these are consonant *sounds*, as in, the shape your mouth makes when you make that sound, not necessarily the spelling of a word. Second, you may have noticed some digits have multiple sounds associated with them. That's only because those sounds are very similar in how they are made with the mouth. A *t* or *d* sound is made with the teeth at the front of the mouth. A *j*, *sh*, or "soft *g*" sound is made at the back of the mouth with the teeth. See what I mean?

Let's encode 324,177 as an example. Using the Major System:

- **32 becomes *mn* → Add an *a* in the middle, and you get "man." (You could also have come up with "mine" or "men" or "moan"; there are multiple options.)**
- **41 becomes *rt* → Add a vowel, and you get "rat." ("Rut," "root," "rate" would also be acceptable.)**
- **77 becomes *kk* → Add vowels, and you get "cake." (Notice that first c is not taken as the letter, but rather the *k* sound it makes.)**

The image for 324,177 would then be a *man* holding a giant *rat* that's munching on a *cake*. Weird? Yes. Memorable? *Absolutely.*

When *decoding* that image, you'll think of *man-rat-cake* and extract the consonant sounds, translating them back to their original digit: 32-41-77.

I'll admit that creating these images on the fly takes practice. But it's definitely doable. I recommend building a personal library of one hundred premade images—one for every two-digit number from 00 to 99. Once you've got your set and committed it to memory, you'll be able to crush any sequence of numbers that comes your way. Any time you're met with a two-digit number, you'll have a go-to image at the ready.

Don't forget that second part of memorization: STORAGE. If it's a four-digit pin code or five-digit zip code, it may not be worth storing in a Memory Palace. But for longer sequences, such as your credit card number, passport number, or social security number, a Memory Palace would be a great place to store them.

EXAMPLE: MEMORIZE PI TO TWENTY DIGITS.

Just for fun, let's look at a longer number: the famous mathematical constant pi. Casually knowing twenty digits of pi is definitely a genius-seeming skill, so let me show you how I'd break down the first twenty digits using the Major System. You can then practice creating your own Memory Palace and storing it.

The first twenty digits of pi (excluding the initial "3")
3.14159265358979323846:

14 → t, r → "tar"
15 → t, l → "tail"
92 → p, n → "pan"
65 → sh, l → "shell"
35 → m, l → "mall"
89 → f, b → "fob"
79 → k, p → "cape"
32 → m, n → "man"
38 → m, f → "muff"
46 → r, j → "rage"

Another quick memory technique to use in a pinch is the Linking Method. The method works by taking each of the images that you have and linking them into a connected narrative or a memorable story—one image linking to the next, in a chain of images.

FOR EXAMPLE:

- **14 (tar): Imagine stepping outside your house and falling on a giant puddle of sticky tar.**
- **15 (tail): As you try to get up, a mischievous cat with a ridiculously long tail walks by and smacks you in the face.**

- 92 (pan): You chase the cat into your kitchen, where you grab a frying **pan** to defend yourself.
- 65 (shell): Inside the pan, there's a massive turtle with a shiny **shell**, looking unimpressed.
- 35 (mall): The turtle jumps out of the pan and scurries toward a tiny shopping **mall** that suddenly appears on your counter.
- 89 (fob): Inside the mall, you find a key **fob** that unlocks a nearby race car.
- 79 (cape): You hop into the car, but it won't start until you wear a superhero **cape** hanging on the rearview mirror.
- 32 (man): As you drive, you almost hit a **man** juggling noisy chain saws in the middle of the road.
- 38 (muff): To drown out the noise of the chain saws, you put on a set of giant ear**muffs** as you drive past him.
- 46 (rage): Because of the near miss, the man bursts into a fit of **rage**, chasing you down the street.

Each wild image and transition keep the sequence locked in your mind. Make sure to test yourself and see how well the story stuck! The encoding/decoding portion of this technique, going from number to consonant sound and vice versa, might take a little practice. But once you have the phonetics down, it will become automatic!

Memorizing twenty digits of pi? That's one surefire way to casually flex your memory genius in any conversation.

MEMORIZING DATES AND APPOINTMENTS

We all have important dates to memorize: anniversaries, birth dates, court dates, appointments, the big game, etc. How can we apply memory techniques here? Well, you have a number system now—so let's use it!

Let's start with how to memorize the kinds of dates that you just want to store in your mind, about or related to some specific event. A person's birthday or anniversary. A famous historic date. An upcoming holiday. Something you'd be able to pull up instantly from your mind.

Unsurprisingly, the process to memorize any date starts with encoding the birth date as an image, using your number system. The two-digit day and the two-digit month (and two-digit year ending if you want) are what you'll need to convert. Convert them using the Major System we learned previously, and there you have it, an image to represent the date.

GENIUS PROFILE: KIM PEEK

If you've ever seen the movie *Rain Man*, you've witnessed a character inspired by the real-life memory savant Kim Peek. Known as a "megasavant," Peek had a brain unlike anyone else's. Born with macrocephaly and other brain abnormalities, he lacked the connective tissue (corpus callosum) that normally links the brain's two hemispheres. But instead of holding him back, this unique wiring gave him a jaw-dropping ability to memorize.

Kim could read two pages of a book simultaneously—one with each eye—and remember nearly everything he read. By the time of his death in 2009, he had memorized around twelve thousand books. His recall extended to facts about history, geography, music, and even zip codes. Give him your birth date, and he'd even tell you what day of the week it fell on (we'll learn this skill in chapter 5, page 149) as well as what day it'll fall on decades from now.

The next step, once you have those images, is to link the image to something about the event the date represents. Just as with memorizing names, you'll want to imagine the encoded numbers attached to or interacting with a feature about the *thing*—in this case, not a face, but an event.

Let's try one out:

EXAMPLE: AUGUST 11, MY DAD'S BIRTHDAY

Simple enough—a parent's birthday. Comes up every year. And you need to remember it instead of letting social media remind you.

First, let's convert August 11 into a number → 08-11.

Then, let's convert it to words with our Major System. 08 → SaFe, 11 → ToT. My image for August 11 is a safe filled with tater tots.

Finally, I need to find a way to link that ridiculous image to my dad. Well, that's easy. He is totally into heist movies, so I'd imagine him being in one, cracking open a safe that's filled with delicious tots. Imagining him doing that every birthday would be enough to lock in that date.

EXAMPLE: AUGUST 26, 1920, THE 19TH AMENDMENT WAS SIGNED INTO LAW, GIVING WOMEN THE RIGHT TO VOTE.

In this example, we have a little bit more to encode for the year. We need the month, day, and presumably the *full* year:

First, encode the date: 08-26-1920 turns into: *SoFa, NuDGe, TaP, NoSe*.

We need to relate that random sequence of images to something about the 19th Amendment and the right to vote. I might imagine a bunch of women heading to a sofa to vote, and the way they vote (instead of by filling in a ballot) is by nudging and tapping their own noses, or each other's noses. Whichever is weirder for you!

If you want to include something about that 19 so that you can remember specifically which amendment number it was, then you need to encode that as well and incorporate it into your image.

You could encode 19 into TaP again and incorporate that extra image into your story. Or you could keep it simple and imagine that the women tap their noses *exactly* 19 times.

GENIUS THINGS TO MEMORIZE

You've got the tools. You know how to create mental images, link ideas, and store them in a way your brain will be able to retrieve them reliably. So, the next question is: *What should you memorize?*

Well, whatever you want, honestly! My personal philosophy on memory training is that you should find something you're interested in memorizing and memorize *that*. Since having a great memory is a skill you need to practice consistently to see real, long-term improvement, finding something that will motivate you to sit down at your desk and memorize is the most important thing. I've generally found that if your brain is a treasure trove of widely recognizable, knowledge-rich topics, there's a higher chance people will think of you as a genius. For whatever reason, knowing geography, rattling off historical facts or pop-culture trivia, or speaking multiple languages on the fly tends to trigger that "genius" label in people's minds.

There are a lot of suggestions below, but you don't need to learn them overnight (or at all, for that matter). Ultimately, memorize what's meaningful to you! Working on these could be a long-term goal: You could tackle one category per month, gradually building up your genius knowledge base.

GEOGRAPHY

If you can mentally map out the world—countries, capitals, landmarks—you instantly have a deeper understanding of history, travel, and global events. The world stops feeling like a list of names and starts making sense.

- **ALL 195 COUNTRIES AND THEIR CAPITALS:** Turn both the country name and the capital name into wild images and then connect them. Bangladesh → Dhaka. *Imagine BANGing a DHUCK over the head.*
- **US STATES AND CAPITALS:** Classic trivia gold. Bonus if you know state nicknames too. Nevada → Carson City. *Imagine the Vegas strip packed with CARS making a cacophony of noises (CAR SOUNDS).*
- **MAJOR RIVERS AND MOUNTAINS:** The Amazon cutting through South America, the Nile running through Egypt, Mt. Everest towering over Nepal—picture them associated with an image for their country, and they'll stick.
- **FLAGS:** Turn colors and symbols into stories and associate them with the country name. *Bhutan's flag has a dragon on it. Imagine the flag dowsed in BUTANE (Bhutan) right before the dragon breathes fire and burns it to a crisp.*

HISTORY

History isn't just a bunch of dates; it's a road map to how the world got to where it is today. The better you remember it, the better you understand *everything*.

- **US PRESIDENTS (OR WORLD LEADERS):** Not just their names, but what happened during their terms. Knowing who did what makes history way more interesting. Use the Linking Method to string together a sequence of images to represent all the president names in order. *For example, to remember the sequence of Buchanan, Lincoln, Johnson, Grant, picture a book canon firing a book at ol' Honest Abe, who is sitting on the john while granting three wishes.*
- **MAJOR WARS AND REVOLUTIONS:** The American Revolution, World War II, the Cold War—picture the events, the battles, the turning points. Create a vivid image for each battle or war, then use the Major System to encode important dates and link them together. *Let's say you want to remember that the Invasion of Normandy (D-Day) happened on June 6, 1944. Break that down into 06-06-19-44, which translates into: SaSH–SaSH–TuB–RoaR. Now tie it all together visually: I picture hundreds of troops storming the beach, each wearing two bright sashes, arriving in oversized bathtubs and letting out thunderous roars as they charge forward.*
- **BIG INVENTIONS AND DISCOVERIES:** The printing press, electricity, the Internet—who invented them, how they changed the world. *Link names to inventions with a silly image—Gutenberg pressing bibles, Edison with a light bulb head, Tim Berners-Lee surfing the Web.*

POP CULTURE AND TRIVIA

Want to dominate trivia night? Or train to be on *Jeopardy!*? Or be the person who knows the obscure fact no one else does? Here are some ideas of things to lock in:

- **OSCAR-WINNING MOVIES:** If you can name every Best Picture winner, you're basically a human IMDb. *Create a Memory Palace where each area represents a decade, and each location is an image that represents the title of the movie.* Forrest Gump *could be an image of a box of chocolates;* Casablanca *could be a white house. If you wanted to add the year these movies won, adjust your image of a box of chocolates to be a box of chocolate balls (BaLL -> 95 -> it won in 1995). Imagine that white house filled to the brim with rum (RuM -> 43 ->* Casablanca *won in 1943).*

- **FAMOUS BOOK QUOTES:** "Call me Ishmael." "It was the best of times; it was the worst of times." Drop a famous line at the right moment, and you'll sound like a genius. *Let's say you wanted to remember "Stay gold, Ponyboy." from S. E. Hinton's* The Outsiders*: Visualize a golden pony hinting (Hinton) at going outside* (The Outsiders). *Combine quote, author, and title in a mini-scene.*
- **RECORD-HOLDERS:** Fastest marathon runner? Tallest building? Most streamed song? These weird facts always come in handy. *Eliud Kipchoge, Burj Khalifa, "Blinding Lights." Imagine Kipchoge sprinting up the Burj Khalifa, chased by a speaker blasting "Blinding Lights." The more absurd, the more memorable.*
- **SPORTS CHAMPIONS:** If you can name Super Bowl winners, World Cup champions, or Olympic gold medalists, you'll never lose a sports debate. *For these, Memory Palaces are your best friend. Create a Memory Palace for each sport, and place images for the winning team names at each location.*

VOCABULARY AND LANGUAGE LEARNING

Memorization alone won't make you fluent in a language, but it will absolutely supercharge your ability to learn one! Vocabulary is the foundation of both native and foreign language fluency. Whether you're expanding your command of your first language or diving into a second (or third), the ability to rapidly memorize words and phrases gives you a powerful edge. And since you now know how to memorize quickly and efficiently, why not apply those skills to language learning?

- **SOUNDING SMARTER IN YOUR OWN LANGUAGE:** Memorizing words isn't just for learning a new language; it can also level up how you speak your native one. A broader vocabulary helps you express thoughts more precisely and confidently (and it also makes you sound smarter). *For example, instead of saying "persuasive," you could say "cogent." And then to remember its definition, you could imagine someone presenting an argument so solid it feels like being hit with a cog from a machine ("cogent" means: clear, logical, and convincing).**
- **THE 1,000 MOST COMMON WORDS:** Word frequency lists are easy to find on the Web, and learning them covers 80 percent of daily conversation in any language. The great thing about memorizing

* We'll dive deeper into the art of more articulate speaking in chapter 8.

foreign words is that it's a simple two-step process: Create an image for the word, create an image for the meaning, then link them together. *Take "comer" (Spanish for "to eat"). Imagine a comet (sounds like "comer") crashing into a giant plate of food. You start eating the food raining down from the sky. Boom—comer = to eat.*

- **NUMBERS AND DAYS OF THE WEEK:** You don't want to be in a foreign country and not know how to count or not understand which days of the week a place you want to visit is closed. *In Swahili:*
    - *Moja = 1 → For moja, imagine one mocha coffee spilling over a giant number one. (mocha → moja)*
    - *Jumatatu = Monday → For Jumatatu, imagine a girl named June ("Juma") is late to work on Monday and steps on a tattoo needle ("tatu") on the floor. Painful start to the week!*
- **VERB CONJUGATIONS:** The hardest part of any language? Irregular verbs. Memorize them early, and everything else gets easier. *For example, in Dutch: "Ik ga" ("I go"), picture yourself being disgusted (ik = ickkk) going on an adventure while saying "ga-ga." Silly? Yes. Effective? Also yes.*
- **COGNATES AND FALSE FRIENDS:** Some words look like English, making them easy to remember. Others trick you. *"Attualmente" in Italian means "currently," not "actually." Just think "attualmente" means "at the moment" (currently) or rather, "At the AcTUAL-mo-MENT-e."*

The world of mnemonics is like a giant treasure chest, full of colorful and mind-blowing techniques. I wish I could pack them all into this book, but we've got to keep things focused. If you can nail the Memory Palace and the Linking Method and start applying it to stuff you want to remember, you'll feel like you've leveled up your brain in no time.

But remember, these techniques take practice. The more you work at them, the faster and more natural they become. When I first started, memorizing a forty-digit number in five minutes felt like climbing Everest. But with practice, I got to a point where I could memorize four hundred digits in the same amount of time. Yes, you read that right—*four hundred digits*.

Like any skill, building a killer memory takes patience and consistency. Treat it like going to the gym for your brain. Even just a few minutes a day can make a huge difference. Stick with it, and you'll be amazed at how quickly your memory transforms!

GENIUS PROFLE:
LYDIA MACHOVÁ

Most people struggle to learn a single foreign language. But Lydia Machová speaks nine! She is a true polyglot. Fluent in languages such as English, German, Spanish, Polish, and French (just to name a few), Machová isn't your typical polyglot. Her approach to learning so many languages was primarily to make it fun. Machová learns through immersion—reading books, watching TV shows, mimicking native speakers. She treats the process like a game rather than a chore. She's living proof that with the right techniques—smart immersion, consistency, and engagement—anyone can learn multiple languages, even as an adult.

THE ALPHABET BACKWARDS

Here's a fun application of memory techniques to practice: the alphabet . . . backwards! A quick way to memorize it is to create a small sequence of mental images that represent a few letters at a time, and then string them into a memorable story (using the Linking Method):

- **ZYX WV - "SIX WAVES" - Imagine a surfer dude surfing on six (sounds like ZYX) gnarly waves (waves will help you remember WV)**

- **UTSR QPON - This surfer surfs all the way to the shores of the USSR (former Russia), only it's UTSR instead of USSR, because it's a discount USSR. Obviously, since it's on sale, there is a coupon (QPON) dangling from it.**
- **MLK JIHG - Then, the surfer encounters a milk (MLK) carton doing a little jig (JIHG) on the shores of Russia.**
- **FED CBA - After the dancing ends, he feeds (FED) a taxicab (CBA, the letters are jumbled around, so maybe it's a confused cab).**

That's it! Remember that silly, nonsensical story, and the alphabet will be a breeze to say backwards.

EXERCISES AND RESOURCES

- **Start by creating three to five different Memory Palaces with twenty locations each. Use these to practice memorizing lists. Use them for your daily to-do lists or your grocery lists, and just keep practicing! I have more than 100 different Memory Palaces, and I am always creating new ones.**
- **You can reuse Memory Palaces, but I'd suggest only reusing ones you've dedicated to storing short-term, replaceable information (like**

a daily to-do list or grocery list). If you want to use a Memory Palace to memorize something big and important (something long-term), I suggest creating a Memory Palace *specifically* for that and only that.*

- When meeting people, take the opportunity to put your new memory skills to work. One of the most impressive reactions I get is when I remember people's names. It might be one of the quickest ways to get someone to start thinking you're a genius. Trust me!
- Take the opportunity to practice memorizing phone numbers. An awesome genius-like skill is to ask someone for their number and NOT write it down. I can't tell you the number of times people were blown away that I had memorized their number on the spot. Genius, indeed!
- Memory breeds confidence. Make the effort to memorize things rather than write them down. The more confident you become in your own memory abilities, the stronger your memory will become. The Pygmalion effect in action!
- Don't ignore the fundamentals. Your brain runs on sleep, exercise, good nutrition (omega-3s, antioxidants), and hydration. Skimp on these and even the best memory techniques won't save you.
- We're not fully done with memory in this book. It will pop up frequently, so make sure to practice the techniques from this chapter!

For more in-depth info on memory techniques, make sure to check out:

BOOKS:

- *Remember It!*—My memory technique book for adults.
- *Memory Superpowers!*—My memory technique book for kids.
- *Moonwalking with Einstein* by Joshua Foer—An amazing overview of the history of the art of memory.

APPS/WEBSITES:

- My YouTube channel: https://www.youtube.com/c/nelsondellis
- The top memory technique discussion forum: https://forum.artofmemory.com/
- A great place to train your memory: https://memoryleague.com

---

* Fun fact: For a memory challenge (and as a complete non-Swiftie), I once memorized Taylor Swift's entire music catalog—all the albums, track names, and track lists. It required multiple Memory Palaces to store each album (twelve in total!), ones that navigated through old homes, mountain trails, and even museums.

CHAPTER 2

SPEED-READING

"BOOKS ARE THE TRAINING WEIGHTS OF THE MIND."
—EPICTETUS

I WAS WELL OUT OF MY LEAGUE.

I HAD SIGNED UP ON A WHIM FOR THE SPEED-READING PORTION OF THE 2016 MEMORIAD COMPETITION—THE OLYMPICS FOR THE MIND—BECAUSE I COULDN'T RESIST THE CHALLENGE.

THE OTHER COMPETITORS CLAIMED THEY COULD READ AT 2,000-PLUS WORDS PER MINUTE (KEY WORD: "CLAIMED." I WASN'T ENTIRELY CONVINCED). MEANWHILE, LITTLE OL' ME WAS CRUISING AT A MEAGER (ALBEIT TOTALLY RESPECTABLE) 400 TO 450 WORDS PER MINUTE; I WAS JOGGING LEISURELY NEXT TO A PACK OF OLYMPIC SPRINTERS.

STILL, I FIGURED I'D SEE WHAT I COULD DO.

THE RULES WERE SIMPLE. READ A PREVIOUSLY UNPUBLISHED, INCREDIBLY DENSE TEXT AS FAST AS POSSIBLE, THEN RECALL AS MUCH INFORMATION AS POSSIBLE BY ANSWERING A SLEW OF QUESTIONS RELATED TO SAID TEXT.

When the event started, I noticed my competitors zipping through at breakneck speed. I remember chuckling quietly to myself when I heard them stopping their timers; meanwhile I had barely made it halfway through the material! I had zero chance against them. But I stuck to my plan. I wasn't going to worry about being the fastest. Instead, I was going to focus on actually understanding what I read and let my memory skills do the heavy lifting during recall.

It worked. While my competitors blazed through the text, I took my time and made sure I absorbed as much as I could. When it came time to recall, I crushed it. Turns out, reading at lightning speed doesn't mean much if you can't remember what you've read. My relatively slow and steady approach earned me a bronze medal, and I walked away feeling as if I had just hacked the system. And just like that, I was a medalist at a speed-reading olympiad.

That experience taught me something important: Speed-reading isn't just about racing through a book, it's about finding the balance between speed and comprehension. It's about learning how to process *and* retain information. That's exactly what this chapter is about. I'm going to show you how to read faster, remember more, and make speed-reading a skill that actually works for you.

I wouldn't say I've always been the fastest reader. If anything, I've considered myself pretty average (maybe slightly above). The average person reads at around 250 words per minute. A "fast" reader clocks in somewhere above 400 words per minute. If you're curious about yours, it's super easy to calculate. Just follow these steps and you'll have your answer in about a minute.

First, pick something to read. Ideally something *new* to you—maybe a novel, an article, or a nonfiction book. Keep it fair by choosing a passage between 300 and 1,000 words. (A typical paperback or hardcover novel has around 250 to 350 words per page, so plan to read about three or four pages.)

Now grab a timer. Set it for exactly *one minute* and find a quiet spot where you won't get distracted.

When you're ready, start the timer and begin reading. Don't rush, don't slow down. Just read at your normal, comfortable pace, as if you were genuinely trying to absorb and comprehend what you're reading. When the timer rings, stop immediately and mark the last word you read.

Now count how many words you read in that one-minute span.* That number is your words-per-minute (WPM) score. Easy as that.

As I said before, speed doesn't mean much if you don't remember what you read. To check your comprehension, jot down *two or three key points* from the passage, then compare them with the text. Or, if you have someone nearby, have them skim the passage and ask you a few questions about it.

In case you're wondering how you measure up, here's a rough breakdown of reading speeds:

- **Average reader: 200–300 WPM**
- **Above average reader: 300–450 WPM**
- **Fast reader: 450–700+ WPM**
- **Speed reader: 1000+ WPM (though comprehension can vary)**

That should give you a solid benchmark. Now that you know your speed, let's be clear on goals: the goal is *not* to crank up your reading speed so high that comprehension goes out the window. The goal is to *read faster while still actually understanding what you're reading.* Speed-reading isn't something you'll always want to do. But by the time you finish this chapter, you'll be able to adjust how fast or slow you read based on the purpose of what you're reading. You'll be in control.

Some books you'll want to savor like a fine wine—read slowly, soak in the beauty, let the words marinate, maybe even read it multiple times. Other books you'll just need to get through them, extract the key details, and move on. Think of it like walking versus running. Sometimes you want a slow, leisurely walk through the park, taking in the scenery, breathing in the fresh air; other times, you're sprinting to catch a train. It all depends on your end goal.

I've seen way too many speed-reading books and courses obsess over WPM as if that's all that matters. They push the idea that faster is always better, but that's the wrong approach. Instead, you need to learn how to control your speed so you can read *smarter.* That's the real skill.

---

* You don't need to count every word. Just pick a random line, count the words, multiply by the number of lines on the page, and then multiply by the number of pages you read. For the last partial page when the timer went off, just estimate or count it roughly. It doesn't have to be perfect.

But you might be thinking, *Why does speed-reading even matter? Why does reading more matter?* Here's my hot take: To be perceived as smart, you need to know a lot. And a simple way to become someone who knows a lot, is by reading a *lot*.

To me, being well-read is one of the strongest signs of intelligence. A few of the genius definitions we discussed in the opening chapter touched on the idea of being knowledgeable across a broad range of topics; having

GENIUS PROFILE: HOWARD BERG

Howard Berg, recognized by the *Guinness Book of World Records* in 1990 as the world's fastest reader, claimed to read at a rate of more than 25,000 words per minute. He gained national attention after appearing on more than 1,100 television programs, including *Live with Regis and Kathie Lee*, where he read full-length books in minutes and accurately answered detailed questions about them.

Berg, who studied biology and psychology at SUNY Binghamton, developed his technique by combining insights from neuroscience and visual processing. His method focused on eliminating subvocalization, expanding peripheral vision, and training the brain to process words in chunks rather than one at a time.

While his exact reading speed has been debated, his core belief was simple: reading is a skill that can be trained and dramatically improved with practice.

a certain degree of mastery; an ability to pull insights from different areas. That kind of intellectual depth and range typically doesn't just appear out of nowhere. It comes from exposure to ideas, perspectives, and information.

And what's the best way to get that exposure? You guessed it. *Reading.**

Before diving into practical tips, it's worth addressing the elephant in the room: the term "speed-reading" comes with a lot of baggage (flashy infomercials, courses promising 2,000+ words per minute, gimmicky apps, etc.). Research is clear that pushing reading speeds far beyond the average range of 200 to 450 WPM usually comes at the cost of comprehension. Reading speed gains *are* possible, but many of the extraordinary claims are unsupported or have been outright debunked.† That being said, I believe much of the research actually *supports* the kinds of strategies I use, ones that lead to modest but meaningful improvements. Typically, the anti-speed-reading studies you'll find are aimed at dismantling the most extreme claims rather than showing that all speed-reading methods are useless.

Either way, to stay in line with both the research and reality (and to pacify the skeptics), I'll use the term "focused reading," instead of speed-reading, from here on out. That's really at the heart of what I'm sharing in this chapter anyways: learning how to control your focus and attention at different reading speeds in order to understand and remember more of what you read. Plain and simple.

TEN TIPS TO READ FASTER

Let's get into the juicy stuff! Follow these tips, and I guarantee you'll be able to boost your reading speed, have better control over it when it matters, and actually retain what you read.

1. INTENT

First, and probably most important, is that you have to actually *want* to read. There's nothing worse than forcing yourself to read a book you're absolutely dreading. Later in this book, I'll talk about defining your *why*, because it's the key to getting anything done with real intensity and focus. The same applies here. Get clear on why you want to read a particular

---

* It's possible to get that exposure through other sources—AI tools, videos, podcasts, conversations—especially in the modern age. But there is something about reading that, from a memory and learning standpoint, simply can't be beat. The act of engaging with written words forces your brain to process information in a deeper way.

† Melissa Dahl, "The Sad Truth About Speed-Reading: It Doesn't Work," *The Cut*, April 18, 2016, https://www.thecut.com/2016/04/the-sad-truth-about-speed-reading-it-doesnt-work.html.

book. What you hope to gain, learn, or change. Once you have that reason locked in, reading becomes something you *want* to do, not just something you're trying to get through.

Now, you're not *always* going to be reading for pleasure. Sometimes you're tackling a book because your professor assigned it (yawn), and other times you're diving headfirst into the latest book in your favorite fantasy series (hell YES!). Some books excite you; others feel like watching paint dry. The trick is to *make the reading session matter to you*. Dedicate time to it. Realize the upsides of why finishing said book would make a difference. Make it a game if you have to—see how fast you can get through a section while retaining as much as possible. But whatever you do, don't procrastinate. *Do the damn thing.*

2. BLOCK OUT DISTRACTIONS

We live in an age where distractions are relentless. If you're the kind of person who compulsively checks their phone the second a notification pops up, that's fine—but *not while reading*. If you're serious about hitting your reading targets, put your phone in another room or turn it off. Your reading environment makes a huge difference. Clear your desk, grab some water, use the bathroom beforehand, put on relaxing music (or go full silence mode), and consider yourself *unavailable* for the next hour or so. Treat your reading session with respect. Allow it to happen in a space that feels inviting and comfortable. You'll be amazed at how much progress you make.

3. DON'T READ ALL THE WORDS

This tip changed *everything* for me. Most people assume reading faster means skimming and missing details—not true! Your brain is wired to see patterns and fill in gaps. Just like you don't need read every letter in word to understand it, you don't need every single word in sentence to grasp meaning.

Hold up.

Go back and read that last paragraph again. Notice anything weird? Probably not. But look again—I removed words. And guess what? Your brain didn't care. It filled in the blanks effortlessly. That's how focused reading works. Your mind is already predicting meaning from structure and context. Once you lean into this, you'll unlock a whole new level of reading speed without sacrificing comprehension.

Aslo, yuo dno't need to raed evrey lteter in a wrod to unedrtsand it. In fcat, as lnog as the frist and lsat ltteres are in palce, yuor bairn wlil sutill mkae snese of it. Tihs is beacuse yuor mnid deosn't raed evrey chracater indiviudlaay. It jummps, pttinog toghteer mnainig basde on cnotext. So, if you've been raeding tihs pragarph wtih no isseus, taht's ecxalty the pniot!

See what I mean? That last paragraph was a jumble, yet you still read it with no problem. That's because reading is about recognizing patterns, not processing every letter. The more you trust your brain's ability to do this, the faster you'll read while still understanding everything.

To train myself to read this way, I use a simple trick. I take a ruler and draw a vertical line about one inch into the left margin and another one inch from the right margin. When I read, I keep my focus between these lines, avoiding the outer edges. Think about how much time your eyes spend traveling from the left to the right side of a page over hundreds of pages. That's a ton of unnecessary movement. By narrowing my focus, I train my brain to process information more efficiently, skipping filler words while still absorbing meaning. And even though you're technically not "reading" the outer words on a line, your brain is still able to fill in the gaps (it can see the words to a certain extent in your peripheral vision as well, so you're not *completely* skipping them).

Now, you might be tempted to move those vertical lines even further inward. Experiment with it, but there's going to be a limit. If you go too narrow, you'll miss a *lot* of the words on a line and your brain will struggle to figure out the context of the words it *did* read. What we're actually training is reducing saccades.

Saccades are the rapid, jerky movements your eyes make when scanning a text. When you read, your eyes will naturally make tiny jumps from word to word (or even phrase to phrase). The fewer saccades per line, the faster your reading speed. Instead of fixating on individual words, you train your brain to absorb chunks of text at a time. This cuts down on eye movement and increases efficiency.

The good news is, you won't always need to draw those margin lines. After a while, it'll just become your natural reading style.

4. DON'T BACKTRACK!

Backtracking on what you've already read is a killer for speed. Ever catch yourself rereading the same sentence or paragraph over and over again because you weren't fully paying attention? Or maybe your eyes keep jumping back instead of progressing forward? That's called regression, and it massively slows you down.

To fix this, *use a pointer.* It sounds basic, like something you were taught in elementary school, but it works. Drag your finger, a pen, or even a toothpick under the words as you read. Your eyes will naturally follow, reducing unnecessary backtracking. It might feel a little awkward at first, but as you get better at it, you'll be able to increase the speed of your pointer. Incredibly, your eyes will keep up.

5. READ FOR LONGER PERIODS (WITH BREAKS!)

When you're first training yourself to read faster, it's going to feel weird. Your brain will resist. Your eyes might get tired.

The solution is simple: *longer* reading sessions.

Give yourself enough time to actually settle into the reading flow. It takes a few pages, but you'll start to feel your brain getting the hang of it. Don't overdo it, though. Pushing too hard can lead to mental fatigue. If you feel your focus slipping, take a short break. Stand up, stretch, grab some water, then dive back in. The goal is to get into the zone, not burn yourself out.

6. PRACTICE, PRACTICE, PRACTICE

At the end of the day, reading is a skill. And like any other skill, the more you do it, the better you get. Focused reading isn't a magic trick, it's a trained ability. Practice using all these strategies, and soon they'll feel completely natural. You'll read faster and you'll be able to adjust your speed as needed.

HOW TO REMEMBER WHAT YOU READ

Remember, focused reading is a two-part process: you want to read faster *and* remember more. Let's talk about the memory part.

VISUALIZE

In chapter 1 (page 27), we learned that one of the most powerful memory techniques is visualization. When you encode something as a mental picture, you give your brain a stronger hook to hang on to. The more vivid and sensory-rich the image, the more likely it is to stick.

Reading is no different. As I read, I'm screening a mental movie. The words aren't just abstract letters on a page. I'm actively translating them into visuals. I picture the scenes, the characters, the concepts. Some of you might be thinking, *Isn't that what reading is?* Actually, a lot of people don't do this but instead process words, understanding them in the moment, and then move on. Instead, try to consciously project what you're reading onto a giant screen in your mind's eye. If you make it as vivid as possible, you make it memorable. This simple shift will enhance your ability to retain what you read.

TAKE NOTES

Don't just passively absorb a book; *interact* with it. For me, reading creates an active conversation between me and the book. I underline things that strike me as important, I box things that jump out, and I circle things I never want to forget. My notes are messy, but that's okay. Physically marking up the page forces my brain to engage *more*, which makes the ideas stick longer. And when I finish a chapter, I can glance back at my notes and have a better recall of the big takeaways. That's a game-changer.

But if you really want to remember what you read, you need more than just margin notes. You need a system; a way to capture and organize your notes so they actually help you later. Leaving all those markups trapped in the margins is *such* a waste of effort. So instead, you can extract them into an organized medium for easier reference.

One of the best methods I've found for doing this is by using a Commonplace Book.

A Commonplace Book is a dedicated place—usually a notebook or a collection of organized notecards—where you collect the best ideas from what you read. It's where you jot down anything that makes you stop and think: quotes, insights, lessons, or reflections you don't want to forget. It can also include things you underline, circle, or write in the margins of a book. Basically, anything worth returning to later. It sounds simple, but it's an incredibly powerful tool. One that has been used by some of history's greatest minds—Thomas Jefferson, Benjamin Franklin, and Ralph Waldo Emerson, to name a few.

When you're done with a chapter (or the whole book, whatever you prefer), write down the best of the best from what you read. It could be every single thing you marked up in your book or it could just be the things that punched you in the gut or made you think, *Whoa, that's good,* after the fact. You decide. Then, summarize these key ideas in your own words, ideally not in an actual book but on a notecard* (this is crucial—don't just copy them, make it your own). Also, do your best to do the note taking by hand, not digitally. You remember things better when you write them out.†

Finally, sort them by theme or topic, so when you need inspiration or want to revisit any of those topics, your best ideas will be waiting for you, and they'll be easy to access.

---

* As the name suggests (and historically), a Commonplace Book is usually some kind of notebook. But I personally think notecards are better, because they are much easier to file and sort. Ultimately, the format doesn't matter. What matters is that your notes and ideas are easy to categorize and find later.

† P. Mueller and D. Oppenheimer, "The Pen Is Mightier Than the Keyboard: Advantages of Longhand over Laptop Note Taking," *Psychological Science* 25, no. 6 (2014): 1159–1168.

But don't just file them away and forget about them—make it a habit to review your Commonplace Book regularly. Set aside time weekly or monthly to flip through your notes. You'll be surprised how ideas that seemed ordinary when you first captured them suddenly spark new connections or solutions to current problems. Regular review keeps your best thinking active and accessible, not buried.

This method is perfect if you read for inspiration, self-improvement, or creative fuel. It gives you a deep well of references to tap into while building your knowledge.

What's even cooler is that once the notes are organized, you can start to think about which notes you'd actually like to extract and mentally store in a Memory Palace (kind of like your own *mental* Commonplace Book). Now, it doesn't have to contain *everything* in your physical Commonplace Book, but it could be a subset of the data—the notes that might be worth memorizing at that time, things that you'd like to keep top-of-mind.

Regardless of your system, one thing is clear: Writing down and reviewing information locks it in your brain. When you pause after reading a section and summarize it *by hand*, you're forcing your brain to engage, as well as forcing yourself to remember way better than if you were only reading. When you either review it from your notes or store it in a Memory Palace and review *that*, you'll be a walking genius filled with knowledge you learned from all the books you read.

I should mention that you don't have to necessarily use the system above. The simple act of taking a moment to write down *anything* you remember after reading a section of a book—that *effort* of recall paired with the physical act of writing—will help transform what you read from words on a page into knowledge that stays with you.

SWITCH LOCATIONS

This is a small suggestion that can sometimes have a huge effect. Reading is an event. And it takes place somewhere: on a couch, in a train, on a plane, in bed, etc. In many circumstances, you may remember where you were when you read something. Research shows that our brains encode environmental context along with information—a phenomenon called "context-dependent memory." Our brain loves to remember novel things. So, if you change up your location when you read, you'll find that you remember certain passages better. Studies have found that people recall information more effectively when they're in the same environment where they learned it, and varying your study locations can create multiple retrieval cues.*

* S. M. Smith and E. Vela, "Environmental Context-Dependent Memory: A Review and Meta-Analysis," *Psychonomic Bulletin & Review* 8 (June 2001): 203–20.

Different sections of the book that were read in unique locations will stick out, and you'll have an extra meta-memory of the text because of when and where you read it. It can be hard to constantly change locations, but if you switch things up from time to time, I guarantee what you read in those new locations will stand out in your memory.

GENIUS PROFILE: BENJAMIN FRANKLIN

Benjamin Franklin was one of the early pioneers of the Commonplace Book. Not just as a collector of interesting quotes, but as someone who used it strategically to fuel his growth. From a young age, he filled his notebook with excerpts from books, arguments that impressed him, and personal reflections.

As a teenager, Franklin began collecting well-written essays in his notebook from publications such as *The Spectator*, a popular eighteenth-century periodical full of sharp, witty essays on society, philosophy, and self-improvement. But instead of just reading them, he would summarize the ideas, hide the original text, then attempt to reconstruct the essays in his own words, sometimes even translating them into poetry and back into prose. Afterward, he'd compare his version with the original and note where he could improve. He was deliberately training himself in rhetoric, logic, and composition, all through his Commonplace Book.

For Franklin, the Commonplace Book helped him think better, write sharper, and live more intentionally. In many ways, it was the blueprint behind the polymath he became.

HOW TO FINISH MORE BOOKS

Practicing focused-reading techniques is one thing, but committing to finishing a book is another beast entirely. With distractions everywhere, it's easy to put off reading in favor of endless scrolling or binge-watching. But if you want to *actually finish books*, here are some strategies that have helped me:

1. PRIORITIZE READING IN YOUR LIFE

This all ties back to intent. If you really want to read and make progress, then *act on it.* Make it a priority. Set aside reading time just like you would for the gym or any other hobby you care about. I also recommend keeping an active wish list of books you genuinely want to read. Seeing them written down will give you a sense of urgency to start tackling them. It will also motivate you to stick to reading consistently so you can make progress down that list.

2. READ EVERYWHERE

Reduce friction. Carry your book everywhere. Even if you only read one page at a time, that's one more than you would've read otherwise. Keep books easily accessible—on your nightstand, in your bag, on your phone as an eBook, or as an audiobook for when you're on the go. The easier you make it to pick up a book, the more you'll actually read.

3. STOP READING BOOKS THAT SUCK

One of the easiest ways to finish books is to *read books you actually enjoy.* You're not obligated to finish a book just because you started it. If a book is a slog, put it down. There's no rule saying you have to suffer through it. If a TV show sucks, do you force yourself to finish it? Hell no! You change the channel. Apply that same ruthless logic to books.

4. READ MULTIPLE BOOKS AT A TIME

I know, I know—some people hate this idea. But hear me out. Sometimes I get *so* immersed in a book that I don't want to read anything else. Other times, I like variety. Reading across different genres—self-help, fantasy, science, history—keeps things fresh. Sometimes spreading yourself across multiple books can slow progress on each individual one, but it keeps the excitement level high. And that's what will keep you reading.

5. READ IMPULSIVELY

If a book sparks my interest, I start it *immediately.* Why? Because my excitement is at its peak. If I add it to a wish list and wait too long, by the time I get to it, my interest might have cooled. I strike while the iron is hot, because I know I'll read fast and voraciously. If you're genuinely excited about a book, dive in quick!

6. MAKE A GOAL OUT OF IT

If you're goal-driven, setting a reading target can be a game-changer. It gives your reading purpose and turns it into something you actively pursue, not just squeeze in when you have time. Your goal could be as simple as X books per year, Y pages per day, or even a time-based goal like twenty minutes before bed every night—whatever keeps you motivated.

Personally, I set a yearly book goal. Not as a strict rule or pressure-filled challenge, but as a friendly motivator. It keeps me consistent. Some years I hit it. Some years I don't. That's not the point. The goal is there to nudge me forward when life gets busy or my motivation dips. Choose a goal that fits your pace and lifestyle. The key is not quantity for its own sake, but building a habit that sticks.

7. BE CALCULATED

Look, if you're still struggling to finish books despite having the best intentions, here's a hack I use to force momentum into my reading routine.

Before the start of a new month, I pick four books I want to read—one per week. Then, I check how many actual readable pages each book has and divide that by seven. That tells me exactly how many pages I need to read per day to finish that particular book in a week. I use small, color-coded stickers to mark these daily targets in the book.

Obviously, you still have to read those pesky pages. But having a clear, visible daily target makes a huge difference. And, often, I actually *pass* my daily markers because I think, *I already hit my goal, why not keep going a little bit more?* That little psychological trick often gets me finishing books even faster.

I also apply this system across different formats. So, in any given month I might be reading:

- *Four physical books* (using the page breakdown method above)
- *Two audiobooks* (I divide total run time by fourteen days to set a daily listening goal)
- *One digital book* (usually my lowest-priority book, read in spare moments on my phone when I'm on the go)

For audiobooks, I listen while driving, running, cleaning—whenever I'm not actively reading a physical book. And yes, I speed them up. I'm comfortable listening at 2× speed, slowing down to 1.5× for dense sections, and bumping up to 3× when it's filler.

This is just one method—but if you're serious about reading more, having a structured system like this helps break down big books into manageable daily chunks. Taking small steps can lead to huge gains.

Reading is an absolute joy. It's taken me to the top of Mt. Everest, taught me about love, languages, chess, fun facts about the world, how to navigate relationships, win friends and influence people, the list goes on. It's an escape from our daily lives into new worlds, as well as our own minds. I've always noticed at times when I've felt stuck, the simple act of opening up a book and committing to reading its pages will *always*, without fail, propel me forward. When I read more, I always have more to say to the people around me (and also to myself). It really gets me thinking.

While I may never enter myself into another speed-reading (sorry . . . er, I mean . . . *focused*-reading) competition again, I will never, ever stop reading. And neither should you.

EXERCISES AND RESOURCES

- Genius hack: *Always* memorize the title and author of every book you read. Sounds simple, but most people don't. Be intentional about learning them before you start the book. Rattling off books and their authors without hesitation is one of the sharpest genius flexes you can have.
- When reading, make sure to pause after every chapter to think back on what you just read. Can you name important characters and/or recap important plot points or ideas? Taking the time to review what you just read in increments will help you remember more in the long run.
- This is one of my favorite go-to reading exercises:
  - Pick an unread nine-page chunk from a book you're reading.
  - Read those pages in three-page groupings, each group with a different goal:
    - First: Comprehension—read at your natural pace.
    - Second: Speed—go as fast as possible, even if you miss things.
    - Third: Balance—split the difference now; aim to read fast *and* understand.
  - As you play around with different reading speeds, you'll become more familiar with how fast you can read in various situations. Over time, you'll gain the confidence to read faster than you normally do, when the need calls for it.

- Here's a thirty-day challenge to boost your genius knowledge base:
    - One Commonplace Book note a day for thirty days. That's it.
    - Every day, write down a single thing worth remembering—a quote, an insight, a lesson, an observation. Anything that makes you think I want to remember this. Preferably from books you read, but it doesn't have to be!
    - Every week, review your last seven entries. Notice any patterns, connections, or ideas that suddenly click.
    - By day thirty, you'll have thirty insights embedded deeper in your memory than when you started.
    - Now scale that up: Keep going for a year, and you'll have 365 curated pieces of knowledge. Three years? More than 1,000 reference points your brain can connect and cross-reference. Imagine all the patterns you'd see that others miss. All the connections you could make on command.
    - Your Commonplace Book doesn't need to be fancy. It just needs to be consistent. Start today!

Here are some focused-reading tools and resources:

BOOKS:

- *How to Read a Book: The Classic Guide to Intelligent Reading* by Mortimer J. Adler and Charles Van Doren—A deep, structured approach to reading for understanding.
- *Breakthrough Rapid Reading* by Peter Kump—Practical techniques to increase reading speed and comprehension.
- *10 Days to Faster Reading* by the Princeton Language Institute and Abby Marks Beale—A quick-start program to boost reading efficiency fast.

APPS/WEBSITES:

- Spreeder—An app that trains your eyes to focus on a single word stream for rapid reading.
- BeeLine Reader—An app with color-gradient text to guide your eyes across lines.
- Reedy—Another option for a focused-reading app.
- Freereadingtest.com—Test your current reading speed.

CHAPTER 3

FOCUS AND CONCENTRATION

"CONCENTRATION IS THE ROOT OF ALL THE HIGHER ABILITIES IN MAN."
—BRUCE LEE

I HAD TAKEN A THREE-YEAR HIATUS. TECHNICALLY, I WAS RETIRED. BUT SOMETHING PULLED ME BACK IN—A VOICE WHISPERING, "YOU'RE NOT DONE YET."

SURE ENOUGH, IN 2024, I FOUND MYSELF BACK IN THE ARENA AT THE USA MEMORY CHAMPIONSHIP. ONE LAST TIME.

I HAD WON MY FIFTH CHAMPIONSHIP TITLE IN 2021, CEMENTING MYSELF AS THE MOST DECORATED MEMORY CHAMPION IN THE HISTORY OF THE COMPETITION. BEFORE THAT, SCOTT HAGWOOD—ONE OF THE MEMORY GREATS—HELD THE RECORD WITH FOUR WINS. WHEN I TIED HIS RECORD IN 2015, I KNEW I COULDN'T STOP THERE. I NEEDED ONE MORE.

BUT THAT FINAL WIN DIDN'T COME EASY. I CAME CLOSE, AGAIN AND AGAIN, ONLY TO KEEP FALLING SHORT. UNTIL 2021. MISSION ACCOMPLISHED. I THEN WALKED AWAY FROM COMPETITIVE MEMORY, CONVINCED I WAS DONE FOR GOOD.

. . . THEN 2024 HAPPENED.

I had an unshakable feeling, a pull. My intuition was screaming: *This is your year. One more win is waiting for you.* So, I signed up. I started training again. And now there I was. Championship day. I had fought my way back to the final round: *Double Deck or Bust*.

Two decks of cards. Five minutes to memorize as many cards as possible. Three finalists, taking turns recalling one card at a time. One mistake, you're out. Last man standing wins the title.

I had been here before. Eight times, to be exact. But this time, something was off. Maybe it was my age (I had just turned forty earlier that year). Or maybe it was the fact that I was out of practice. Three years is a long time to step away from this level of competition.

Whatever it was, my nerves were on fire.

It was down to just me and two other finalists, and we were given a fifteen-minute break before the final event. Soon, we'd be back onstage, locked in a battle of pure mental endurance.

I can't screw this up.

The thought kept looping in my head. I had clawed my way back to the finals—was I really going to choke now? Maybe I should have stayed retired. The more I thought about it, the more my focus slipped. My heart was pounding. My hands, shaking.

I needed to get it together—*fast*. So, I closed my eyes, and went through my focus routine . . .

THE MONROE INSTITUTE

A few months before the competition, a strange series of synchronistic events led me to a weeklong meditation retreat in a small town outside of Charlottesville, Virginia. But this wasn't just any retreat; this was at the Monroe Institute: a research center dedicated to exploring altered states of consciousness, human potential, and expanded awareness through meditation, proprietary sound technology, and out-of-body experience training.

It was called the Gateway Experience, a program designed to help you expand your mind and discover that "you are more than your physical body." Whatever that meant.

I was deeply skeptical. It all sounded like some New Age fluff wrapped in vague metaphysics. But despite my doubts, I kept an open mind. Since 2021, I had started exploring consciousness, altered states, and the unseen layers of reality, leaning more into the spiritual (you'll hear more about that in chapter 9). What I found at the Monroe Institute was eye-opening. Mind-bending. Transformational. It changed me in ways I didn't expect; primarily, by giving me an entirely new approach to calming and focusing my mind.

In the past, I had always said I didn't meditate. When asked whether I used meditation to sharpen my focus and memory, I'd shrug it off. *No need—I train my memory,* I would say. *My memory training* is *my meditation.*

But that week at the Institute literally and figuratively changed my mind. I learned that training my focus—quieting my thoughts, controlling my breathing, dropping into deep concentration—was a skill I could practice and hone. And that practice paid off in a big way.

Back at the championship, during that fifteen-minute break before the final event, I closed my eyes and ran through the techniques I had learned at the Institute. My breathing slowed. My nerves settled. I locked in. I had made it to the finals eight times before—nine, including that championship. And I can honestly say I had never walked onto that stage as calm and collected as I did that day.

You can probably guess how it turned out. I won. (Otherwise, I wouldn't be telling you this story.)

Winning reminded me of the profound importance of focus and concentration. They aren't abstract skills. They're a real, tangible advantage. The ability to control your attention on demand is a genius superpower. In this chapter, I'm going to show you how to develop it.

HOW FOCUS WORKS

Most people think they have a motivation problem when they actually have a *focus* problem.

You've probably been there—you sit down to work, and within minutes, you've checked your phone twice, clicked on a random YouTube video, and somehow ended up googling "How tall was Napoleon?" Forty-five minutes later, you realize you've done absolutely nothing.

It's not your fault. The modern world is designed to hijack your focus at every turn. But why does your brain seem to actively resist staying on task?

At its core, focus is controlled by dopamine—the neurotransmitter that makes us seek out rewards. Every time you scroll social media, check notifications, or jump between tasks, you're giving yourself tiny dopamine hits. Your brain loves this instant gratification, so it becomes conditioned to crave distraction. And with distractions just a tap away, it's never been harder to stay focused.

Meanwhile, *deep* focus—what's often called *flow state*—requires delayed gratification. It takes effort to lock in, and there's no instant reward. This is why most people never actually experience deep focus in their daily lives.

They're constantly switching tasks, or *task-switching*, before their brain has time to fully engage.

Task-switching (also known as context-shifting) refers to when your brain rapidly jumps between different tasks, topics, or modes of thinking—and it's one of the biggest enemies of deep focus.

Cal Newport, author of *Deep Work*, defines work in two categories:

- ***Shallow work*—Low-value, low-focus tasks that don't push you forward (checking email, responding to messages, jumping between tabs).**
- ***Deep work*—High-value, deeply focused tasks that require zero distractions and lead to breakthroughs.**

Most people live in shallow work mode all day and wonder why they aren't getting anything done. The key to elite-level concentration is training yourself to drop into deep work mode on command. This begins with training your brain to stop switching tasks.

HOW TO STOP SWITCHING TASKS

Context-shifting can absolutely kill your focus. Research shows that even brief interruptions create "attention residue"—where part of your attention remains stuck on the previous task, significantly degrading your performance on the new task.* These days, everything around us is designed to grab our attention in tiny, fragmented bursts—emails, social media, text messages, notifications, all pulling us in different directions. And each time we shift between these things, our brain has to reset and reorient itself. This is why so many people feel as if they've been working hard all day but have nothing meaningful to show for it.

Let's say you're reading a book, but you stop every ten minutes to check your phone. Even though it may feel like a much-needed quick break, your brain has to reload the book's context every time you return. That constant resetting dramatically slows you down.

So how do you train your brain to stop craving these dopamine-fueled distractions? Here are some of my best strategies.

---

* Sophie Leroy, "Why Is It So Hard to Do My Work? The Challenge of Attention Residue When Switching Between Work Tasks," *Organizational Behavior and Human Decision Processes* 109, no. 2 (2009): 168–81.

GENIUS PROFILE:
NIKOLA TESLA

Nikola Tesla was a visionary inventor and electrical engineer, best known for his groundbreaking work in electricity and magnetism. One of the things that set him apart from the rest was his ability to enter states of deep, undistracted focus. In 1882, while walking through a park in Budapest reciting lines from Goethe, Nikola Tesla suddenly saw a vision of a fully functional electric motor in his mind—complete with rotating magnetic fields. He immediately drew a diagram in the sand with a stick, capturing the design of what would become the AC (alternating current) induction motor, a breakthrough that would eventually power the modern world. Tesla later claimed he could mentally test and refine inventions with such detail that he didn't need to build prototypes until they were perfect in his head. He stated: "It is immaterial to me whether I run my machine in my mind or test it in my shop."

1. REDUCE "OPEN LOOPS"

Every unfinished task or thought is mental clutter. When you have too many loose ends, your brain constantly jumps between them, trying to remind you of what's unfinished.*

The fix is what I call a "Brain Dump."

* The Zeigarnik effect. See footnote on page 75.

I sit down, let my thoughts spill out onto paper, and just write. No structure, no filter—just a free-flowing purge of whatever is taking up space in my head. After a few minutes, I usually have a full page of this stuff; mostly noise. But when I'm done, I feel a million times lighter. Suddenly, my actual work target becomes clearer.

But I don't stop there. Once the mental clutter is out, I comb through the mess to find what matters. Sometimes I spot actual important to-dos, clear, actionable items I can pull and prioritize. Other times, the dump is just noise: random thoughts, worries, distractions. But even then, the act of spilling it all out clears the fog in my mind. It's only once it's on the page that I can decide what truly needs my attention.

From there, I make a list. Not a rigid schedule but a simple breakdown of priority tasks that deserve focus, and smaller to-dos that were taking up mental bandwidth. Writing them down doesn't mean I have to do them all right away, though. It's more about off-loading them so my brain knows they're handled. They're no longer bouncing around in my head, demanding attention. Approaching my thoughts in this way, I'm not just reacting to whatever pops up; I'm choosing what to focus on, with a clearer mind.

This is just one method, but there are plenty of ways to do the same thing (journaling, to-do lists, note-taking systems, etc.). The key is to clear your mental storage so you can focus on what's in front of you.

2. ELIMINATE POTENTIAL DISTRACTIONS

This one's obvious, but let's be honest, you already know exactly what's going to distract you. The goal here is to plan and remove those distractions before they sabotage you.

- If your phone is a problem, *put it in another room.* Or turn it off entirely. Research finds that you're better off with your phone out of reach.*
- If you're on your computer, *close all your extra or unnecessary tabs.* Use a website blocker,† or even turn off your Wi-Fi if you can.
- If your environment is noisy, *use noise-canceling headphones or move somewhere quiet.*
- If your kids or roommates interrupt you, *set boundaries.* Make it clear when you're unavailable and make yourself harder to reach.

---

* Adrian F. Ward et al., "Brain Drain: The Mere Presence of One's Own Smartphone Reduces Available Cognitive Capacity," *Journal of the Association for Consumer Research* 2, no. 2 (April 2017); Chelsea M. Cutino and Michael A. Nees, "Restricting Mobile Phone Access During Homework Increases Attainment of Study Goals," *Mobile Media & Communication* 5, no. 1 (January 2017): 63–79.

† See the end of the chapter (page 80) for specific recommendations for some of these tools.

- If your workspace is a mess, *clean it up*. Clutter can cause more cognitive overload.

Listen, I get it. Some distractions can't be eliminated entirely. But if you *know* something derails your focus, and you know it's preventing you from making real progress, then *do something about it*. It might be uncomfortable at first, but once you start getting deep, uninterrupted work done, you'll realize it's worth it.

3. FIND YOUR "FOCUS ZONE"

Create a *dedicated place* for deep work. If you always work in the same spot, your brain will start associating it with focus, making it easier to drop in.

For this to work, your Focus Zone needs to be used *only* for deep work. If you start answering emails or scrolling social media in that space, the effect is ruined. Keep distractions *out*.

You can also create additional focus cues. For example, wear the same hoodie or sit in the same chair every time you work. Over time, these triggers will signal your brain: *Time to lock in*. Think of it as a Pavlovian response to productivity.

4. CUT THE JUNK WITH AN "ATTENTION DIET"

Just as your body performs better with a clean diet, your brain performs better when you limit junk inputs. If your day is filled with social media, clickbait, and endless notifications, your brain gets stuck in *shallow focus*.

Try a 30-Day Attention Diet:

- Cut social media. If that's too much, drastically limit it.
- Only consume high-quality content. Books, long-form podcasts, documentaries—things that awaken your brain and move the needle for you.
- Spend at least one hour a day in deep focus. Reading, writing, learning a skill—something that requires full attention.

Do this for a month, and you'll feel like your brain has rebooted. Focus will come easier, and distractions won't feel as irresistible.

5. THE POMODORO TECHNIQUE

The Pomodoro Technique is a simple but powerful way to stay focused while avoiding burnout. Developed by Francesco Cirillo in the 1980s, it's based on the idea that short, structured bursts of work—followed by brief breaks—allow you to sustain concentration for longer periods.

How it works:

1. Set a timer for twenty-five minutes—work on a single task with no distractions (it can be a different length of time, but twenty-five minutes seems to be the sweet spot).
2. When the timer goes off, take a five-minute break—step away, stretch, breathe.
3. Repeat this cycle three to four times, then take a longer break (fifteen to thirty minutes).
4. Repeat as needed.

This method works because it creates urgency (forcing you to start) while also giving your brain just enough recovery time to avoid burnout.

An interesting study from 2019 found that using a cell phone during a break lead to greater mental depletion and poorer performance on subsequent tasks, compared with other break activities (suggesting that phones may not provide the mental recharge other types of breaks offer).* So when taking your five-minute break, try doing something that doesn't involve your phone or checking your email. Do a lower-intensity task. You just worked hard for twenty-five minutes, why overstimulate your mind even further during your break? Your mind should be doing less during the break, not more. The best results (in terms of staying in that focused mindset) will happen if you limit your breaks to things like going for a walk, snuggling with your dog, getting a snack, staring out the window, stretching—in other words, *relaxing*. Things that lower the bar of what is interesting for your mind—boring even—so that when it gets back to work, your mind is ready to go, interested, and motivated again.

Anyone can focus for twenty-five minutes, right? That's why this works. It's short enough to feel manageable but long enough to make real progress. If you're locked in and don't want to break your flow after twenty minutes, you can stack multiple Pomodoros together for longer deep work sessions:

- Work fifty minutes → Take a ten-minute break.
- Work seventy-five minutes → Take a fifteen- to twenty-minute break.

Find a rhythm that works for you. And instead of relying on a phone timer (which can tempt you to check notifications), use a kitchen timer, an hourglass, or a distraction-free Pomodoro app.

---

* Sanghoon Kang and Terri R. Kurtzberg, "Reach for Your Cell Phone at Your Own Risk: The Cognitive Costs of Media Choice for Breaks," *Journal of Behavioral Addiction* 8, no. 3 (September 2019): 395–403.

6. MAKE YOUR WORK AUTOTELIC

One of the best ways to stay focused is to make your work *autotelic*—to do it for its own sake. Think about the things you love: playing guitar, sketching, running, whatever it may be. Those things don't require a reward dangled in front of you to keep going. You do those things because the acts themselves are satisfying. If you can train your brain to find that same spark of enjoyment in the more challenging tasks you're trying to focus on, suddenly they'll stop feeling like chores. They'll become little challenges, games, or chances to improve. That shift in mindset will keep you locked in and focused far longer than willpower or external motivation ever could.

Finding joy in the task itself is easier said than done, though. A helpful trick is to break your big goals into smaller, simpler steps that can feel more autotelic, more rewarding in the *doing* rather than just in the *finishing*. For example, instead of thinking *I need to clean the entire house*, break it down into micro-tasks like wiping down one counter, folding five shirts, or sweeping a single room. Each of these smaller actions can be satisfying on its own, almost like leveling up in a game.

7. CREATE A "SHUTDOWN RITUAL"

A lot of context-switching comes from unfinished work lingering in your brain after hours. If you don't properly shut down your brain at the end of the day, it stays in "open loop" mode, making it harder to focus the next morning.*

A shutdown ritual doesn't need to be fancy. Just a simple end-of-day routine to signal to your brain that work is done:

- Review what you accomplished. Take note of progress.
- Plan your top priorities for the next day. Write them down.
- Close your laptop, put your phone away, and walk away.
- No more work until the next day or scheduled deep work session. Honor that boundary.

This tells your brain: *We're done. Time to recharge.*

If you never set clear boundaries between work and nonwork time, your brain will always be "on." This leads to more task-switching, more distractions, and less progress. If you train yourself to properly shut down right before bed (not just after you complete the task), you'll focus better when you restart.

---

* This idea aligns with the Zeigarnik Effect, a psychological phenomenon where people remember uncompleted tasks a lot more than completed ones, leading to mental tension. Bluma Zeigarnik, "On Finished and Unfinished Tasks," *Psychological Research* 9, no. 1 (1927): 1–85.

THE MULTITASKING MYTH

Let's take a moment to talk about multitasking. Because that's *really* what we're talking about when we say task-switching. And I know what some of you are thinking: *But, Nelson, I can multitask really well!*

No, you can't. No one can. And there's plenty of research to back that up.

Most people swear they're great at multitasking. They can listen to a podcast while responding to emails or scroll through social media while working on a project. But your brain isn't *actually* multitasking; it's task-switching. And it's doing a terrible job at it.

I should clarify that multitasking comes in two main forms: task-switching and *dual-tasking*. Dual-tasking is when you're genuinely doing two things at the same time that draw on different resources—say, one motor and one verbal. Those can overlap with little interference. Walking on a treadmill while having a phone conversation is a good example; the tasks don't really trip each other up. But when both activities demand the same resource, like trying to write an email while listening to a podcast, performance tends to suffer quickly. In that case, you're not handling both at once (even though it may feel like you are); you're actually task-switching. Focusing on your email for a moment, then flipping to the conversation, then back again, bouncing between the two.*

The research is clear; our brains are not wired to handle multiple cognitive tasks at once. You think you're multitasking, but actually, your brain is rapidly switching between tasks, and each switch comes at a cost. A Stanford University study† found that people who consider themselves "high multitaskers" performed worse on cognitive tasks than those who focused on one thing at a time—they were more prone to distractions, struggled with information retention, and had difficulty switching between tasks.

So why do so many people think they're good at multitasking? Because they mistake busyness for productivity. The small hit of dopamine from switching tasks is mistaken for progress. Really, you're doing each task more poorly and inefficiently.

Have you ever typed out an email while half listening to a meeting, only

---

* There are a few people, however (about 2.5 percent of the population), who can efficiently switch their attention between different, complex activities. Odds are you are not one of these people, though. Most brains just aren't set up that way. Jason M. Watson and David L. Strayer, "Supertaskers: Profiles in Extraordinary Multitasking Ability," *Psychonomic Bulletin & Review* 17, no. 4 (August 2010): 479–85.

† Eyal Ophir, Clifford Nass, and Anthony D. Wagner, "Cognitive Control in Media Multitaskers," *Proceedings of the National Academy of Sciences* 106, no. 37 (2009): 15583–87.

to realize you absorbed none of the discussion? Or tried reading a book while watching TV, then suddenly realized you have no idea what you just read? That's proof that your brain can't fully process multiple high-level tasks at once.

Multitasking has high costs. You're more likely to make mistakes. Studies show that switching between tasks can reduce productivity by up to 40 percent; you're actually working slower.* And when your focus is split, your brain doesn't encode information properly, meaning you retain less (and you know I hate *that*).

So, if you really want to work more efficiently and focus better, the solution is simple: Stop multitasking and commit to deep, single-tasking work.

Task-switching may feel like productivity, but it drains mental energy, slows you down, and kills deep focus. Train yourself to stay locked into one task longer, and you'll get more done, in less time, at a higher quality.

Oh, and one more thing: Research shows people who constantly media multitask have physically smaller gray matter in the part of their brain responsible for focus and self-control. We can't prove multitasking caused it, but maybe don't test that theory with your own brain.†

MEDITATION AND BREATHING

Once you've eliminated distractions and master staying on task, how do you actually lock in? Just because you're not physically jumping between tasks, that doesn't mean your mind isn't wandering.

This is where meditation and focused breathing help. These techniques train your brain to hone your attention and silence mental noise.

When I first started training for the USA Memory Championships, I competed in an event called 5-Minute Numbers. It's pretty straightforward: memorize as many digits as possible in five minutes.‡ At first, I focused on getting faster at encoding the numbers into mental images (just like we talked about in chapter 1). But eventually, I hit a wall. My speed maxed out.

That's when I realized that the only way to get faster was to eliminate the mental noise that slowed down my mind while creating the images.

---

* Joshua S. Rubinstein, David E. Meyer, and Jeffrey E. Evans, "Executive Control of Cognitive Processes in Task Switching," *Journal of Experimental Psychology: Human Perception and Performance* 27, no. 4 (2001): 763–97.

† Kep Kee Loh and Ryota Kanai, "Higher Media Multi-Tasking Activity Is Associated with Smaller Gray-Matter Density in the Anterior Cingulate Cortex," *PLoS One* 9, no. 9 (September 2014): e106698.

‡ At one point I had the US record: 339 digits. It may sound impressive, but the current world record sits at a whopping 642 digits, achieved by Wei Qinru of China.

Even though I thought I was locked in, my brain would stray—just for a moment—in between encoding those sets of numbers, and tiny lapses in attention added up. So, whenever I caught my mind wandering, I'd immediately bring it back to the numbers. Over and over. Just as in meditation, where you train yourself to notice when your mind drifts.

GENIUS PROFILE: BRUCE LEE

Bruce Lee was a master of the mind. His ability to eliminate distractions, refine his training, and sharpen his focus made him one of the most disciplined thinkers of his time.

One lesser-known but essential aspect of Bruce Lee's genius was his relentless commitment to refined repetition. He trained hard, with surgical precision. For example, he would spend hours practicing the exact same punch or kick, obsessively fine-tuning every micromovement until it was fast, clean, and automatic. Lee understood, intuitively, the power of muscle memory and deliberate practice long before it was widely studied. His famous quote, "I fear not the man who has practiced ten thousand kicks once, but the man who has practiced one kick ten thousand times," perfectly captured this mindset. His speed and accuracy were so refined that he could reportedly snatch a coin from a person's open palm before their fingers could close—a feat of timing and reaction that stunned even those who trained with him.

I didn't call it meditation but instead thought of it as mental training for memory competitions. Years later, though, after my time at the Monroe Institute, I realized that's exactly what I had been doing all along.

Meditation sometimes gets a bad rap for being New Agey, with critics pointing to methodological problems in the research and concerns that many studies show overly optimistic interpretations of modest results.* But the research is far more nuanced. In fact, many recent studies show the opposite, that meditation can be remarkably effective for focus and attention. Regular practice has been linked to positive changes in brain structure, stronger emotional regulation, and greater stress resilience. It has also been shown to sharpen how quickly we can direct attention, reduce mind-wandering, and improve overall attentional control.†

Studies show that just four days of brief meditation training—twenty minutes per day—can improve concentration, cognitive control, and working memory.‡ If you want laser focus, meditation is a tool you can't ignore.

There are *countless* ways to meditate, and entire books dedicated to the practice. But here are two simple things I do before deep work sessions that have made a huge difference.

1. BREATHWORK—THE PRE-FOCUS RESET

Before I start any serious focus work, I do this simple breathing exercise to reset my brain:

- **Inhale deeply through your nose for about five seconds.**
- **Hold for three to five seconds.**
- **Exhale slowly through your mouth for about fifteen to twenty seconds (super slowly), until your lungs are completely empty.**
- **Repeat for two to three minutes.**

That's it.

This kind of controlled breathing sends a signal to your brain to calm down, refocus, and let go of distractions. It's also a great way to reset your focus anytime you feel your attention slipping. It's simple and easy to try!

---

* N. T. Van Dam et al., "Mind the Hype: A Critical Evaluation and Prescriptive Agenda for Research on Mindfulness and Meditation," *Perspectives on Psychological Science* 13, no. 1 (January 2018): 36–61.

† Andy Jeesu Kim, et al., "The Effects of Mindfulness Meditation on Mechanisms of Attentional Control in Young and Older Adults: A Preregistered Eye Tracking Study," *eNeuro* 12, no. 7 (July 2025), https://doi.org/10.1523/ENEURO.0356-23.2025.

‡ Fadel Zeidan et al., "Mindfulness Meditation Improves Cognition: Evidence of Brief Mental Training," *Consciousness and Cognition* 19, no. 2 (2010): 597–605.

2. SHORT DAILY MEDITATION—TRAINING YOUR ATTENTION MUSCLE

I'm not sitting on a mountain in lotus pose for hours a day, I promise. I keep it simple. Just five to ten minutes a day is enough to see results.

Here's the protocol:

- **Find a relaxing area, ideally removed from noise. Sit comfortably and close your eyes.**
- **Focus on your breath. Feel it come in, feel it go out.**
- **When your mind wanders, bring it back to your breath. *Always* to your breath.**
- **Repeat for a pre-decided amount of time.**

At first, your mind will wander constantly. You'll think about work, random memories, song lyrics, what's making that noise upstairs, whether penguins have knees—anything but your breath. That's totally normal, and okay. The whole point isn't to *never* get distracted. It's to notice when you *do* and train yourself to bring your focus back.

Be consistent with this practice and you'll find that you'll be able to hold focus for longer stretches. Not just in meditation but in every aspect of your life.

Even if you can manage only one or two minutes at first, don't get discouraged. Monks spend entire lifetimes mastering this skill. You just need to tap into it frequently enough to make a difference in your ability to focus.

Meditation is something that takes practice; you won't become a Zen master overnight. But you will feel the benefits of it almost immediately. And it's one of the oldest and most battle-tested techniques for sharpening focus, reducing distractions, and improving mental clarity. There's a reason why people have been doing it for thousands of years. Learning to quiet the noise trains your mind to stay present and can unlock that holy grail of unwavering, unrelenting focus.

There's no single way to master focus. You have to find what works for you. Experiment. Try out some of the strategies in this chapter. Find what gets you in the zone. Once you do, lock in and use it.

Focus is what separates the doers from the dreamers. You can't show even a glimmer of genius without it.

EXERCISES AND RESOURCES

- **Try a Pomodoro session next time you sit down to get work done: 25 minutes on, 5 minutes off. Repeat four times, then take a longer break. Simple. Proven.**

- **Sounds insane, but try this: Draw a black dot on paper. Stare at it for 60 seconds. Do nothing else. Eliminate any other thoughts. Feel how hard that is? Good. You're training focus. Can you master 60 seconds? Then try 5 minutes.**
- **Single-Task Timer: Pick one task. Set a 10-minute timer. Your goal is to not switch tasks. Not even once.**
- **As an alternative to the breathing pattern I suggested earlier in this chapter, try box breathing: Inhale 4 seconds, hold 4 seconds, exhale 4 seconds, hold 4 seconds. Do this for a few minutes before a deep work session. It's designed to calm the mind and body by regulating the breath and activating the parasympathetic nervous system.***
- **Try 5 minutes of focused-attention meditation, just on your breath. Whenever your mind drifts, gently bring it back. Over time, increase the duration.**

Here are some focus/meditation resources:

BOOKS:

- ***Deep Work* by Cal Newport—The playbook for getting into the zone.**
- ***Indistractable* by Nir Eyal—For mastering your attention in the digital age.**
- ***The Practicing Mind* by Thomas M. Sterner—Zen-like wisdom on staying present.**

APPS/WEBSITES:

- **Forest App (www.forestapp.cc)—Grow a tree every time you stay focused. Break concentration? The tree dies. Guilt-powered productivity.**
- **The Monroe Institute's Expand App (https://info.monroeinstitute.org/get-expand-app)—A fantastic meditation app that uses the sound science developed at the Monroe Institute.**
- **Pomofocus.io—A minimalist Pomodoro timer to help structure study/break cycles.**
- **Brain.fm—Music app scientifically designed to boost focus.**
- **Cold Turkey (https://getcoldturkey.com)—Hardcore website blocker. (Not for the faint of heart.)**

---

* The parasympathetic nervous system is your body's built-in focus enhancer. Slow, steady breathing activates it, quieting stress and boosting concentration.

CHAPTER 4

LEARNING MASTERY

"LEARNING NEVER EXHAUSTS THE MIND."
—LEONARDO DA VINCI

IT'S SEPTEMBER 21, 2016—COINCIDENTALLY, WORLD ALZHEIMER'S DAY—AND I'M SITTING AT A DESK, FACING THREE JUDGES. BEHIND ME IS A GIANT SCREEN DISPLAYING TEN THOUSAND DIGITS OF PI. I'M MID-ATTEMPT AT TRYING TO BREAK A MEMORY RECORD BY RECALLING SECTIONS OF ITS DIGITS. WITH SEVERAL MORE RECALLS TO GO, THE WORLD RECORD IS CLOSE TO BEING MINE.

ONE OF THE JUDGES CALLS OUT, "6-5-3-1-9."

I PAUSE. FOR THE FIRST TIME, I'M STUMPED. I'M SUPPOSED TO REPLY WITH THE NUMBERS SURROUNDING THIS SEQUENCE. AS THE STOP-WATCH TICKS ON, I'M BECOMING INCREASINGLY MORE FRANTIC, WILDLY SEARCHING MY BRAIN FOR THIS FIVE-DIGIT SEQUENCE, SOMEWHERE BURIED WITHIN THOSE FIRST TEN THOUSAND DIGITS OF PI.

Pi is an irrational number, meaning it can't be expressed as a simple fraction. Its decimal representation goes on forever without repeating. Most people know just the first few digits (3.14), which is more than enough for any practical use. I've memorized the first *ten thousand.*

Memorizing and reciting a lot of digits of pi has recently become a common practice for number enthusiasts, or anyone who wants to flex their memory abilities.*

But my record attempt is a bit different. It's a memory matrix record, meaning that I need to know ten thousand digits inside and out, not just in one order. The record description officially reads as: *The first ten thousand digits of pi are divided into two thousand five-digit blocks. The testers call out one of these five-digit sequences, and the candidate must reply with the five-digit numbers on either side of the number chosen. This happens fifty times.* The record is the cumulative time it takes to correctly answer all fifty (any mistakes, and the attempt is over).

I was panicking. I'd narrowed down 65319's location to somewhere in the five thousand to seven thousand digits of pi, but I couldn't seem to get any more clarity. In my wild world of mnemonics, this particular sequence translates to the image of Steve Vai (the virtuoso guitar player made famous in the eighties and nineties) kickflipping a skateboard. The image of him doing this was incredibly clear in my mind, and I was sure it was in a Memory Palace that is either inside or outside of my parents' Miami home, which spans the five-thousandth to seven-thousandth digit range. I just couldn't find the exact location.

I looked over at the clock and I saw the seconds ticking by. I had a chance to beat the current record of 16 minutes and 38.35 seconds, but the timer had just turned over the fourteen-minute mark and I still had about eight more recalls to go. It wasn't looking good.

My eyes were closed as I mentally zipped through the locations in my parents' Memory Palace. I scanned the rear portion of their home, walking through the back door and out onto the back patio.

Okay, the outside table, that's Jermaine from Flight of the Conchords *dodging bullets. Next to that, by the back Ping-Pong table, it's* a Lord of the Rings–*style orc slap shotting a hockey puck. And then next it's . . . AHA!*

---

* Genius fact: In 2006, Akira Haraguchi of Japan claimed 100,000 digits of π (later saying he reached 111,700 in 2015), though these were never recognized by Guinness due to his requiring multiple breaks, as well as other verification issues. The current Guinness World Record belongs to Rajveer Meena of India, who officially recited 70,000 digits on March 21, 2015, in nine hours and twenty-seven minutes under full Guinness oversight. Just months later, fellow Indian memorist Suresh Sharma recited 70,030 digits in seventeen hours and fourteen minutes, a feat recognized by the Limca Book of Records and the Pi World Ranking List but not Guinness.

There he is! It's Steve Vai in all his eccentric glory, doing kickflips by the BBQ grill!

"The five digits before are 3-4-3-1-4," I recalled to the judges.

The judges nodded.

"The five digits after . . . are 7-7-7-7-5," I continued.

Silence. Too long of a silence . . .

The judges looked at each other.

"I'm sorry, Nelson. That ends your attempt. The correct five digits following the number were 7-7-7-7 . . . - **4**. You were off by one digit . . ."

I was crushed. Of *course* it was a 4! The image for 77774 is my undergraduate physics professor, Dr. Gunderson, rigging a mouse trap. Ending that sequence with a 5 instead would have been Gunderson ogling over a shiny jewel, which isn't an image that exists in my palace. Frustratingly, the mental flub boiled down to a mental decoding error, rather than an actual recall error.

In an instant, my attempt at one of the most prestigious memory records in existence had come crashing down. I knew I *knew* those ten thousand digits, but that day was not my day. The record would have to wait for another time.

Still, as I sat there processing the defeat, a strange calm washed over me. I wasn't angry. I wasn't devastated. Because deep down, I knew why I was doing this. That clarity—that *why*—is what had driven me to spend countless hours building my Memory Palaces, encoding all those digits of Pi, and chasing what most would consider an insane goal.

So, before we go any further, let's rewind and look at how I got here in the first place. It all started with a "why."

YOUR WHY

Whether it be memorizing thousands of digits of pi, learning how to fix and maintain your car, or becoming a walking encyclopedia for ancient Egyptology, mastering whatever field you want to be regarded as a genius in (or even simply knowledgeable about) isn't all that complicated. At least, the road map getting there isn't too complicated to understand.

But the first step is probably the most crucial.

Whatever it is that you want to learn and master, I would presume (and hope) that you actually *want* to learn it. For example, sure, I'd *love* to be able to speak Russian, but do I want to? Do I want to take time out of my already busy schedule and devote it to learning Russian? Not really. Not now, anyways. So, diving into Russian right now probably wouldn't pan out the way I'd want.

The key is: *You need to have the desire to achieve said learning goal.* You need a reason *why* you will repeatedly, continuously work on this particular skill or knowledge set.

This may sound obvious to some, but not many people take the time to think about it at depth. Sometimes your *why* may be obvious, other times it may need a moment or two to make itself known. Either way, it needs to be defined.

GENIUS PROFILE:
ADA LOVELACE

In 1843, Ada Lovelace (who is now widely recognized as the world's first computer programmer) was asked to translate a paper by Italian mathematician Luigi Menabrea on Charles Babbage's proposed Analytical Engine. She did far more than translate it, she added a series of extensive notes that ended up being three times longer than the original paper. In these notes, she described how the machine could follow a sequence of instructions to manipulate symbols, essentially outlining the world's first computer algorithm.

But what truly set her apart was her vision. Ada had a WHY. She believed the Analytical Engine could go beyond mere calculation. She imagined it composing music, processing language, even generating art—decades before the first real computer came into existence. That deep sense of purpose is what fueled her genius.

DEFINE YOUR WHY

STOP right now. Go grab a pen and a sheet of paper.

Next, write down the thing you're keen on learning or learning about. Anything! Once you've done that, next to that thing, write *why* you want to learn it. Be honest with yourself. Once you've written *that* down, go back and ask yourself *why** you want that why.

For example's sake, let's say I want to learn to play the trumpet. On my first pass, my *WHY* might be: *because I love the way jazz trumpet sounds.*

Okay, that's a fine first pass, but not a great *WHY*. Why not? Think about this future scenario: You've committed yourself to learning the trumpet. You've bought yourself a trumpet, you've set up trumpet lessons with a local teacher, you've even invested in some books and accessories. You are all set and super excited to start. A few weeks pass, you've had multiple weekly lessons, you've been practicing diligently—all is good.

But then, after a few months, you notice that the rapid progress you were making at the beginning isn't as drastically noticeable anymore. You're becoming a bit bored with the monotony of practicing your scales and playing the same dull introductory pieces of music. *Why am I not Miles Davis yet?!* you might think to yourself.

This is when you remember your *WHY*. You remember that you started learning the trumpet because jazz trumpet sounds cool. Well, dang. Surprise, surprise. That doesn't really give you any added motivation to pick up the trumpet and practice. In fact, maybe the funk you're in frustrates you even more because it just reminds you of how far you still have to go.

What if your WHY had been this instead: *I love the way jazz music sounds because it reminds me of my father, who passed away recently. And when I hear the music, I feel like he is still with me. I want to learn the trumpet because it will keep a piece of my father alive within me.*

Now THAT! *That's* a WHY!

Next time you feel a bit of a drag picking up that trumpet, you'll remember why you started learning in the first place, be deeply inspired to honor your father, and it will be such a purer, more powerful motivator. If you can't come up with substantial *WHY* for your goal, then it's probably a good indication that you don't really want to learn that thing, deep down. Because true learning starts with this clear defining of purpose; it starts with defining your *WHY*. That's not to say you can't learn something without it. But when it comes to deep, lasting learning—the kind that sticks and grows over time—it's much harder without that underlying reason driving you forward.

* To avoid confusion, I'll capitalize the bigger WHY, so you know when I'm referring to the core reason, not just the word "why."

So that's why, before I tackle any learning or skill-acquisition endeavor, I always tackle this question first. Without it, I'm destined for failure. Having a strong *WHY* becomes the superpower that carries you through your knowledge-learning quests.

Once you've defined your *WHY* and it's set in stone, it's time to start going after the dang thing. Where do we start?

HOW TO STUDY BETTER

It's no secret why this book started off with a chapter about memory techniques, followed by a chapter on reading, and then a chapter about focus and concentration after that. Arguably, mastering memory techniques, reading, and focus will allow you to learn *anything*, much more efficiently and infinitely faster (including ten thousand digits of pi . . . or more!), while also retaining it.

There's really nothing genius about memorizing so many digits of pi. In fact, there's generally nothing genius about memorizing a lot of *any* particular thing. People have been memorizing large amounts of data since the dawn of civilization. That being said, we still need to learn how to integrate all our skills together. To truly learn anything, we need to be better (and smarter) at reviewing.

THE BRAIN'S TWO LEARNING SYSTEMS

Our brains like to forget. We retain information in levels of priority. If it's something you don't ever use, then why would your brain waste any of its processing power to keep it? While that may be true, there are plenty of instances when retaining less-used information is just as important as (if not more important than) remembering frequently used information. To be seen as a genius, you need to be able to access information that you've mentally stored, quickly, no matter how much time has passed since you first learned it.

We haven't gone deep into brain science in this book, but here's a quick breakdown that'll help this next idea make sense. When it comes to memory, your brain handles information in two main ways: declarative and procedural. *Declarative* memory is the stuff you *know*—facts, figures, names, places—the kind of things you can intentionally recall, write down, and as the name suggests, declare (like the techniques we covered back in chapter 1). The other way is *procedural*. This is akin to things that are "muscle memory"—things you know, but you don't really have to think about to recall them. Think of your fingers dancing across the piano keys, almost having a life of their own, as they play a piece you practiced for hours on end as a child but has somehow never left your memory.

One way to tell if something is procedural is this: The moment you try to slow down and *think* about it, it actually becomes harder to do. Procedural memory works best when you're not consciously analyzing it; it's automatic, almost invisible. You use it every day without realizing it, whether it's riding a bike, typing, or tying your shoes. Declarative memory, on the other hand, works differently. It's the kind of memory you *do* think about—facts and information you consciously try to remember. This kind of data typically moves from your short-term or working memory into long-term storage through a more deliberate process, one we can actively train and improve.

While the declarative system may seem a little more reliable to use (in the sense that you can consciously go retrieve things), it can be a slower lookup/retrieval process. One benefit to using the declarative system is that there are many quick and powerful techniques that work so well with it. The other benefit is that once you've learned some information, you can store it away, and potentially review it enough to the point that that declarative information *becomes* procedural.

You may, for example, memorize a poem declaratively, and then after practicing it extensively, you eventually might get to a point where you just *know* it and can say it without having to mentally look *anything* up at all, without thinking. That's procedural.

Procedural sounds like the goal, doesn't it? To be able to instantly recall something without any effort or awareness of how we're doing it? Most definitely! The downside to procedural memory is that it takes *a lot* of time and effort to get information to that point. Remember that last step I taught you in chapter 1 to remember anything? It was all about review. In other words, declare! Declare all the stuff! Do it! Constantly. Over and over again. So that said *stuff* becomes procedural. Unfortunately, there is no *quick* hack to do this. But there are two well-studied methods for jump-starting our brain into this ideal recall mode: spaced repetition and interleaving.

SPACED REPETITION

Imagine you're learning something new—a language, a complex theory, or even a dance routine. You dive in, absorb the basics, use some declarative techniques, and feel pretty good. Now it's time for some *active recall*. Active recall is the act of retrieving information from memory without looking at your notes or materials. Instead of passively rereading, you force yourself to produce the answer: What were the key points? How does this concept work? What's the formula? This retrieval process itself strengthens memory far more than passive review. Before anything, actively recalling what you're trying to learn is the place you need to start. Yes, it's hard (obviously it's much easier to look back at your notes and say "Ah yes, there it is" and convince yourself you know it), but that's the whole point. When you're feeling challenged while recalling something, your memory is actually working out, building the neural pathways to make future recall of that information better and more reliable. You're actually making it stick for the long term.

This is a prime example of what psychologists call a "desirable difficulty": something that feels harder in the moment but produces dramatically better long-term retention. Any time you can insert some desirable difficulty (key word here: desirable—don't make it undesirable!), you're doing the proper work to make something memorable long-term. The harder you have to work to pull something from memory, the stronger that memory becomes.

Spaced repetition takes active recall a step further by suggesting that you should repeat this retrieval process spaced out over time. That is to say, not all in the same session.

When you first learn something new, your brain works to build fresh pathways between neurons. That's how learning occurs. At first, these pathways are weak and inefficient, which is why new information often feels confusing or harder to recall. But giving your brain a break helps. During rest, your brain starts to consolidate what you just learned, reinforcing those pathways and making the connections stronger and more efficient. The real magic happens when you revisit the material after that break. Repeat this over time, initially with shorter breaks between study sessions, then longer breaks as the information becomes more familiar, and you'll have a recipe for *really* retaining that information for the long term.

Back in the late 1800s, Hermann Ebbinghaus, a German psychologist who studied memory, discovered the forgetting curve, which is a model of the exponential loss of information from memory without any recall; a curve we all (as humans) have to deal with. Through meticulous self-experimentation, Ebbinghaus memorized lists of nonsense syllables and tracked how quickly he forgot them. He found that forgetting occurs rapidly

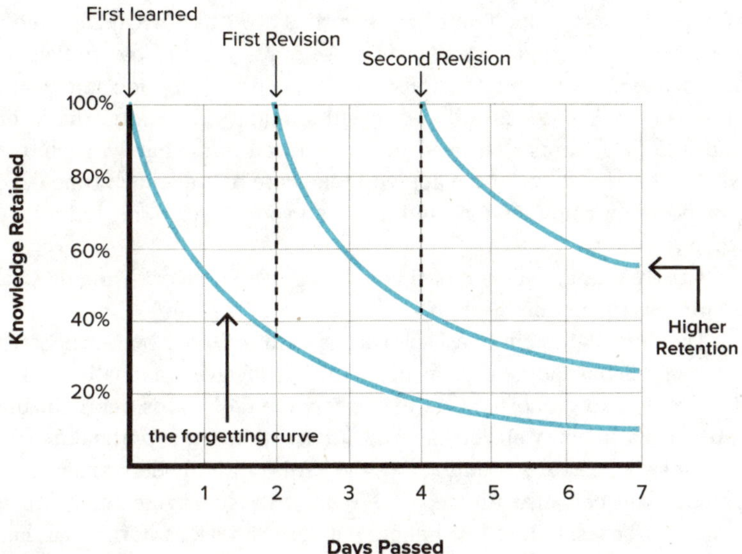

at first and then levels off over time. He also discovered that with spaced repetition, he was able to combat that natural tendency to forget. Each time he reviewed the information (after a certain period of time without review), the forgetting curve appeared to level out at a higher and higher level of retention (see the chart in next page).

In other words, Hermann's results gave us the permission to spread out our study sessions with time, instead of having to cram all our studying into one lengthy marathon session (we've all been there, fueled by caffeine and sheer willpower, right?). This way, your brain can organize the information with a better system before you revisit it.

Turns out the science backs this up in a big way too. Spaced repetition isn't just a nice idea; it's been tested again and again, and the results are impossible to ignore. A 2025 meta-analysis in math education showed that when students spread out their study sessions over time, their learning stuck far better than when they crammed it all at once.* And it's not just kids in classrooms. In one of the largest studies ever run on this, more than twenty-six thousand physicians used spaced review to keep critical medical

* E. Murray et al., "A Meta-analytic Review of the Effectiveness of Spacing and Retrieval Practice for Mathematics Learning." *Educational Psychology Review* 37, no. 1 (2025): Article 75.

knowledge fresh. The results were stronger recall and, even more importantly, an improved ability to apply what they learned when it mattered.*

So how do you practice spaced repetition? Luckily, there are plenty of apps that can help. Two of my favorites are Anki or Quizlet (see page 101 for a more exhaustive list). In these apps, you can create flash cards and designate whether the information is something you know, sort of know, or don't know at all, and it will automatically group the information into flash cards that need to be reviewed immediately, soon, or in a while. The algorithm in the app will take care of how much time needs to pass between study sessions and will send you notifications reminding you when to study.

A more manual version of this (and a personal favorite analog strategy of mine) is the Leitner System.

The Leitner System is a flash card system invented by German science journalist Sebastian Leitner in the 1970s. It involves manually organizing flash cards into groups and, as you review the flash cards, reorganizing the cards based on how well you know the information at that particular moment.

Typically, a box is used to store the cards, with dividers to separate the groups (you can also use separate boxes). Let's imagine there are three groups, or boxes. In Box 1 you might put flash cards for information that you may *not have learned yet*, in Box 2 flash cards you know pretty well, and in Box 3 flash cards you know *really* well. All cards start in Box 1, and as you review them, if you get any right, you promote those cards to Box 2. Anything you get wrong stays in Box 1. Cards in Box 1 get reviewed more often (based on a predefined schedule), while those in Box 2 get reviewed less often (and Box 3 even far less or rarely at all). When you review the cards from Box 1 and get them correct, they advance to Box 2; the same with those from Box 2 to Box 3. If incorrect, those cards go all the way back to Box 1 (see the chart opposite). Determining a review schedule for each box is also important. You might, for example, decide that Box 1 gets reviewed daily. Box 2 every couple of days, and Box 3 once a week (or even every other week).

Any number of Leitner boxes can be used, but traditionally, a five-box Leitner System is most common (and what I like to use). The idea is simple: Box 1 holds newly learned material. As you correctly recall an item, it moves up to the next box. The higher the box, the less frequently you review it (because you're more confident with it). Box 5 is your "I know this cold" tier. The following is the Leitner review schedule I use, optimized for a one-month study period (which you can then reset and repeat): I review Box 1

---

* David W. Price et al., "The Effect of Spaced Repetition on Learning and Knowledge Transfer in a Large Cohort of Practicing Physicians," *Academic Medicine* 100, no. 1 (2025): 94–102, https://pubmed.ncbi.nlm.nih.gov/39250798/.

MY PREFERRED LEITNER REVIEW SCHEDULE

Day 0 Box 1		
Day 1 Box 2, Box 1	**Day 11** Box 2, Box 1	**Day 21** Box 2, Box 1
Day 2 Box 3, Box 1	**Day 12** Box 5, Box 1	**Day 22** Box 3, Box 1
Day 3 Box 2, Box 1	**Day 13** Box 4, Box 2, Box 1	**Day 23** Box 2, Box 1
Day 4 Box 4, Box 1	**Day 14** Box 3, Box 1	**Day 24** Box 1
Day 5 Box 2, Box 1	**Day 15** Box 2, Box 1	**Day 25** Box 2, Box 1
Day 6 Box 3, Box 1	**Day 16** Box 1	**Day 26** Box 3, Box 1
Day 7 Box 2, Box 1	**Day 17** Box 2, Box 1	**Day 27** Box 2, Box 1
Day 8 Box 1	**Day 18** Box 3, Box 1	**Day 28** Box 5, Box 1
Day 9 Box 2, Box 1	**Day 19** Box 2, Box 1	**Day 29** Box 4, Box 2, Box 1
Day 10 Box 3, Box 1	**Day 20** Box 4, Box 1	**Day 30** Box 3, Box 1

every day, Box 2 every other day, Box 3 eight times a month (roughly every fourth day), Box 4 four times a month, and finally Box 5 twice a month. The goal, of course, is to get all the cards into Box 5.

Here is the core of the Leitner System broken down step-by-step:

STEP 1: Prepare all your cards, empty boxes, and a schedule for the upcoming month (see previous page for my preferred schedule).

STEP 2: Begin by studying a new set of flash cards. After reviewing, place all these new cards in Box 1, representing the first level.

STEP 3: On Day 0, review the cards in Box 1. If you remember a card, move it to Box 2. If you forget, keep it in Box 1.

STEP 4: Repeat this process daily, always moving correctly remembered cards to the next box. Each day, review the cards from different boxes according to your schedule.

STEP 5: If you forget a card from any box (2, 3, 4, or 5), it always goes back to Box 1.

STEP 6: **When you remember a card in Box 5, congratulations! You've mastered it. You can keep it there for occasional review.**

STEP 7: **When you need to add new cards, always add them to Box 1.**

That's it! Over time, you'll be reviewing cards from all levels, ensuring consistent practice. Just stick to the schedule and don't miss your learning days. Voilà!

If you're thinking, *Hey, Nelson, this sounds like a ton of work!*, you're absolutely right. Apps can do all of this for you automatically. Which is nice for saving time. But there is something incredibly powerful when you work on something analog. Writing everything down by hand is, as we've seen, a great technique for further enhancing your memory!

INTERLEAVING

We've seen that spacing out your study sessions helps you strengthen neural connections for newly learned information. So now, let's talk about the other effective procedural memory hack: interleaving.

Imagine you're in the kitchen, trying to whip up a culinary masterpiece. Instead of focusing on chopping onions all day (cue the tears!), you switch it up—chopping onions, slicing tomatoes, and dicing peppers all at once. That's what interleaving is like—mixing it up like a master chef (of learning, in our case). Rather than tediously repeating the same information over and over again in one sitting, it's actually *more* beneficial as you study to mix similar but distinct material (the kind the brain could confuse). That's interleaving.

Now, quick clarification: *This is not multitasking.* Multitasking is when you try to do multiple things at once—like reviewing flash cards while texting a friend—and it splits your attention, making both tasks worse. Interleaving, on the other hand, is *intentional switching* between similar (but different) things. You're still focusing on one thing at a time, and importantly, you're giving each task your full attention for a meaningful amount of time before switching to the next. It's deliberate and structured.

This approach works because it forces your brain to stay active and spot the subtle differences between things that look alike. In math, for example, that might mean blending fractions, decimals, and percentages in the same set instead of drilling each one at a time. Recent research backs this up: In a massive classroom trial across fifty-four algebra classes, students who practiced with interleaved problem sets outperformed their peers who stuck to blocked practice.* And the effect wasn't small, either; it was huge. Meta-analyses echo

* Doug Rohrer et al., "A Randomized Controlled Trial of Interleaved Mathematics Practice," *Journal of Educational Psychology* 112, no. 8 (2020): 40–52.

this, showing that interleaving consistently helps learners to recognize the differences and similarities between related concepts. Interleaving trains your brain not just to remember better, but to flexibly apply knowledge in different contexts, something rote repetition can't always do.*

While interleaving may not seem as structured as spaced repetition, it doesn't need to be. The key is to mix up what you're studying *within* a single session, switching similar concepts at intervals rather than sticking with just one thing the entire time. And yes, it might *feel* like you're learning less, because it's harder. You're bouncing around, struggling to recall, potentially making more mistakes. But that effort is exactly what makes it work. It's what researchers call "desirable difficulty." That intentional, slower-paced shifting helps your brain stretch, adapt, and draw deeper connections between concepts. It feels messier, but it leads to stronger, more flexible learning in the long run.

WAYS TO SPICE UP YOUR STUDY SESSIONS

It's clear by now that learning and long-term retention require repetition, and the more effort you put into that repetition process, the better that information will stay with you. Repetition signals significance, and the brain tends to hold on to what it believes matters. Now, I'm sure your initial reaction to all this suggested review was probably an internal (or an external, auditory) groan. I mean, who likes to review? It's time-consuming and often boring. With that in mind, let me share a few other study techniques that make the often dry and boring recall portion of learning much more engaging and effective.

THE FEYNMAN METHOD

Named after the physicist Richard Feynman, this method engages with the idea that teaching someone else forces you to truly understand a concept. Feynman was nicknamed "the Great Explainer" and believed that learning happens when you explain and use information in different situations. This technique is another form of active recall, and it involves four simple steps to help you clarify difficult topics in your mind.

1. **CHOOSE A CONCEPT: Select a topic or concept you're learning and trying to master.**

* Matthias Brunmair and Tobias Richter, "Similarity Matters: A Meta-Analysis of Interleaved Learning and Its Moderators," *Psychological Bulletin* 145, no. 11 (2019): 1029–52.

2. **EXPLAIN SIMPLY:** Pretend you're teaching the concept to someone unfamiliar with it. Use plain language and analogies to simplify complex ideas.
3. **IDENTIFY GAPS:** Struggling to explain a part of the concept indicates areas where your understanding is weak. Go back to your materials and review those sections.
4. **REPEAT AND REFINE:** Continuously refine your explanation until you can articulate the concept clearly and concisely.

The Feynman Method not only reinforces your understanding through active engagement but also helps identify and fill knowledge gaps effectively.

MIND MAPS

Mind maps are great visual tools that let you organize ideas around a central theme in a branching, easy-to-follow layout. They're especially useful for brainstorming, note-taking, and problem-solving because they break complex information into clear, colorful, connected visuals, making it easier to understand, learn, and remember.

Here's what you need to make one:

- A large sheet of plain white paper.
- A selection of colored pens or pencils.
- A subject that you want to learn.
- Your imagination and creativity.

STEP 1: In the example in the chart on page 98, I'm mind-mapping the plays of William Shakespeare. First, orient your paper horizontally (landscape). Then, in the center, start by drawing a colorful image that represents your subject. For Shakespeare, that could be his portrait, a quill, or any simple symbol. You can also write a word if you prefer, but make sure it's bold and multidimensional.

STEP 2: Pick another color and draw a *thick* branch coming away from the central image. I like to let my branch curve organically, as this leads to a more visually engaging map that is more interesting to the brain, making it more likely you'll remember the information on the branch. The thickness of the branch symbolizes the weight of the association in the hierarchy of your map.

GENIUS PROFILE: RICHARD FEYNMAN

Richard Feynman was a world-class teacher. Ask any student who sat in one of his lectures, and they'll tell you: he had a real knack for explaining things and making you remember them. He understood how memory works; how stories, analogies, and hands-on logic help information stick. Not only that; he was also incredibly smart.

But what made him truly unforgettable was how cleverly he used his smarts in everyday life. One of my favorite examples goes like this: Feynman was eating alone at a small restaurant when a Japanese man entered selling abacuses. The man challenged the waiters to a speed calculation contest, but they deferred to Feynman instead. They began with addition. Feynman lost. Multiplication was next. He was closer, but still the abacus won. Then long division—this time, it was a tie. Finally, the man suggested cube roots. He wrote down a number: 1729.03. While the abacus salesman worked rapidly, Feynman relaxed, sat back, smiled and said, "12.002." The salesman was stunned. Feynman then explained that he remembered 1728 is 12 cubed, so the cube root of 1729.03 had to be just slightly more than 12. He used a quick mental approximation to estimate the decimal. The man, realizing he'd been beaten, packed up and left. Genius!

STEP 3: Label the branch with a single word in capital letters. Since this Mind Map is about Shakespeare's plays, I might label this first branch *COMEDY, TRAGEDY*, or *HISTORY*. Alternatively, instead of writing a word, I might decide to draw a comedic mask, a dagger, or a crown—as long as it's symbolic of the word.

STEP 4: Draw secondary-level offshoots from the main branch. Then draw third-level branches that spread out from these secondary branches (again, in a different color). Write keywords on all those branches as well (or draw symbols, or a combination of both). Give each symbol its own branch.

STEP 5: Pick yet another color and create your next main branch, working around the central image. I often suggest that beginners work clockwise around the middle. As before, draw secondary and tertiary branches from this new branch and label them. Keep adding main branches until you have about five or six.

STEP 6: Now you have your main branches all set up! Move freely around your mind map, leaping from branch to branch, filling in any gaps and adding new sub-branches as ideas and associations arise.*

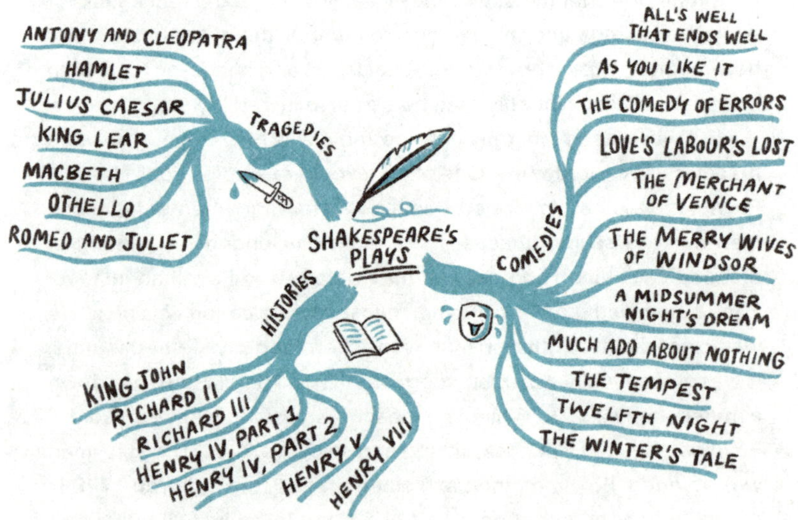

* You can add arrows, curving lines, extra flourishes, and links between your main branches to reinforce their connections. The more visual and colorful, the better.

Congrats! You have just created your first mind map.

The example mind map that I've included above is by no means complete. It's still a work in progress and could grow to include all of Shakespeare's plays, his sonnets and poems, key biographical facts, and memorable themes or details from each work. I've kept it simple here just to give you a general idea (and maybe inspire you to create your own).

Try completing your own version of this mind map (or create a new one with a topic you are more interested in). I suggest first memorizing the information using our methods from chapter 1 (page 27). Then, to start the process of review, create your mind map to really cement the recall process. The cool thing about creating mind maps is that they push you to actively link ideas together, which makes the material more meaningful and can improve understanding and recall.* Also, a finished map can double as a powerful study reference for later.

VARY STUDY LOCATIONS

Whether it's a café, library, or park, changing scenery can sharpen focus and memory recall. It keeps things fresh, but more importantly, your brain is always picking up contextual cues, even when you're not aware of them. Those "where you were" details become part of the memory itself.

If you usually study at a desk but then finish the session under a tree, you've now tied that material to a biographical memory: studying under that tree. Later, recalling the fact will be easier because the location itself acts as a cue.

Smith, Glenberg, and Bjork (1978) showed that students who studied in multiple environments recalled more than those who studied in the same one.† Varying the context during learning enriches encoding and creates multiple retrieval pathways. When you study the same material in different settings, each location becomes associated with what you're learning, giving you more mental "hooks" to pull the information back later.

So mix up your study locations. You're not just breaking routine; you're stacking helpful contextual cues into your memory.

---

* Yinghui Shi et al., "Effects of Mind Mapping–Based Instruction on Student Cognitive Learning Outcomes: A Meta-analysis," *Asia Pacific Education Review* 23 (March 2022): 615–32.

† Steven M. Smith, Arthur Glenberg, and Robert A. Bjork, "Environmental Context and Human Memory," *Memory & Cognition* 6, no. 4 (July 1978): 342–53, doi:10.3758/BF03197465.

Remember my pi memory-competition record attempt? Well, as I sulked down the hall, defeated, Mary, one of the judges, ran over to me.

"You know . . . that was one of the most impressive memory feats I've ever seen," she began. "Everyone in the audience seems to think so as well. They can't stop talking about it! Some lady was even telling her friend what a genius you are!"

It was nice to hear. I had spent so many months studying those numbers that it hurt to be thwarted by a momentary lapse in memory. As terrible as I felt, I began to perk up. I am—we are—only human, and memory isn't perfect. Even if you apply all the techniques in the world and study until your eyes bleed, you can still forget. As I collected my thoughts, I picked myself up, straightened my back, and looked again at Mary, straight into her eyes.

"You're right. It was impressive. I'll make sure to get the record next time," I told her, firmly.

And I meant it. With a stronger strategy, a clearer purpose, and my WHY to carry me, I knew that whenever I tried it again, I'd get it.

EXERCISES AND RESOURCES

Here are a few tips and suggestions to remember when studying:

- **Don't cram. Space out your study sessions. Use spaced repetition to review material over gradually increasing time intervals.**
- **Mix it up. Interleave similar but different topics instead of blocking them.**
- **Focus beats multitasking. Give one task your full attention, then intentionally switch.**
- **Hard = helpful. When active recall feels challenging, that's when the real memory gains happen.**
- **Vary your study locations. A change of scenery can boost recall by creating stronger context cues.**
- **Write out what you've studied by hand. Using analog tools (pen and paper) can deepen encoding and slow you down just enough to think.**
- **Add challenge or risk (within reason). Introduce mild distractions or mild pressure—like a time limit or a public quiz—to simulate real-world retrieval.**

- Chew gum before studying (not during). Some research suggests mastication (genius word, FYI) of gum can increase alertness and improve attention.*
- Take a topic you're learning and spend five minutes explaining it out loud—to someone else or even yourself in the mirror—to take advantage of the Feynman method.

Here are some other resources:

BOOKS:

- *Make It Stick* by Peter C. Brown—A must-read on how real learning happens.
- *Ultralearning* by Scott Young—A tactical deep dive into how to teach yourself anything efficiently.
- *Peak* by Anders Ericsson—Explores the science of expert performance, including memory, deliberate practice, and retrieval.
- *How We Learn* by Benedict Carey—A fun, science-backed guide to optimizing how your brain absorbs information.
- *Range: Why Generalists Triumph in a Specialized World* by Dave Epstein—On the topic of how wide learning builds flexible minds.
- *Start With Why* by Simon Sinek—If you're looking for help in defining your WHY, look no further.

APPS/WEBSITES:

- Anki—The gold standard for spaced repetition (SR) flash cards.
- SmarterHumans.ai—AI-infused study tools designed for smart, adaptive learning.
- Brainscape—A user-friendly SR flash card system with premade decks.
- RemNote—Great for mixing notes and SR review.
- Notion or Obsidian—For building your own modular learning systems and note archives.
- Memrise.com—A great platform for learning languages (and built by another grandmaster of memory, Ed Cooke!).
- Let AI quiz you—ChatGPT and similar tools make excellent study partners. They can generate unlimited practice questions, adjust difficulty on the fly, and give instant feedback. Use them.

---

* Andrew Smith, "Effects of Chewing Gum on Cognitive Function, Mood and Physiology in Stressed and Non-stressed Volunteers, *Nutritional Neuroscience* 13, no. 1 (February 2010): 7–16.

PART II

GENIUS IN ACTION (THE TRICKS & STRATEGIES)

85²
8x8
+1
8x9
+25
72
7225
$= \frac{t'}{\sqrt{1-\frac{V^2}{C^2}}}$
05
11
16
22
33
39
44
50

You know that moment when someone does something so impressive, so seemingly impossible, that you have to ask: *How the hell did they do that?*

That's what this part of the book is about: the skills, tricks, and techniques that make you *seem* like a genius, not because you're pulling off magic, but because you've learned something most people haven't.

You're about to learn how to do things like:

- Calculate math problems in your head faster than someone can grab a calculator.
- Memorize a shuffled deck of cards and count cards in blackjack.
- Solve a Rubik's Cube in minutes.
- Read people like Sherlock Holmes—analyzing body language and predicting thoughts through cold reading.
- Think creatively, solve problems intuitively, and develop razor-sharp mental skills.
- Be more creative.

Whether it's improving your social intelligence, making faster decisions, or blowing someone's mind with a seemingly impossible mental feat, these aren't just party tricks (though they can make for amazing party tricks at times). They're skills that give you an edge in everyday life.

but powerful tricks that make it *seem* like you have superhuman intelligence. None of them require innate talent, by the way. It's all a bit of know-how and some practice. That's it.

When you see someone solve a Rubik's Cube in under ten seconds, you might think they're some kind of genius. But in reality, they've just memorized a few key patterns. When you meet someone who can tell you what day of the week April 23, 2075, falls on, it might seem like magic. But actually, they're just using a system that's easy to learn.

As you read this section, pick and choose what excites you! Maybe you want to sharpen your social intuition. Maybe you want to get better at chess. Maybe you just want to impress people with lightning-fast mental math. And remember, in a world where any answer is a click away, what matters isn't what you can look up—it's how quickly you can think, how well you can read situations, and how creatively you can solve problems. Whatever draws you in, you'll find something in here that makes you feel smarter, think faster, and pull off abilities most people assume are innate or take years to master.

This is your genius tool kit. Use it wisely.

CHAPTER 5

MENTAL CALCULATION

"MATHEMATICS BEGINS
IN WONDER AND ENDS IN WISDOM."
—VICTOR HUGO

I HAD JUST FINISHED MY MEMORY CHALLENGE ONSTAGE AT A FOX NETWORK STUDIO LOT IN LOS ANGELES. THE SHOW WAS CALLED *SUPERHUMAN*, A COMPETITION FEATURING PEOPLE WITH SEEMINGLY SUPERHUMAN ABILITIES. FROM MEMORY EXPERTS (ME, OBVIOUSLY) TO FROG-CALL IDENTIFIERS, FIRE BREATHERS, MENTAL CALCULATORS, SPEED CUBERS, AND EVEN CONTORTIONISTS (JUST TO NAME A FEW), THE SHOW SHOWCASED SOME OF THE MOST MIND-BLOWING TALENTS ON THE PLANET.

MY CHALLENGE WAS SOMETHING STRAIGHT OUT OF *MISSION: IMPOSSIBLE*.

I WAS HARNESSED UP AND LOWERED FROM THE CEILING, STOPPING JUST INCHES ABOVE A CIRCULAR PLATFORM WHERE TEN LOCKED SAFES SAT WAITING. EACH SAFE HAD AN EIGHT-DIGIT PIN, ALL OF WHICH I HAD MEMORIZED MOMENTS BEFORE. MY TASK WAS TO CRACK THEM OPEN IN JUST A FEW MINUTES . . . ALL WHILE DANGLING IN MIDAIR.

To be honest, it wasn't difficult. Memorizing eighty digits in a few minutes was nothing compared with some of the feats I had to complete in real memory competitions. But it *looked* impossible, and that's what mattered.

The judges ate it up. Even Mike Tyson (yes, *the* Mike Tyson) told me it was one of the most impressive things he had ever seen. Christina Milian flashed a smile and complimented my flawless performance. I felt good. *Really* good. If I could win over the crowd as well, I had a real shot at the $50,000 prize.

Then came the final act.

A teenager named Javen Ho.

Javen was quiet, polite, almost shy. We had tested him backstage, throwing random math problems at him just to see what he could do. And let me tell you, he was a number-crunching *machine*.

His method was fascinating, to say the least. He used a mental Soroban, or, as most people know it, a mental abacus.

No calculators, no notes—just pure visualization. He could see the beads of an imaginary abacus in his mind, flicking them from rod to rod with lightning speed to arrive at his answers. Addition, subtraction, multiplication, division—even square roots and exponents—it didn't matter. He could do it all. No hesitation. No second guesses. All at blinding speeds.

It was, hands down, one of the most impressive things I'd ever seen. So I wasn't surprised when the crowd absolutely lost their minds at his performance. The judges were feeding him random three-digit numbers, and he had to add each number to another random three-digit number, as fast as possible, over and over again.

He was so quick that the verifying calculators couldn't even keep up.

Even crazier was that he didn't say the numbers like we normally do—"one thousand three hundred twenty-four," "two thousand six hundred forty-eight." That actually slowed him down. Instead, he rattled off the raw digits: one-three-two-four, two-six-four-eight—rapid-fire, no pauses, just so that he could vocalize his answers as fast as his brain computed them.

The crowd was hooked. It didn't seem like math at all. Javen was pure magic. And he didn't even break a sweat.

I've always been fascinated by people who can effortlessly crunch numbers in their heads. I wouldn't say I'm bad at numbers, but mental math has never come naturally to me. Over the years, though, I've met some incredible human calculators who have inspired me, shared their techniques, and proven that that skill isn't just for the mathematically gifted—it's for *everyone*.

I'll admit, some people are naturally wired for numbers. There's definitely a genetic component to it. But I also believe it's a skill in which we can be trained. And in this chapter, I'm going to show you how.

THE ART OF NUMBER SENSE

If you've ever watched someone casually estimate the total at a restaurant or figure out the best deal at a grocery store without pulling out their phone, you've witnessed strong number sense in action. It's that intuitive feel for numbers that makes calculations smoother, estimations more natural, and problem-solving faster.

But number sense isn't only about being good at math. It's about *understanding* numbers. People with strong number sense don't see math as rigid equations; they see numbers as flexible, adaptable, and—believe it or not—enjoyable.

At its core, number sense includes a few key abilities:

- *Grasping quantity and magnitude*: Knowing that 900 is much closer to 1,000 than it is to 500, without even thinking about it.
- *Recognizing patterns and relationships*: Seeing connections, such as realizing that doubling one side of a multiplication problem while halving the other gives the same answer (e.g., 4 × 12 is the same as 8 × 6).
- *Flexible thinking in math*: Breaking numbers apart and recombining them in easier ways. If you need to add 48 + 37, you might see 50 + 35 to get there faster with easier numbers to compute.
- *Quick estimation and approximation*: Getting a rough answer before even calculating, so you instantly know if a final answer "feels" right or wildly off.
- *Mental math fluency*: Performing calculations in your head using logic and intuition instead of relying on a calculator.

These all build *confidence* with numbers. People with great number sense aren't scared of math; they lean into it; they play with it. Now, some of these abilities might come naturally to you, and others might feel more difficult. That's fine. With some of the tips and tricks in this chapter, you'll be able to improve until you're a confident number cruncher.

Having a good number sense *matters* in your daily life. Whether you're splitting the bill at a restaurant, estimating how much a discount actually saves you, figuring out how many bags of soil you need for a garden, or even just knowing when someone's math seems *off*—numbers are *everywhere*!

People who struggle with number sense tend to rely on memorized formulas, get lost in long calculations, and second-guess themselves even when they're right. But when you understand how numbers behave, you don't have to memorize anything. Instead, you *intuit* your way forward.

You break problems apart, spot shortcuts, estimate with confidence, and adjust on the fly. You adapt not by following rules but by *thinking*. That kind of thinking makes you faster, more accurate, and far more flexible.*

The good news is you can train your number sense just like any other skill.

In this chapter, we'll build up your calculation speed, learn mental math tricks that make solving problems easier, sharpen your estimation skills, explore number patterns, and challenge you with some problems to test your progress. Before long, you'll be the person at the table who *knows* the bill is wrong before anyone even pulls out their phone.

HOW TO MENTALLY ADD FAST

Every other math operation builds from addition. Yup. Basic, first-grade-level arithmetic—that's it! So let's start there.

I'm going to assume you already know how to mentally add single-digit numbers. But what about multiple digits? There's a counterintuitive idea that actually works super well:

We're going to calculate from left to right, instead of right to left.

In grade school, we're taught to add right to left when solving problems on paper. That's fine when you're writing things down, but in your head, it's slow. It forces you to hold onto unnecessary details while waiting to carry numbers over.

When calculating mentally, left to right is the way to go. It aligns with how your brain naturally processes numbers.

Think about it: when you see the number 573, you don't think of it as *three, then seven, then five*—you see it as *five, then seven, then three*, or *five hundred seventy-three*. That's how we naturally read and understand numbers. But in most languages, numbers flow from big to small.† So why not add that way too? When you do mental math the same way, you keep your brain in sync with how it already understands numbers.

---

* By the way, you can absolutely be a genius without being great at number crunching—plenty of geniuses are terrible at math. But if this book is meant to be a toolbox of techniques to elevate your thinking, then number sense *has* to be part of it. So don't be scared of the numbers you're about to see in this chapter! Embrace the challenge!

† Genius fact: Some languages do exactly that. Dutch, for example, says 56 as "zesenvijftig," literally "six and fifty." Weird, right? French takes it even further. The number 77 is "Soixante-dix-sept," or "sixty-ten-seven." And don't even get me started on 98: "quatre-vingt-dix-huit," which translates to "four twenties ten eight." Bavarian German is another funky one—256 might be said as "sechs und fuchzig und zwoa hundert"—literally, "six and fifty and two hundred." Always gives me a good chuckle.

LEFT-TO-RIGHT ADDITION: THE BASICS

Let's walk through some two-digit sums using the left-to-right method. Once we bump up to larger numbers, the benefits will be obvious.

We'll start with a problem that doesn't require carrying (meaning both columns add up to 9 or less).

EXAMPLE: 32 + 24

1. **Start with holding 32 in your mind.**
2. **Notice that from left to right, 24 breaks into 20 (in the tens column) + 4 (in the ones column).**
3. **Add the 20. 32 + 20 = 52.**
4. **Then, add the remaining 4. 52 + 4 = 56.**

Simple, right? Let's try a problem that requires carrying.

EXAMPLE: 78 + 27

1. **Start with 78 in your mind.**
2. **Add the 20 → 98.**
3. **Add the 7 → 105.**

Try one on your own:

85 + 66*

If you got 151, awesome. If the carrying still feels tricky, don't worry—like everything else in this book, it just takes a bit of practice. I'll include more exercises at the end of the chapter (page 156).

THREE-DIGIT ADDITION: SAME APPROACH, JUST ONE MORE STEP

For three-digit numbers, it's the same approach as above except we add the hundreds first, then the tens, then the ones.

---

* The steps:
1. 85 + 60 = 145
2. 145 + 6 = 151

EXAMPLE: 438 + 514

1. Start with holding 438 in your mind.
2. Notice that 514 breaks up into 500 + 10 + 4.
3. Add the 500 → 938.
4. Then, add the 10 → 948.
5. Finally, add the 4 → 952.

Final answer: 952

Let's try one more (they don't really get much harder than this one, by the way).

EXAMPLE: 788 + 523

1. Start with 788 in your mind.
2. Add 500 → 1288.
3. Add 20 → 1308.
4. Add 3 → 1311.

Final answer: 1311

WHEN NUMBER SENSE KICKS IN

As your number sense improves, you'll start seeing shortcuts inside problems. When you notice a pattern that makes the calculation easier—use it!

Take the following problem:

EXAMPLE: 689 + 398

Looks tricky, right? But what if you recognize that 398 is simply (400 – 2)?

Instead, you could do this:

1. Turn 398 into (400 – 2).
2. 689 + 400 = 1089
3. 1089 – 2 = 1087

Much easier, right? This is the kind of number sense that we're hoping to hone! The more comfortable you get with numbers, the more you'll start to naturally see these kinds of shortcuts.

HOW TO MENTALLY SUBTRACT FAST

For most people, subtraction is trickier than addition. But if we apply the same approach we used for addition, it's almost as easy.

Let's start simple—no borrowing needed. We'll break down the problem the same way we did with addition.

EXAMPLE: 75 – 44

1. **Start with holding 75 in your mind.**
2. **Notice that 44 breaks down into 40 + 4.**
3. **Subtract the 40 first: 75 – 40 = 35**
4. **Then, subtract the 4: 35 – 4 = 31**

Nice. Clean and simple. But what about when borrowing *is* required?

EXAMPLE: 76 – 39

If we do it the normal way:

1. **76 – 30 = 46**
2. **46 – 9 = . . . *ugh.***

My brain doesn't like that part. But what if we reframed 39 as (40 – 1) instead of (30 + 9)?

Now, we can do this instead:

1. **Start with 76 in your mind.**
2. **76 – 40 = 36**
3. **Then *add* 1 → 37.**

Much easier.

Wait, but Nelson, why do we add 1? Because if we rewrite 39 as 40 – 1, then 40 – 1 brings the same result as subtracting 40, *then* adding 1.

Since we now have two ways to approach our subtraction problems, how do you know which method to use? Well, for any two-digit subtraction problem that requires borrowing, here's the rule:

Round the second number up to the nearest multiple of 10, subtract that, then add back the difference.

If you're wondering why we wouldn't ever round down, well . . . think about it. If the problem requires borrowing, then that second digit must be five or larger. If it were smaller, then there wouldn't be any need to borrow and we can stick to our normal way of subtracting.

EXAMPLE: 64 – 37

1. **Round 37 up to 40.**
2. **64 – 40 = 24**
3. **Add back 3 → 27.**

Try one yourself:

84 – 59*

Did you get 25? If so, nice! If not, no worries—it takes a bit of practice. There are more problems at the end of the chapter (page 156) to drill even further.

THREE-DIGIT SUBTRACTION: THE POWER OF COMPLEMENTS

Let's bump up the difficulty a little bit, to three-digit subtraction. Before we dive in, though, let's talk about something called complements.

No, not: *"Hey, nice shirt!"*—I mean mathematical complements.

A complement is a number's counterpart that brings it up to the next power of 10.

- **The complement of 7 is 3, because 7 + 3 = 10.**
- **The complement of 67 is 33, because 67 + 33 = 100.**

The trick to finding complements quickly?

1. **Start with the leftmost digit and find how far it is from 9.**
2. **Continue the same method for all digits of the number until the last.**
3. **For the last digit, find how far it is from 10.**

That's it! Let's try some.

Find the complements of these numbers:
55 → 45 *(5 is 4 away from 9, 5 is 5 away from 10)*
81 → 19 *(8 is 1 away from 9, 9 is 1 away from 10)*

---

* The steps:
1. Round 59 up to 60.
2. 84 – 60 = 24
3. 24 + 1 = 25

37 → 63
689 → 311
302 → 698
74 → 26
5099 → 4901

Not too difficult, right?

WHY COMPLEMENTS MATTER

When subtracting three-digit numbers, we use the same rounding trick as before—but instead of rounding to the nearest 10, we round to the nearest 100 and use the complement to adjust the answer.

EXAMPLE: 726 – 478

1. Round 478 up to 500.
2. How far is 478 from 500? Use the complement trick on 78 → 22
3. We now rewrite 478 as (500 – 22).
4. Now do 726 – 500 = 226.
5. Add back 22 → 248.

If you can do that last step in one go, great. If not, no problem. Break it down like before:

1. 226 + 20 = 246
2. 246 + 2 = 248

Final answer: 248

Let's do one more example before we move on. There will be a lot more examples at the end of the chapter (page 156).

EXAMPLE: 219 – 176

1. Round 176 up to 200.
2. Complement of 76 → 24.
3. 219 – 200 = 19
4. Add back 24 → 19 + 24 = 43

Final answer: 43

With a touch more practice, you'll be well on your way to becoming an adding and subtracting *machine*, just like Javen Ho.

HOW TO MULTIPLY IN YOUR HEAD

Now we're getting to the fun stuff! Multiplication is one of the coolest mental math skills to master. It's flashy and impressive, and when you get good at it, you genuinely *feel* like a genius.

There are plenty of tricks for specific numbers, which we'll get into. We'll also cover multiplying one-digit numbers by two-digit and three-digit numbers, learn how to square numbers quickly, and pick up some powerful mental shortcuts along the way.

MULTIPLYING A TWO-DIGIT NUMBER BY A ONE-DIGIT NUMBER

Let's start with something simple:

EXAMPLE 1: 34 × 6

Just like addition and subtraction, we're going to go from left to right.*

1. **Start with 30 × 6 → 180.†**
2. **Multiply the last digit: 4 × 6 = 24.**
3. **Add the two results: 180 + 24 = 204.**

Another one!

EXAMPLE 2: 69 × 7

1. **60 × 7 = 420**
2. **9 × 7 = 63**
3. **420 + 63 = 483**

What's truly great about multiplying like this in your head is that since we're going left to right, we can *start* to say the answer as we're calculating it; we don't actually need to be finished calculating in order to start spitting out the answer. To anyone watching you do this, it'll seem as if you're calculating faster than you actually are. Cool!

---

* Don't forget, from left to right, 34 is 30 (in the tens column) and 4 (in the ones column).

† When numbers end in zeros, ignore them temporarily, multiply what's left, then add the zeros back. 30 × 6 = 3 × 6 = 18 → 180. Same with multiple zeros: 400 × 30 = 4 × 3 = 12 → 12,000.

MULTIPLYING A THREE-DIGIT NUMBER BY A ONE-DIGIT NUMBER

Going up to three-digit numbers isn't much harder; we just extend the same approach.

EXAMPLE: 326 × 7

1. **300 × 7 = 2100**
2. **Do 20 × 7 = 140.**
3. **Add 2100 and 140 → 2240.**
4. **Do 6 × 7 = 42.**
5. **Add 2240 and 42 → 2282.**

The trick is to keep track of each step in your head, speaking the answer out loud if needed. As you practice more of these problems, you'll realize that when you start to say the answer out loud, digit by digit, you'll need to make sure a carry-over number isn't coming into play. Not a problem if you say the answer slow enough; you can still sound super fluid.

NOTICING SHORTCUTS: USING NUMBER SENSE

Multiplication problems often have built-in shortcuts. The more you practice, the more you'll spot them naturally. Remember, the ultimate goal here is to become *flexible* with our approach to numbers. If we see a shortcut, we should take it. Let's take a look at some of these kinds of shortcuts.

EXAMPLE: 998 × 3

Instead of multiplying 998 × 3, we might notice that 998 is really close to 1,000 and do the following:

1. **Reframe 998 as (1,000 – 2)**
2. **Do 1,000 × 3 = 3,000**
3. **Multiply the difference of 2 by 3 to get 6***
4. **Subtract 6 from 3,000 → 2,994**

Final answer: 2994

Much faster. Here's another.

---

* We can't just subtract 2 at the end here, as we did for straight-up subtraction. We're doing multiplication by 3 here, so our subtracted 2 is actually 3 times that; hence the 6.

EXAMPLE: 46 × 4

Instead of multiplying by 4 directly, realize that multiplying by 4 is just doubling twice:

1. **46 × 2 = 92**
2. **92 × 2 = 184**

Maybe that's quicker for you, maybe that's harder. There are always going to be shortcuts that feel easier than others, the important thing is to notice them and take advantage of them when they feel right.

Here are some tricks to keep in mind when you're multiplying by any of the single-digit numbers (excluding 0 and 1, because those are trivial):

Multiply by 2	Just double it.
Multiply by 3	Double it, then add the original number.
Multiply by 4	Double it twice.
Multiply by 5	This one is fun, just halve the number and then add a zero.

EXAMPLE: 422 × 5

1. **Half of 422 is 211**
2. **Add a zero → 2110**

If the number is odd, the result will end in 5 instead of 0:

EXAMPLE: 421 × 5

1. **Take 1 away from your odd number → 421 becomes 420**
2. **Half of 420 is 210**
3. **Add a 5 → 2105**

Multiply by 6	Multiply by 3, then double it. This isn't always easier, but it's nice to have as an alternative approach in certain cases. Multiplying by 6 can also be done by multiplying by 5 and then adding the original number.

The above uses a method called "factoring." Most numbers (except primes*) can be factored. This means I can break them up into the product of smaller numbers. These may not always be obvious upon a quick glance, but in other cases they might be. Say we had 32 × 12. I might

* A prime number is a number that can be divided evenly only by 1 and itself.

notice that 12 is 2 × 6, and 6 is 2 × 3. So, we could triple our number (× 3) and then double it twice. 32 × 3 is pretty easy; it's just 96. Then double that, you have 192, double that again, you have 384. Remember, if 192 × 2 isn't obvious to you, that's okay! We have other tools for that. I might notice that 192 is close to 200. So, what if I did 200 × 2 (easy, that's 400) and then subtract the difference of 192 from 200, doubled. That's, 8 × 2 = 16. So 192 × 2 is the same as 400 – 16, which is 384. Look at them math moves!

Multiply by 7	No real advantageous trick for this one, unfortunately; just use standard methods.
Multiply by 8	Double it three times. Or multiply by 10, then subtract double the original number.

EXAMPLE: 62 × 8

1. Change the 8 to (10 – 2).
2. Multiply 62 × 10 first → 620.
3. Then subtract 62 × 2 from your answer → 620 – 124.
4. For 620 – 124, I might start with subtracting 120 first → 620 – 120 is 500.
5. Subtract that remaining 4 → 500 – 4 = 496

Multiply by 9	Triple your number two times. Or multiply by 10, then subtract the original number.

EXAMPLE: 68 × 9

1. Multiply by 10 → 680
2. Subtract 68 → 680 – 68 = 612

MULTIPLYING A TWO-DIGIT NUMBER BY A TWO-DIGIT NUMBER

Now we're going to look at two-digit by two-digit multiplication. For these kinds of problems, you really want to have a mixed bag of tricks to tackle what the situation calls for. I'm going to show you a bunch to help you master these, and then one final method to help you out with all the rest.

MULTIPLYING BY 11

This method is surprisingly easy! For a two-digit number, first add together the digits of the number being multiplied by 11. Then, place it in between the original two digits. Make sure to carry, if that middle number needs to carry.

EXAMPLE: 32 × 11

1. Add the digits together: 3 + 2 = 5
2. Place the sum in the middle: 352

That's it. 32 × 11 = 352.
It works for any two-digit number.

EXAMPLE: 78 × 11

1. 7 + 8 = 15
2. Write the 5 in the middle and carry the 1 → 858

For larger numbers, just keep adding pairs of digits, from left to right. And make sure to keep the original digits on the outer edges (the leftmost digit might need adjusting if a carry is in order). Here's a problem that looks ridiculously hard but is easy with the 11s trick:

EXAMPLE: 324215 × 11

1. Keep the leftmost digit: 3
2. Add pairs going left to right:
   - 3 + 2 = 5
   - 2 + 4 = 6
   - 4 + 2 = 6
   - 2 + 1 = 3
   - 1 + 5 = 6
3. Keep the last digit: 5

Final answer: 3566365

This trick will also help you multiply numbers that are a multiple of 11 (22, 33, 44, etc.). For example:

EXAMPLE: 54 × 33

1. Notice that 33 is 3 × 11
2. First, do 54 × 3 → 162
3. Apply the magic of 11 to 162

a. **Keep the leftmost digit 1**

b. **Add pairs going left to right:**
   - **1 + 6 = 7**
   - **6 + 2 = 8**

c. **Keep the rightmost digit 2**

Final answer: 1782

You're basically a calculator at this point!

MORE FACTORING AND MANIPULATING NUMBERS

Always keep in mind factoring tricks, as well as the technique of rounding to numbers that may be easier to work with. *Always* take advantage of any time you see a number that you know can break down into easier numbers! I've already listed some multiplying tricks for single-digit numbers but here are some for a few bigger numbers as well:

Multiply by 12	Multiply by 3 and then double two times (× 4). Or use the magic of 11 trick and then add the original number to that answer.
Multiply by 15	Multiply by 3 and then by 5. Or add a zero to your number, then add that number to half of itself.

EXAMPLE: 24 × 15

1. **Add a zero to your number → 240**
2. **Add that number to half of itself → 240 + 120 = 360**

Multiply by 16	Double your number 4 times.
Multiply by 18	Multiply by 6 and then by 3. Or multiply by 20 and then subtract 2 times the original number.
Multiply by 21	Multiply by 20 and then add of the original number.
Multiply by 22	Multiply by 2 and then use the magic of 11!

You get the idea!

Most numbers you can fiddle with to be something easier. And even if you can't, it's worth playing around with different ways to view a multiplication problem. This builds up your number sense and can come in handy with harder problems.

QUICK TRICK FOR MULTIPLYING ANY 2-DIGIT NUMBERS UP TO 19 × 19

This trick works for any two-digit number multiplied by another two-digit number between 10 and 19. Here's how it works:

1. **Add the ones place digit from the smaller number to the whole larger number.**
2. **Add a zero to the end.**
3. **Multiply the ones place digits of the two numbers together.**
4. **Add the results of steps 2 and 3.**

Watch it in action:

EXAMPLE: 17 × 12

1. **Notice that 12 is the smaller number, so we take the 2 and add it to the bigger number 17 → 19**
2. **Add zero to the end → 190**
3. **Next, multiply the 2 × 7 → 14**
4. **Add 190 + 14 = 204**

Final answer: 204

Most of us know our multiplication tables up to 10 × 10 (or even 12 × 12 in some cases). This quick trick will take you up to 19 × 19.

EXAMPLE: 18 × 14

1. **14 is the smaller number, so we take the 4 and add it to 18 → 22**
2. **Add zero to the end → 220**
3. **Next, multiply the 4 × 8 → 32**
4. **Add 220 + 32 = 252**

Final answer: 252

EASILY MULTIPLY ANY NUMBER BY 25

This one is quick and easy: Multiply the number by 100, then divide it by 4 (or halve it twice).

EXAMPLE: 42 × 25

1. Multiply 42 by 100; that's 42 × 100 → 4200
2. Half of that is 2100.
3. Half of that again is 1050.

Final answer: 1050

NUMBERS CLOSE TO 100

Problems involving numbers close to 100 are easier than you might think. Here's how to approach them:

1. Find the difference between each number and 100.
2. Add those differences together.
3. Subtract the result from part 2 from 100. This is the first part of your answer.
4. Multiply the two differences from step 1, and those are your last digits.

EXAMPLE: 97 × 92

1. First, find out how far each number is from 100, 3 and 8 respectively.
2. Add those values together to get 11.
3. Subtract that from 100; 100 – 11 → 89 (this is the first part of our answer).
4. Multiply the two numbers from step 1 → 3 × 8 = 24 (the is the second part of our answer).

Final answer: 8924

EXAMPLE: 98 × 99

1. These numbers are 2 and 1 away from 100
2. Adding those values together: 2 + 1 → 3
3. Subtract that from 100: 100 – 3 = 97
4. Multiply 2 × 1 → 2 (we need this answer to be two digits, so 02)

Final answer: 9702

HOW TO MULTIPLY THE REST—THE VERTICALLY AND CROSSWISE METHOD

I discovered this technique while studying Vedic math, a system of mental math techniques that originated from ancient Indian scriptures (the Vedas). It provides fast and efficient methods for arithmetic operations, based on sixteen Sutras (formulas) and thirteen sub-Sutras (corollaries) that help simplify calculations. And while at first it probably would be best to practice on paper (to see how it works visually), eventually you'll be able to do this process entirely in your head.

For any two-by-two multiplication (or any-size multiplication, for that matter), you can follow the following approach:*

EXAMPLE: $\begin{array}{r} 35 \\ \times\ 22 \end{array}$

1. **Start by multiplying the first column of digits (vertically); that's 3 × 2 → 6. Remember, we're going left to right on this as well. This is the first digit of your answer (unless there is a carry in the next step).**
2. **Next, multiply digits diagonally in both directions and add the result, so (3 × 2) + (2 × 5) = 6 + 10 → 16. Since there is a carry here, that 1 gets added to your first digit from step 1. So the first digit of your answer is actually 7, followed by the 6 from 16.**
3. **Then, the final digit is found by multiplying the last column vertically: 5 × 2 → 10. There is a carry there, so that 1 gets added to the previous digit. 76 now becomes 77 . . . then the last digit is the 0 from the 10.**

Final answer: 770

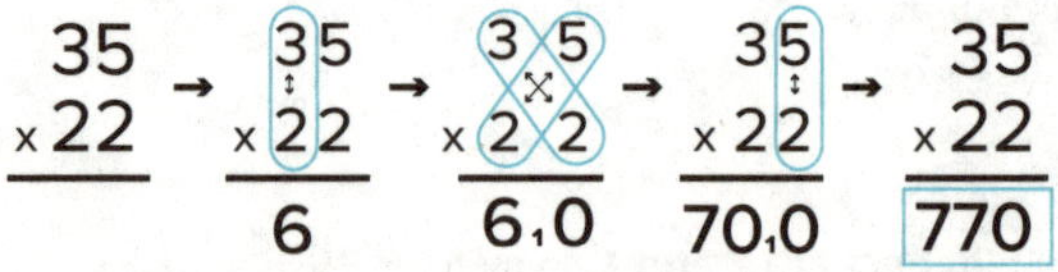

$$\begin{array}{r} 35 \\ \times\ 22 \\ \hline \end{array} \rightarrow \begin{array}{r} 35 \\ \times\ 22 \\ \hline 6 \end{array} \rightarrow \begin{array}{r} 35 \\ \times\ 22 \\ \hline 6_{1}0 \end{array} \rightarrow \begin{array}{r} 35 \\ \times\ 22 \\ \hline 70_{1}0 \end{array} \rightarrow \begin{array}{r} 35 \\ \times\ 22 \\ \hline \boxed{770} \end{array}$$

The same process occurs with a three-by-three problem, except there are more steps. Watch this in action:

* The little 1s you see in the answer lines are there to signify that there was a carry involved in that step of the calculation.

EXAMPLE:

451
× 211

1. First, vertical on the left: 4 × 2 → 8
2. Then, moving left to right, we take care of the left two-digit columns by multiplying crosswise and adding: (4 × 1) + (5 × 2) → 14.
3. Then all *three* columns: crosswise again, but vertical for that middle column, add it all together: (4 × 1) + (2 × 1) + (5 × 1) → 11.
4. Then the last two columns: (5 × 1) + (1 × 1) → 6.
5. Finally, the last column vertically: 1 × 1 → 1.
6. Put all the digits together from left to right (accounting for any carry-overs) and you get . . .

Final answer: 95161

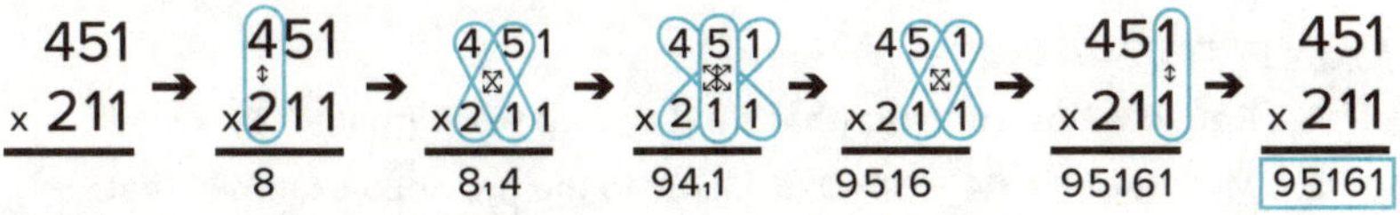

451 × 211	→	451 × 211 8	→	451 × 211 8,4	→	451 × 211 94,1	→	451 × 211 9516	→	451 × 211 95161	→	451 × 211 95161

SQUARING TWO-DIGIT AND THREE-DIGIT NUMBERS

Squaring a number means multiplying it by itself. Now, of course you can use any of the tools we've learned previously for multiplication, but there is a super-neat trick you can apply for squaring that's quite easy to do mentally. Here's the process:

1. Round the number to the nearest multiple of 10 (either up or down, whichever is closest).
2. Whatever that difference is, also apply that difference to the original number but in the opposite direction.
3. Do the multiplication of *those* two numbers instead of the original.
4. Then, when you're done, square the difference you took away from the original number and add that to your answer.

Let's see it in action.

EXAMPLE: 47^2

1. Round 47 up to 50 (that's +3) and down to 44 (that's –3).
2. Multiply 50 × 44 → 2200 (I know that 50 may look intimidating, but it's not. It's just a 5 followed by a 0. So, treat it as if you're multiplying by 5—which you know how to do already—then add the 0 at the end of your calculation. (Remember, multiplying by 10 is the same as just adding a 0.)
3. Add the square of the difference ($3^2 = 9$) → 2209

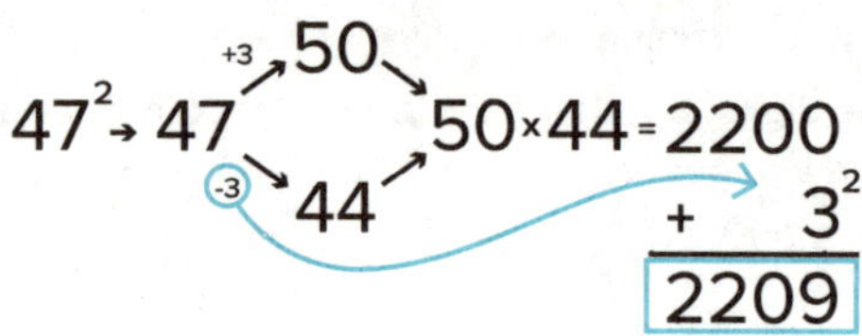

EXAMPLE: 62^2

1. Round 62 down to 60 (that's –2) and up to 64 (that's +2).
2. Multiply 60 × 64 → 3840 (similarly to the previous example, that 60 is just multiplying by 6 and then adding a 0 at the end of your calculation)
3. Add the square of the difference ($2^2 = 4$) → 3844

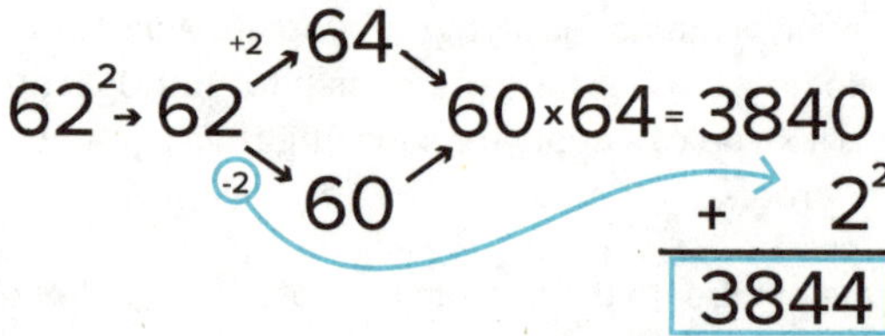

For squaring two-digit numbers ending in 5, there's an even *easier* trick. Whatever the number is, 35, 65, 75, etc. you take the first digit and multiply it by 1 higher. Then the last two digits of your answer will always be 25. So . . .

EXAMPLE: 85^2

1. Multiply 8 × (8 + 1) → 8 × 9 = 72
2. Add 25 at the end → 7225

Simple as that! This works for any two-digit number that ends in 5.

Now, if you *really* want to seem like a genius, showing off that you can mentally square a three-digit number is *really* powerful. It can be challenging, but as with everything in this book, practice can make things become effortless.

The approach is similar to the two-digit problems, except we round to the nearest hundred.

EXAMPLE: 506^2

1. **Round down to 500 (that's –6) and up to 512 (that's +6).**
2. **Multiply 500 × 512 → 256000**
3. **Add the square of the difference ($6^2 = 36$) → 256036.**

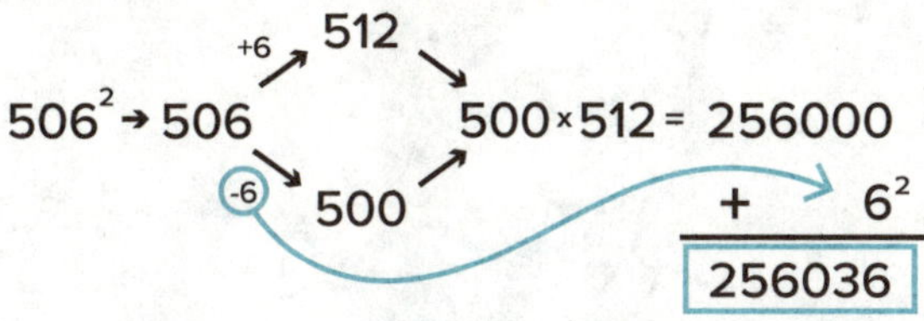

For that example, we got lucky, given that 506 was *very* close to 500. But what if rounding down (or up) is much farther away? Well, as you might guess, your brain has to work a little harder. But it's still doable.

EXAMPLE: 439^2

1. **Round down to 400 (that's –39) and up to 478 (that's +39).**
2. **Multiply 400 × 478 → 191200**
3. **Add the square of the difference (39^2 = ???)**
4. **Calculate 39^2 using the same technique, but for two-digit numbers → 1521**
5. **Add it to 191,200 → 192721**

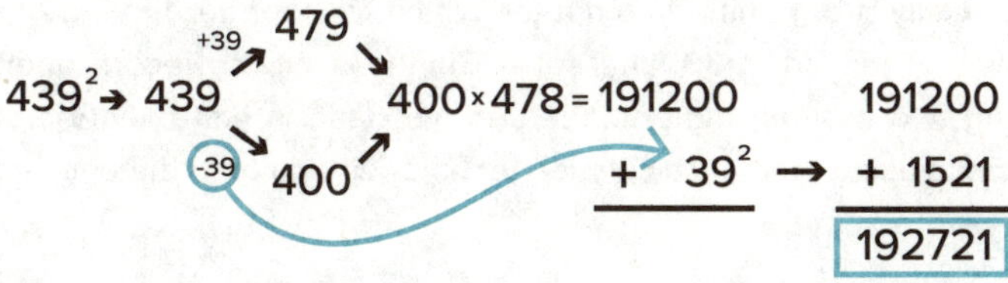

I'll admit, that one is tricky, especially because you have to remember the first answer while working on the second. Keep practicing—and the more efficient you get with these steps, the less memory you'll need.

That said, it shouldn't be too hard to memorize all one hundred squares (from one to ninety-nine). We have the number memory techniques from chapter 1 to do that. Spoiler alert: I have them all memorized! It makes the second part of a large problem like the previous one much, much easier.*

GENIUS PROFILE:
SHAKUNTALA DEVI

Shakuntala Devi was dubbed "the Human Computer" because no machine at the time could keep up with her mental calculation abilities. Born in India in 1929, she demonstrated extraordinary math skills from a young age, despite having no formal education. By the time she was a teenager, she was traveling the world, performing complex mental calculations onstage that stunned mathematicians and scientists alike.

For one of her most jaw-dropping feats, in 1977, she found the twenty-third root of a 201-digit number in fifty seconds—faster than a specially programmed computer, which took longer to verify her answer. Then, in 1980, she set a Guinness World Record, multiplying two thirteen-digit numbers in her head in just twenty-eight seconds using mental calculation techniques similar to the ones you just learned.

* If you want to see a truly mind-blowing mental calculation feat, make sure to watch this video of Art Benjamin on YouTube: He's a well-known mental calculator and is known for squaring five-digit numbers live. It's incredible to see! ("Faster than a calculator," Arthur Benjamin, TEDxOxford, www.youtube.com/watch?v=e4PTvXtz4GM.)

HOW TO DIVIDE IN YOUR HEAD

Division doesn't get nearly as much love as multiplication, but it's just as important—maybe even more. We divide things constantly in real life, whether we realize it or not.

We use division when we're splitting the bill at a restaurant with friends—how much does each person owe? Or figuring out travel time—if a road trip is 360 miles and you're driving 60 miles per hour, how long will it take? Or cooking and baking—if a recipe calls for three cups of flour but you're making half the amount, how much do you need?

These are all division problems in disguise. And the faster you can divide numbers in your head, the easier life gets.

But division always feels like the "harder" operation to most people. There's good news, though: division is the only math operation we were originally taught from left to right. So, if anything, with your newly learned mental math skill sets, it should actually feel more intuitive than everything we've done so far.

MENTAL LONG DIVISION

Let's start with a classic long division problem:

EXAMPLE: 169 ÷ 6

We approach this just as we did in grade school:

1. **How many times does 6 fit into the leftmost digits?**
   - **6 doesn't fit into 1, so we extend to 16.**
   - **6 fits into 16 twice (2 × 6 = 12).***
   - **2 is the first digit of our answer. So we can say "twenty . . ."**
2. **Subtract:**
   - **16 – 12 = 4, bring down the 9, making 49.**
3. **How many times does 6 go into 49?**
   - **8 times (8 × 6 = 48).**
   - **8 is our next digit, so we can finish saying "twenty . . . eight!"**
4. **Remainder:**
   - **49 – 48 = 1, so the remainder is 1.**
   - **Final answer: 28 remainder 1, or 28⅙.**
   - **As a decimal, ⅙ = 0.1666 . . . , so we could say → 28.1666 . . .**

* Since 6 doesn't go into 1 but does go into 16, and there's one digit left (the 9), our answer must have 2 digits.

```
           2          2          28          28
6)169 →  6)169 →  6)169 →  6)169 →  6)169 →  28R1
          -12        -12        -12         -12
                      49         49          49
                                -48         -48
                                              1
```

***EXAMPLE:* 497 ÷ 15**

1. **Does 15 fit into the 4? No. How about 49? Yes!**
    - **3 times (3 × 15 = 45). 3 is the first digit of our answer.**
    - **Same logic as before; we know our answer is two digits, so we can say "thirty . . ."**
2. **Subtract:**
    - **49 – 45 = 4, bring down the 7, making 47.**
3. **How many times does 15 go into 47?**
    - **3 times (3 × 15 = 45).**
    - **We can finish saying "thirty . . . three!"**
4. **Remainder:**
    - **47 – 45 = 2, so the remainder is 2.**

Final answer: 33 remainder 2, or 33 2/15

```
              3           3          33          33
15)497 →  15)497 →  15)497 →  15)497 →  15)497 →  33R2
             -45         -45        -45         -45
                          47         47          47
                                    -45         -45
                                                  1
```

Sadly, there aren't any magical tricks for super-fast division as with multiplication. *This* is the way. But with practice, you can start to mentally divide numbers as easily as you multiply them.

TURNING REMAINDERS INTO DECIMALS

What really makes mental division impressive is being able to say the decimal places from a division problem instead of a remainder or fraction. This, my friend, is all memory. I have a lot of these memorized (at least for single-digit divisors).

Let's go through some of the most useful decimal equivalents. Most of these you probably already know:

Fractions of 2, 3, and 4:

½	0.5
⅓	0.333 . . .*
⅔	0.666 . . .
¼	0.25
2/4 = ½	0.5
¾	0.75

Fifths have an easy pattern:

⅕	0.2
⅖	0.4
⅗	0.6
⅘	0.8

The sixths are mostly recognizable when reduced, with two new ones you have to memorize:

⅙	0.1666 . . .
2/6 = ⅓	0.333 . . .
3/6 = ½	0.5
4/6 = ⅔	0.666 . . .
⅚	0.8333 . . .

Eighths seem tricky, but they're not:

⅛	0.125 (memorize this one)
2/8 = ¼	0.25
⅜	0.375 (this is just 3 × ⅛ = 3 × 0.125)
4/8 = ½	0.5
⅝	0.625 (this is just 5 × ⅛ = 5 × 0.125)
6/8 = ¾	0.75
⅞	0.875 (you guessed it, it's 7 × ⅛ = 7 × 0.125)

The ninths have their own special thing going on. Every fraction over 9 is just the numerator repeated:

* Any time I put a trailing ". . ." after a decimal, it means that everything repeats from that point on.

1/9	0.111 . . .
2/9	0.222 . . .
3/9	0.333 . . .
4/9	0.444 . . .
5/9	0.555 . . .
6/9	0.666 . . .
7/9	0.777 . . .
8/9	0.888 . . .

Tenths are obvious:

1/10	0.1
2/10	0.2
3/10	0.3
4/10	0.4

. . . and so on.

We don't really need to know more than this, but the elevenths are interesting. All you need to know is that 1/11 = 0.0909. With that, the rest is a breeze. Just multiply that by the numerator:

2/11	0.1818 . . .
3/11	0.2727 . . .
4/11	0.3636 . . .
5/11	0.4545 . . .

. . . and so on.

Notice the pattern? It's just the 9 times tables repeated!

Now for the sevenths. These ones follow a special *cyclic pattern*. The key to mastering them is memorizing just *one*:

1/7	0.142857 . . .

Notice it's just 14 (which is 7 × 2), then 14 doubled (28), then 28 doubled (well, not quite but almost. It's 56, but let's say it is but rounded up to 57). The decimals 142857 repeat forever. But here's the trick: Every multiple of 1/7 is just the same sequence, just shifted around.

2/7	0.285714 . . .
3/7	0.428571 . . .
4/7	0.571428 . . .

5/7	0.714285 . . .
6/7	0.857142 . . .

Once you know 1/7, you know all of them! And if you can't memorize these, no worries. Whatever the numerator is (the top number), multiply it by the first two digits, 14, and you should roughly get the two starting digits of that seventh's decimal sequence, and that will give you the rest.

So, if someone asked you, *hey, what's 151 ÷ 7?* You'd say *hold on a minute.*

Then, you'd say *twenty* . . . (because 7 goes into 15 twice). Then, you would continue with your mental calculation, thinking *2 × 7 = 14, subtract 140 from 151 and get 11. And 7 goes into 11 once, with a remainder of 4.* Got it!

Then you'd finish saying *twenty . . . one*. And then instead of saying *remainder 4 or 4/7,* you would say *twenty-one point five seven one four two eight* (and then keep repeating that decimal over and over until people's minds melt right off).

HOW TO LOOK LIKE A DIVISION FREAK

Mental calculators like to show off by dividing numbers that are *cyclic*, or numbers that create patterns of repeating decimal places when the cyclical number is the divisor. Seven, as seen above, is one of those numbers, with six repeated decimals.

Now, in the previous example dividing by seven, I said you could repeat the decimals until your audiences' minds melted. But, if you recited those six digits repeatedly, eventually they'd realize you're just repeating the same six digits. If you used a *bigger* cyclic number, you'd have more digits to list before they repeated.

The numbers 7, 17, 19, 23, 29, 47, 59, 61, 97, 109, and 113 are all cyclic. And they each have x – 1 repeating digits (where x is the cyclical number you're using). So 29 has twenty-eight repeating decimal numbers, 17 has sixteen, and 109 has one hundred and eight.

Here are the values for reference:

1/7	0.142857 . . . (6 digits)
1/17	0.0588235294117647 . . . (16 digits)
1/19	0.052631578947368421 . . . (18 digits)
1/23	0434782608695652173913 . . . (22 digits)
1/29	0.0344827586206896551724137931 . . . (28 digits)

1/47	0.0212765957446808510638297872340425531914893617 . . . (46 digits)
1/59	0.0169491525423728813559322033898305084745762711864406779661 . . . (58 digits)
1/61	0.016393442622950819672131147540983606557377049180327868852459 (60 digits)
1/97	0.010309278350515463917525773195876288659793814432989690721649484536082474226804123711340206185567 (96 digits)
1/109	0.009174311926605504587155963302752293577981651376146788990825688073394495412844036697247706422018348623853211 (108 digits)

First, you must have one of these sequences memorized beforehand (or as many as you want). But then, as with 7, whether it's 2/61 or 15/23, all you need to do to figure out where in the sequence of digits that particular fraction begins. To do that, take the numerator and multiply it by the first few digits of the original decimal you memorized for that cyclic number.

So, if you were doing 2/59, you would look at 1/59's decimal value (which you would have pre-memorized) and know that it starts with 0.0169. Then you would multiply 2 (the numerator) × 0.0169 = 0.338. Searching through the sequence you memorized, you'd find it about halfway through (sometimes you may need to round the last digit up, but it should be clear where it is in the sequence). Just start your answer reciting there and cycle around and repeat as long as you like. So, 2/59 = 0.3389830508474 . . .

This isn't necessarily the easiest of mental tricks to show off, but the effect is wild. People will think you can calculate super-difficult divisions in mere seconds!

FINDING DIVISORS: A QUICK-CHECK SUPERPOWER

Knowing whether a number is divisible by another number, without *actually* dividing, is a game changer. It saves time, helps you spot patterns, and makes you look like a math genius.

Here are some fast divisibility tests you can use instantly.

DIVISIBILITY RULES (THE EASY ONES)

- **Divisible by 2 → If the last digit is even (0, 2, 4, 6, 8), the number is divisible by 2. That's it. Super simple.**
- **Divisible by 4 → If the last two digits form a number divisible by 4, then the whole number is divisible by 4.**

EXAMPLE: 1024 → Last two digits are 24, which is divisible by 4.

So, 1024 is divisible by 4.

- Divisible by 8 → If the last three digits form a number divisible by 8, then the whole number is divisible by 8.

EXAMPLE: 4096 → Last three digits 096 are divisible by 8.

You could also halve the number three times. If the result is still a whole number, it's divisible by 8.

EXAMPLE: 846 → Half = 423 → Half again = 211.5 (not whole!) → Not divisible by 8.

DIVISIBILITY BY 3, 6, AND 9 (ALL DIGIT SUM TRICKS)

- Divisible by 3 → Add up all the digits. If the sum is divisible by 3, so is the original number.

EXAMPLE: 3261 → 3 + 2 + 6 + 1 = 12 → 12 is divisible by 3 → Hence, so is 3261.

- Divisible by 9 → Same rule as 3, but for 9. If the sum of the digits is a multiple of 9, the whole number is divisible by 9.

EXAMPLE: 5832 → 5 + 8 + 3 + 2 = 18 → 18 is divisible by 9 → So is 5832.

- Divisible by 6 → A number is divisible by 6 if it's divisible by BOTH 2 and 3.

EXAMPLE: 432 →

- Last digit is even (divisible by 2)
- Sum of digits: 4 + 3 + 2 = 9 (divisible by 3)
- So, 432 is divisible by 6.

DIVISIBILITY BY 5 AND 10 (EVEN FASTER!)

- Divisible by 5 → If a number ends in 0 or 5, it's divisible by 5

EXAMPLE: 2345 → Ends in 5 → Divisible by 5.

- Divisible by 10 → If a number ends in 0, it's divisible by 10.

EXAMPLE: 7890 → Ends in 0 → Divisible by 10.

THE COOLER ONES: 7, 11, AND 37

- Divisibility by 7 (a little trickier) → If you can add or subtract a multiple of 7 to the original number so that the result is a multiple of 7, the original number is divisible by 7.

EXAMPLE: IS 119 DIVISIBLE BY 7?

- Notice that 7 × 7 = 49. I like to think of a multiple of 7 that results in the same last digit of my original number (so when I subtract it from the original number, my result ends in a 0).

- 119 – 49 = 70, which is clearly a multiple of 7.
- So, 119 is divisible by 7.

- Divisibility by 11 (Alternating Sum Rule) → Alternate subtracting and adding digits from left to right. If the result is 0 or a multiple of 11, the number is divisible by 11.

EXAMPLE: 8492 → 8 – 4 + 9 – 2 = 11 → Divisible by 11.

EXAMPLE: 314162 → 3 – 1 + 4 – 1 + 6 - 2 = 9 (not a multiple of 11) → Not divisible by 11.

DIVISIBILITY BY 37 (THE ULTIMATE PARTY TRICK)

Okay, this one is wildly specific and works only for the prime number 37. But it's super fun to show off.

1. Memorize all multiples of 37 up to 1,000 (don't worry, they're easy to recognize and there aren't all that many).
2. Break the number you want to test for divisibility into 3-digit chunks from left to right.
3. Add up those chunks—if the sum is a multiple of 37, the original number is too.
4. Since you've memorized them all up to 1,000, it will be easy to check!

EXAMPLE: IS 1121796 DIVISIBLE BY 37?

- Break it up: 001, 121, 796*
- Add them together: 1 + 121 + 796 = 918
- Is 918 a multiple of 37? Referencing with your memorized multiples of 37 up to 1,000 will tell you *nope*. So, 1121796 is NOT divisible by 37.

Why 37, though? Well, it's prime and has a cool pattern with repeating decimals when dividing by it.†

Here's the list of multiples of 37 (for memorization):

37, 74, 111, 148, 185, 222, 259, 296, 333, 370, 407, 444, 481, 518, 555, 592, 629, 666, 703, 740, 777, 814, 851, 888, 925, 962, 999‡

---

* Notice that the first digit got chunked with two zeros, since it didn't have other numbers to fill out its 3-digit chunk.

† Genius fact: If you ask someone to think of a random number between 10 and 100, most people will say 37, because it feels random.

‡ You don't even need to really memorize them, just be able to recognize them. A lot of

MENTAL SQUARE ROOTS

Remember when we were squaring two-digit numbers? Well, what if someone gave you the squared result and you had to find the square root?

These are surprisingly easy to mentally calculate.

For example, if someone gives you 6889, you should be able to figure out that the original number was 83—without a calculator.

To do this, you first need to memorize the squares of numbers from 0 to 10:

0^2	0
1^2	1
2^2	4
3^2	9
4^2	16
5^2	25
6^2	36
7^2	49
8^2	64
9^2	81
10^2	100

If you don't already know these, take a second to burn them into your brain. Then, apply the following steps.

STEP 1:

- **Take the leftmost two digits of the given number.***
- **Find where that number falls in your list of memorized perfect squares.**
- **Choose the lower one. This is the first digit of your answer.**

STEP 2:

- **Look at the last digit of the given number.**
- **Compare it with the last digits of the squares you memorized and find the ones that match.**

---

these are very memorable numbers!

* The given number should have four digits. In some cases, there may only be three. If so, just take the leftmost single digit.

- If it's 5, you're done. That's your second digit. Otherwise, there will always be two possible answers—and we'll need one more step to decide which one is correct.

STEP 3:

- A quick midpoint check helps pick the correct answer.
- Find the midpoint between the two possible options and compare.
    - For example, if you've narrowed your answer to be either 83 or 87, choose a midpoint of 85.
    - We know how to calculate 85^2 quickly—it's 7225.
    - Check whether that answer is greater or less than your original number.
    - If it's greater, go with the smaller number. If less, go with the larger.

EXAMPLE: $\sqrt{6889}$

- Look at the first two digits → 68.
- 68 is between 8^2 → 64 and 9^2 → 81.
- That means the first digit of our answer is 8.
- Notice our given number ends in 9.
- Looking at our memorized table, only $3^2 = 9$ and $7^2 = 49$ end in 9. So, our answer must end in either 3 or 7 → meaning it's 83 or 87.
- Figure out the midpoint → 85.
    - $85^2 = 7225$, which is greater than 6889.
    - So, our answer must be the smaller one → 83.

Final answer: 83

EXAMPLE: $\sqrt{1936}$

- Look at the first two digits → 19.
- 19 is between 4^2 → 16 and 5^2 → 25.
- That means the first digit of our answer is 4.
- Notice our given number ends in 6.
- According to our table, only $4^2 = 16$ and $6^2 = 36$ end in 6. So, our answer must end in either 4 or 6 → meaning it's 44 or 46.
- Figure out the midpoint → 45.
    - $45^2 = 2025$, which is greater than 1936.
    - So, our answer must be the smaller one → 44.

Final answer: 44

MENTAL CUBE ROOTS

Finding cube roots is even easier than square roots, because each cube has a unique last digit—meaning there's only one possible answer!

A cube means multiplying a number by itself three times:

- $2^3 = 2 \times 2 \times 2 = 8$
- $3^3 = 3 \times 3 \times 3 = 27$

The process for mentally cube-rooting is similar to squaring. We need to start by memorizing all the cubes for numbers 0 to 10:

0^3	0
1^3	1
2^3	8
3^3	27
4^3	64
5^3	125
6^3	216
7^3	343
8^3	512
9^3	729
10^3	1000

Unlike the list of squares, notice that each one has a unique last digit—this will be key for solving cube roots quickly (even quicker than square roots). Here are the steps:

STEP 1:

- **Separate the number into two parts: the leftmost digits (first chunk, before the comma) and the last three digits (second chunk).***
- **The first chunk determines the first digit of our answer.**
- **The last digit of the second chunk gives us the second digit.**

STEP 2:

- **Find the first digit in the same way as for square roots. Look at the leftmost chunk and find where it falls on your memorized cube roots list. Choose the lower number. This is the first digit of your answer.**

---

* Most of the given numbers will be 6 digits, but they can also be 5 or 4 digits. Either way, there will be a comma. The leftmost digits are all the digits left of the comma. The rightmost digits are the three digits after the comma.

STEP 3:

- Look at the last digit of the given number and match it to the correct one from your memorized list that also ends with the same digit. This is the second digit to your answer.

EXAMPLE: 262144

1. Break it up into chunks 262 and 144.
2. Find the first digit:
   - 262 is between $6^3 \rightarrow 216$ and $7^3 \rightarrow 343$
   - That means the first digit is 6.
3. Look at the last digit of the cube (144).
4. Find which cube number ends in that digit. That's 4, because $4^3 = 64$
5. So, the second digit must be 4.

Final answer: 64

THE MAGIC SQUARE

Magic squares are one of those math tricks that feel straight-up impossible when you see them; solving one can dazzle anyone. At first glance, they just look like a random grid of numbers—but hidden inside is a perfectly balanced system where every row, column, and diagonal (even the four corners, as well as any 2 x 2 square) add up to the same total!

Ancient mathematicians were obsessed with these. Da Vinci sketched them, mathematicians in China used them more than two thousand years ago, and even Benjamin Franklin toyed with them. There is a *trick* to them, which I'll explain below, and the following is just one of many ways to do it.

Before performing the trick, you'll need to memorize the following 4 × 4 grid layout:

A	1	12	7
11	8	D	2
5	10	3	C
4	B	6	9

If that's tricky for you, there's actually a pattern hidden inside that makes it way easier to commit to memory:

- **The bottom-left half of the first column is 5 and 4.**
- **The top half of the second column is 1 and 8.**
- **The bottom half of the third column is 3 and 6.**
- **The top half of the fourth column is 7 and 2.**

GENIUS PROFILE:
SRINIVASA RAMANUJAN

Ramanujan was known for seeing deep mathematical patterns where others saw none. One of the most famous stories about his genius comes from a hospital visit by British mathematician G. H. Hardy. Trying to make small talk, Hardy remarked that he had arrived in a taxi with the unremarkable number 1729. Without missing a beat, Ramanujan replied, "No, it is a very interesting number. It is the smallest number expressible as the sum of two cubes in two different ways." And he was right:

$$1729 = 1^3 + 12^3 = 9^3 + 10^3$$

Impressively, that kind of intuitive insight into numbers was typical for Ramanujan. Despite having little formal training, he produced groundbreaking work in number theory, infinite series, continued fractions, and modular forms. Many of his notebooks contained results that mathematicians are still proving to this day.

These form 54, 18, 36, and 72—which are all multiples of 9 and add up to 9.

The bottom-right corner always holds a 9. Then there's a final zigzag of 10, 11, and 12. Once you get this locked in your head, you're ready to perform.

When you're in front of an audience, draw an empty 4 × 4 grid. Then, ask someone to give you any two-digit number between 20 and 100.

This will be the total that every row, column, and diagonal adds to.

Next, we need to calculate A, B, C, and D. Here's the only part you have to calculate on the fly:

- **A = Audience's number – 20**
- **B = A + 1**
- **C = A + 2**
- **D = A – 1**

EXAMPLE: If the audience's number was 38, A would be 18, B would be 19, C would be 20, and D would be 17.

These four numbers are the secret sauce. They are what make the magic work. Once you've figured out A, B, C, and D, plug them into your original memorized grid. You can fill them in any order, but make sure A, B, C, and D are in their correct spots—they control the final total.

That's it. You're done. Try adding up every row, every column, every diagonal, every 2 × 2 box, even the four corners. You'll see it's magically the same answer, every time.*

HOW TO ESTIMATE ANYTHING

Some questions seem impossible to answer off the top of your head. How many piano tuners are there in Chicago? How many gallons of water does an elephant drink in a year? How many blades of grass are in Central Park?

Most people would shrug and say they have no idea. But physicist Enrico Fermi would probably have taken a minute, broken the problem into parts, and come up with a surprisingly accurate estimate—without needing Google, a calculator, or any hard data.

That's exactly what Fermi Estimation is: a way to get a quick, reasonable answer to a big question using logic, simple math, and a few reasonable

* There are many ways to do a magic square—some more magical than others—but this version does the trick.

assumptions. Fermi estimations aren't concerned with getting the exact number. They just want to get a ballpark figure, something close enough to be useful.

Fermi's approach relied on simple mental calculations that allowed him to estimate almost anything relatively quickly, and with surprising accuracy.

But why does this matter? Well, estimations are needed all the time. Scientists, engineers, and business leaders use them to make quick, informed decisions when exact numbers aren't available. You can use them too—to estimate how long a project will take, how much a road trip will cost, or even how many people will show up to your event. Whatever you want!

There are many ways to make approximations for things, but I find Fermi's method to be the easiest and quickest way (and often the most accurate). There isn't a strict, step-by-step formula to it, but the general idea is this: Start by making rough assumptions that feel reasonable, then build a chain of logic to estimate the thing you're trying to figure out. The key is to base your guesses on *orders of magnitude*—that is, ballpark figures that are in the right range of scale.

An order of magnitude refers to powers of ten. So, if something is in the hundreds (whether it's 200 or 732 or 999), it's on the same order of magnitude as 10^2; if it's in the thousands, that's 10^3, and so on. You don't have to use exact numbers—that's not the point; you don't *know* the exact numbers—but we do want to use the correct order of magnitude.

For example, you might ask yourself how many people live in New York City. If you just had to guess based on orders of magnitude, would you say there are 100 people in NYC? No way, way too few! What about the next order of magnitude, 1,000? Nope. How about 10,000? No. 100,000? We're getting there, but that still feels too small. 1,000,000? Now we're talking. I'm probably in the range. Now, I think you probably have an instant feeling that while the true answer might be in the millions, that the answer is *not* 1,000,000. So, let's scope out the next order of magnitude: 10,000,000? Hmm, that feels like too much, but I would lean toward the answer being closer to 10,000,000 than 1,000,000. Okay, so if that's our gut guess, we would use the number 10,000,000. The real answer, by the way, is 8.2 million! Not too far off, eh?

Here's a random question to try this on: *How many spoons are there in America?*

At first glance, this seems impossible to answer. There's no database that tracks the number of spoons in every household, restaurant, or factory. But with Fermi Estimation, we don't need exact data; we just need to break the problem into logical steps, make reasonable assumptions, and get a good enough answer.

Let's think it through.

STEP 1: DEFINE THE QUESTION

Are we counting all spoons ever made? Only spoons currently in use? What about disposable spoons? Let's assume we're estimating the number of spoons currently in existence, meaning both in homes and businesses, but ignoring spoons that have been lost, melted down, or destroyed.

STEP 2: BREAK IT DOWN

Instead of thinking about the whole world at once, let's start with a smaller unit, like an average household, and then scale up.

We'll also need to account for spoons in restaurants, cafés, hotels, and other businesses.

STEP 3: MAKE REASONABLE ASSUMPTIONS

Spoons in households:*

- **The world has about 8 billion people.**
- **The average household might have 4 people (some have more, some fewer).**
- **That gives us about 2 billion households worldwide.**
- **An average household probably has at least 10 to 15 spoons (including teaspoons and tablespoons). Let's assume 12 spoons per household as a middle ground.**
- **So, in households alone: 2 billion households × 12 spoons = 24 billion spoons.**

Spoons in restaurants, cafés, and businesses:

Households aren't the only places with spoons—restaurants, cafés, hotels, and workplaces also stock them.

- **Let's estimate 1 restaurant or café per 500 people (since some areas are dense with them, while others have few).**
- **That's about 16 million restaurants worldwide (since 8 billion ÷ 500 = 16 million).**
- **If each restaurant has around 100 spoons (including spares), that's: 16 million × 100 = 1.6 billion spoons**
- **Hotels, office cafeterias, and other businesses likely add *another* billion spoons.**

---

* Notice I'm going for more specific numbers instead of just powers of 10. You have the flexibility here to do that if you feel confident about your guesses. As long as they are in the ballpark, you're good!

GENIUS PROFILE:
ENRICO FERMI

Fermi was one of the sharpest scientific minds of the twentieth century. He was a nuclear physicist who worked on the Manhattan Project and was behind the first controlled nuclear chain reaction. One of the things that truly set him apart from other scientists at the time was his uncanny ability to make fast, accurate estimates from limited data.

In 1950, during lunch at Los Alamos, the topic turned to the idea that the universe should be teeming with alien life. Fermi famously asked, "Where is everybody?" Given the age of the universe and number of stars, we should've seen signs of intelligent life by now. So where was it?

Rather than leaving the question as unanswerable, he broke it down. How many stars? How many had planets? How many could support life, and how many of those might develop intelligence? Even using conservative guesses, the math pointed to thousands—if not millions—of space-faring civilizations. And yet, silence.

That question sparked what we now call the Fermi Paradox. The reasoning needed to explore it—breaking down the probability by considering stars, planets, and conditions for life—would later be formalized in the Drake Equation. Fermi's approach showcased what we now call Fermi Estimation: a method of taking something wildly uncertain and breaking it down into smaller, solvable steps.

Disposable spoons:

- **If we factor in plastic spoons used for takeout, flights, and events, we're looking at billions more in circulation.**
- **The world produces hundreds of billions of plastic utensils yearly, but since many are thrown away, we won't count them as "existing" spoons in the long run. A reasonable estimate is that at any given time, 3 to 5 billion disposable spoons exist in storage, shipments, or active use.**

STEP 4: DO THE MATH

Now let's add it all up:

- **Households: ~24 billion spoons**
- **Restaurants and businesses: ~2.6 billion spoons**
- **Disposable spoons in circulation: ~4 billion spoons**

Total estimate: ~30 billion spoons worldwide.

STEP 5: REALITY CHECK

Does 30 billion spoons sound reasonable?

- **That's about 3 to 4 spoons per person on Earth when averaging across all places (homes, restaurants, businesses).**
- **Given how common spoons are and how long they last, this seems plausible—not too high or too low.**

Final answer: about 30 billion spoons.

And just like that, from almost nothing but guesses, we have a tangible answer! That's the power of Fermi Estimation. Could we be off by some factor? Possibly. But is this order of magnitude correct? Almost certainly. And that's the goal—to get close, fast, without needing exact data. I'll provide some more examples for you to try on your own at the end of the chapter (page 156).

USEFUL CONVERSION TRICKS

There are seemingly endless calculations and conversions in daily life. We could probably whip out our cell phones and fetch the answer in just a few seconds, but being able to do a quick, rough calculation is sometimes even faster (and a great mental exercise). Keep in mind that these calculations aren't always *exact* but are close enough to make the calculations mentally easier as well as accurate *enough*.

MILES TO KILOMETERS (AND BACK)

If you need to convert miles to kilometers, you have to multiply by 1.6. That's easy to do in your head:

- **Add half your miles to the original miles.**
- **Add 10% of your original miles (remember, 10% is just moving the decimal of your number over by 1. So, for example, if you had 17, 10% is 1.7. If you had 5, 10% is 0.5).**
- **You can also just do the first step, and that would be equivalent to multiplying your miles by 1.5, very close to the right answer as well.**

EXAMPLE:

- **17 miles → ½ that is 8.5, add that back to 17 and get 25.5, add 1.7 (10% of the original 17), that's 27.2.**

To go the other way (kilometers to miles), multiply by 0.6.

- **Halve your kilometers and add 10% of the original kilometers.**
- **Even just halving your kilometers is close enough.**

EXAMPLE:

- **22 km → ½ is 11, then add 2.2 = 13.2.**

METERS TO FEET (AND BACK)

I use this one all the time when climbing in the mountains. The true conversion from meters to feet requires a multiplication of 3.281. But for our purposes, we can just call that 3.3 and it makes our life a whole lot easier.

- **Multiply your meters by 3 and then add 10% of your answer to itself.**

EXAMPLE:

- **4,590 meters → I would first round to 4,600 meters to make my life easier. Then 4,600 × 3 = 13,800 + (10% of 13,800 which is 1,380, or roughly 1,400), 13,800 + 1,400 = 15,200.**

The real conversion is 15,059.06. Not too far off!

Going the other way from feet to meters? Dividing by 3.281 is difficult. So, instead . . .

- **Drop the last digit from your feet, multiply your answer by 3. Voilà!**

EXAMPLE:

- **12,500 feet → drop the last digit, 1,250, then times 3 = 3,750. Not exact (the exact answer is 3,810 meters), but so simple I'll take it.**

POUNDS TO KILOGRAMS (AND BACK)

To convert pounds to kilograms:

- **Divide pounds by 2 and subtract 10%.**

EXAMPLE:

- **200 lbs. → divide 200 by 2 to get 100, then take off 10%, that would be an extra 10, to get 90 kg**
- **150 lbs. → 150 ÷ 2 = 75 → take off 10%, which is 7.5 → gives 67.5 kg**

Going from kilograms to pounds?

- **Double it and add 10%.**

EXAMPLE:

- **50 kg → 50 × 2 = 100 → add 10% (10) → 110 lbs.**
- **80 kg → 80 × 2 = 160 → add 10% (16) → 176 lbs.**

TIP CALCULATION

This all depends on how well you tip, but as a former restaurant server myself, in America you should be tipping at least 20 percent.* It's also super easy to calculate the tip that way!

- **20% → Just move the decimal one place left and double it.**

EXAMPLE:

- **$45 bill → Move decimal: $4.50 → Double it: $9.00 tip**
- **$72 bill → Move decimal: $7.20 → Double it: $14.40 tip**

If you only need 10%, just move the decimal left once. If you need 15%, take 10% and add half of that.

EXAMPLE:

- **$60 bill → 10% is $6**
- **$60 bill → 10% is $6 → Half of that is $3 → Total tip: $9 (that's 15%)**

---

* Here's a general percentage calculation tip: Flip them to make mental math easier. For example: 12% of 25 is the same as 25% of 12.

FAHRENHEIT TO CELSIUS (AND BACK)

The exact formula is clunky, so here's the fast mental math version:

Fahrenheit to Celsius:

- **Subtract 30, then halve it.**

EXAMPLE:

- **90°F → 90 – 30 = 60 → Half of 60 = 30°C**
- **50°F → 50 – 30 = 20 → Half of 20 = 10°C**

Celsius to Fahrenheit:

- **Double it, then add 30.**

EXAMPLE:

- **20°C → 20 × 2 = 40 → 40 + 30 = 70°F**
- **10°C → 10 × 2 = 20 → 20 + 30 = 50°F**

These calculations aren't exact, but they're fast and good enough for everyday use.

HOW TO CALCULATE ANY DAY OF THE YEAR

When I was living in Miami, I became aware of a local getting a lot of press for a very different (and *really* cool) mental ability: remembering calendar dates (or, more aptly, *calculating* days of the week). His name was Yusnier Viera, a Cuban migrant who had made a name for himself by being super quick with numbers. He gravitated to the Doomsday Calculation, which is the algorithm one can follow to figure out what day of the week any day falls on in history, relatively quickly. He tweaked this well-known formula to fit his speed-calculation prowess and soon after became a world record holder in the mental calculation of calendar dates.*

Originally, most of the world used the Julian Calendar, which was introduced in 45 BCE (thanks, Julius Caesar!). It didn't accurately account for leap years, though, as it added a leap day every four years (which is too frequent). Our current calendar, the Gregorian Calendar (invented by Pope Gregory XIII), was introduced in 1582 to rectify this issue by adding a small adjustment: that century years (1600, 1700, 1800, etc.) be considered a leap year *only* if they're divisible by 100 *and* 400. Before, it would

* He once held the world record for calculating the most dates in one minute: 109, to be exact . . . *wow*!

have allowed 1700, 1800, and 1900 to be given a leap day. But no more! Only 1600, 2000, 2400, etc.

Why does this matter? Well, the Earth doesn't perfectly rotate around the sun in exactly 365 days. It's actually 365.242374 days. The Julian Calendar was an approximation of 365.25, while the Gregorian Calendar boosted that a bit closer at 365.2422. Not perfect, but pretty darn close!

When different countries started to switch their calendar, they had to skip some days. Catholic countries such as Spain, Portugal, Italy, and France all switched over immediately by skipping ten days to make up for all those extra leap days. Can you imagine what that must have been like? People went to sleep one night, on October 4, 1582, and when they woke up, the date was October 15. Other countries joined later. For example, the Protestant British (and subsequently, the American colonies) switched over on September 2, 1752 (two hundred years later!). If you look at an (accurate) American calendar, you'll see it jumps from September 2 (a Wednesday) to September 14 (a Thursday). *Weird.*

In 1973, an incredibly bright mathematical genius named John Conway devised the famous Doomsday Algorithm* for mentally calculating any day of the week as per the Gregorian Calendar. Supposedly, he drew inspiration from Lewis Carroll's (yes, the author of *Alice in Wonderland*) perpetual calendar algorithm, which he published in March 1887. While Yusnier's algorithm isn't exactly like theirs, it draws inspiration from them and has been optimized to make the mental calculation easier and faster. In other words, *you're welcome*!

Being able to quickly say on what day of the week a particular date falls may look impossible, but it's actually relatively easy and is a dazzling skill.

Let's dive into the *actual* optimized algorithm that Yusnier developed so that you can learn this genius trick too.

The calculation is easy, grade school arithmetic. It's helpful to just learn the code for the current year (plus or minus a few, to have on hand). Then, if you want to delve a little further (it's really not *that* much more difficult), you can learn how to do it for *any* year—past or future. Even though I refer to this genius skill as "memorizing the entire calendar," it really isn't much of a memory skill at all, but rather an easy mental-math skill.

---

* His method: Certain dates fall on the same day of the week each year, called "doomsdays." These include 4/4, 6/6, 8/8, 10/10, 12/12, plus "working 9-to-5 at the 7-11" (5/9, 9/5, 7/11, 11/7), 1/3 (1/4 in leap years), 2/28 (2/29 in leap years), and 3/14 (pi day!). Once you know the doomsday for a given year (2025 is Friday), you can calculate any date by counting days from the nearest doomsday. The doomsday shifts forward/backward one day each year, or two in leap years. It's a fast method once you know the year's doomsday—but calculating that is the tricky part, which is why Yusnier's method may be faster overall. If you want to know how to calculate any doomsday for any date in history using Conway's method, check it out here: www.everydaygeniusacademy.com/book/calendardates.

Let's get to the codes!

For recent years, all you need to know are the following codes:*

2020 is a 5
2021 is a 6
2022 is a 0
2023 is a 1
2024 is a 3
2025 is a 4
2026 is a 5
2027 is a 6
2028 is a 1
2029 is a 2
2030 is a 3

For the month, remember the following list (I've included a quick mnemonic to help you commit them to memory):

January	5	imagine 5 inches of snow in winter
February	1	the 1 month that has the fewest days
March	1	1 man marching
April	4	"Aprrrrrrril" has an r; so does "fourrrrrrr"
May	6	MAY[be] if you're lucky, you'll have sex [6]
June	2	June is way 2 hot
July	4	July 4, Independence Day!
August	0	think of A GUST of wind blowing through a hole 0
September	3	start of the school year, 3-year-olds going to preschool
October	5	think of 5 scary ghosts for Halloween
November	1	1st cold month of fall/winter
December	3	3 kings for Christmas

The code for each month will *never* change over time. So, learn these once and you'll be set!

Finally, one last easy list to memorize for the days of the week:

Sunday	0 or 7
Monday	1
Tuesday	2
Wednesday	3
Thursday	4
Friday	5
Saturday	6

* See the pattern? It moves forward by one day each year. Except on a leap year, when it jumps ahead by two. I'll constantly update this list for later years, even well before and past the date of this book's publication, in case you want to look it up! (www.everydaygeniusacademy.com/book/calendardates)

Now for the math.

First, during our calculation, every addition we do, whenever we spill *over* 7, we go back down to 0 (and in our weird world of math, 7 is synonymous with 0).

For example, say I have the number 2 and I add 2, that's 4. Duh.

But say I have 4 + 4. That would typically be 8, but that spills over 7 by 1, so my answer is 1. If we start on a bigger number like 28, just divide by 7 and keep the remainder. That's essentially what we're doing here: finding the remainder.

So, say we have 28 + 4. I can always simplify any large-ish number by figuring out its remainder when divided by 7, and then add from there. So, I take 28 and divide it by 7 and keep the remainder: 0. Now it's just 0 + 4, that's 4.

Yusnier's calendar date calculation goes as follows:

- **Take the number code for the year.**
- **Take the number code for the month.**
    - **NOTE: If you're dealing with January or February, always check if it's a leap year. If it is, subtract 1.**
- **Take the number of the day.**
- **Add them together (making sure to always divide by 7 and keep the remainder).**
- **Translate your answer, which will be a number between 0 and 6, into a day of the week: Sunday to Saturday.**
- **Be told you're a genius!**

EXAMPLE: FEBRUARY 6, 2019

- **2019's code is 3.**
- **February's month code is 1 (and 2019 is not a leap year).**
- **6th is 6.**
- **That's 3 + 1 + 6 = 10. Divide by 7 and keep the remainder, that's 3.**
- **3 is the code for Wednesday.**

So . . . February 6, 2019, was a **Wednesday**.

EXAMPLE: DECEMBER 25, 2027

- **2027's code is 6.**
- **December's month code is 3.**

- **25th is a 25 but dividing by 7 gives us 21, with a remainder of 4, so → 4.**
    - **NOTE: You can divide by 7 as you go through each step or wait until you have the final total at the end. It doesn't matter! I personally like to get rid of big numbers along the way, so I do it in stride.**
- **That's 6 + 3 + 4 = 13. Again, divide by 7 and take the remainder, which is 6 (Saturday).**

So . . . Christmas Day in 2027 is a **Saturday**!

Pretty sweet, right? You don't have to check a calendar anymore! You'll know almost instantly what day of the week a certain date falls on.

One small detail you'll have to keep in mind is leap years (a year where there is one extra day in the calendar year). The most recent leap years were in 2016, 2020, and 2024. The next few will come in 2028, 2032, and 2036. For those cases, you need to subtract 1 *only if* your month is January or February. For a year to be a leap year, the two-digit year ending needs to be divisible by four (that means you can halve it twice perfectly). If it's a century year (like 1700 or 2000), you also need to check whether the full number is divisible by 400. So, 2000 was a leap year, but 1900 was not, and the next century leap year will be 2400.

ALL THE OTHER CALENDAR DATES

Now, what if you want to do *any* year in history, not just the years I provided the codes for previously? There *is* a way to do this, but it requires a little more memorization and math. Use of the Gregorian Calendar that we know so well began in the late sixteenth century, so anything before that doesn't really make sense. But you can still apply the following method.

For the year code calculation, we will split it up into century code + 2-digit ending code.

There is a simple code list you need to learn for the century:

1600s	0
1700s	5
1800s	3
1900s	1
2000s	0
2100s	5

Notice that every four hundred years, the century code resets to 0, then it's 5, then 3, then 1, and then 0 once again. (For example, 1685 would have a century code of 0, 2021 a 0, 1905 a 1.) If you're doing any modern twenty-first-century date (2000s), you're always going to be dealing with a 0, which is easy for calculation.

In the examples above, I gave you the codes for the years 2020 to 2030 (just to get you started for some of the more recent twenty-first-century years), but we need to know *all* two-digit year endings. Those previous codes were derived from what I'm about to show you but ultimately are calculated from a century code (see above) and a year code (see below). It may seem tricky to memorize all these codes, but it's not.* Here is the list categorized by similar code:

Code	Year endings
0	05, 11, 16, 22, 33, 39, 44, 50, 61, 67, 72, 78, 89, 95
1	00, 06, 17, 23, 28, 34, 45, 51, 56, 62, 73, 79, 84, 90
2	01, 07, 12, 18, 29, 35, 40, 46, 57, 63, 68, 74, 85, 91, 96
3	02, 13, 19, 24, 30, 41, 47, 52, 58, 69, 75, 80, 86, 97
4	03, 08, 14, 25, 31, 36, 42, 53, 59, 64, 70, 81, 87, 92, 98
5	09, 15, 20, 26, 37, 43, 48, 54, 65, 71, 76, 82, 93, 99
6	04, 10, 21, 27, 32, 38, 49, 55, 60, 66, 77, 83, 88, 94

As you can see from the table above, there are seven possible codes for years. My recommended way of memorizing these is by choosing seven big Memory Palace rooms (refer back to chapter 1 for a refresher if you need it).

Then, with your number system (also, chapter 1), imagine the corresponding image for that number hanging out in that room. For example, room 0 (perhaps your kitchen, say), we would picture SOIL (05), TOT (11), TUSH (16), and everything else on that list for the 0 code, interacting and living in that room. That way, when you see a two-digit year, you'll instantly remember what room they were in and remember the code associated with

* There is a way to calculate them on the fly (but honestly, I think memorizing them is faster/easier). The formula is: year code = ([year / 4] + year + 1) % 7. Take the two-digit year ending, divide it by 4 (half it twice), and ignore any decimal places (that's what the square brackets mean). Add the original two-digit year ending, add 1 more, then do that division-by-7-but-keeping-the-remainder business from earlier (that's what the % means).

that room (just make sure to somehow LINK the 0 through 6 code digit to the room, so you know which room is which number).

Okay, back to the calendar calculation steps. What's next? The process is the same as before except you're adding two more numbers, the code for the century and the code for the year. Let's do some examples for the whole shebang:

EXAMPLE: JULY 4, 1776

- **1700s' century code is 5**
- **76's year code is 5**
- **July's month code is 4**
- **4th is 4**
- **Add it all together (dividing by 7 when you spill over):**
  - **5 + 5 + 4 + 4 = 18, dividing by 7 and taking the remainder gives you 4 (Thursday)**

And now you know: The Declaration of Independence was signed on a **Thursday**!

EXAMPLE: MAY 29, 1953

- **1900s' century code is 1**
- **53's year code is 4**
- **May's month code is 6**
- **29th is 1**
- **Add it all together (dividing by 7 when you spill over):**
  - **1 + 4 + 6 + 1 = 12, dividing by 7 and taking the remainder gives you 5 (Friday)**

May 29, 1953, was a **Friday**!

This was also the historic day that Tenzing Norgay and Edmund Hillary first summited Mt. Everest. I guess Fridays are great for big adventures!

As with anything, practice makes perfect. Whenever anyone tells you their birthday, try to mentally figure out what day of the week they were born. Once you feel confident in your answer, blurt it out and wow them! This simple mental feat will really convince people you're a genius.

Throughout this chapter, we explored how to make mental math faster, easier, and more intuitive by strengthening your number sense. One of the key takeaways was that math doesn't have to be slow or rigid. It can be flexible, intuitive, and surprisingly fun.

The best part is that mental math is a skill that compounds over time. The more you work at it, the more natural it becomes. Instead of seeing numbers as obstacles, you'll start seeing them as tools that can help you navigate the world more efficiently, think more clearly, and even impress the people around you.

So next time you need to do a quick calculation, do everything in your power not to reach for your phone. Instead, try doing it in your head first. The better you get at these techniques, the more you'll realize that number sense isn't just useful—it's everyday genius.

EXERCISES AND RESOURCES

- Make sure to take some time to practice all the skills you learned in this chapter. I've uploaded a collection of example problems (and solutions) from each section in this chapter to help sharpen your skills: www.everydaygeniusacademy.com/book/mentalcalculation.

BOOKS:

- *Secrets of Mental Math* by Arthur Benjamin—Fun, digestible tricks for fast math in your head. Great intro to number sense.
- *The World According to Wavelets* by Barbara Hubbard—A phenomenal book about numbers and patterns in the world.
- *Here's Looking at Euclid* by Alex Bellos—A playful journey through the quirks and wonders of math around the world.
- *The Essentials of Vedic Mathematics* by Rajesh Kumar Thakur—Ancient Indian shortcuts for faster mental calculations and number sense.
- *The Great Mental Calculators* by Steven B. Smith—Profiles of history's fastest human computers and how they did it.

APPS/WEBSITES/VIDEOS:

- Memoriad: www.memoriad.com—A great tool for training your mental calculation skills.
- Mathemagics: Mental Math App—A visual app for learning and training classic mental math tricks.
- Mental Calculation World Cup—If you ever plan to showcase your mental calculation skills on the world stage!
- Numberphile—One of my favorite YouTube channels about math and numbers. All about wildly engaging math ideas, patterns, and number curiosities.
- The Power of Ten: www.youtube.com/watch?v=0fKBhvDjuy0—An amazing visual representation of scale and orders of magnitude.

CHAPTER 6

PROBLEM-SOLVING AND CREATIVITY

"IN THE MIDDLE OF DIFFICULTY LIES OPPORTUNITY."
—ALBERT EINSTEIN

I WAS EDITING A VIDEO IN MY ROOM, SHARING THE SPACE WITH MY FRIEND TREVOR RAINBOLT.

WE WERE IN AFRICA, ABOUT TO HIKE KILIMANJARO—A TRIP I'D PUT TOGETHER AND WAS GUIDING. THE HIKE WOULD START TOMORROW, BUT TONIGHT WE WERE CRAMMING IN SOME LAST-MINUTE WORK BEFORE SHUTTING OUR COMPUTERS OFF FOR THE WEEK.

TREVOR AND I HAD MET EARLIER THAT YEAR, AND HE'D AGREED TO JOIN MY ANNUAL KILIMANJARO CLIMB UNDER ONE CONDITION: WE'D COLLABORATE ON SOME YOUTUBE CONTENT. OUR IDEA? TO TEACH HIM ALL THE US AREA CODES, THEN GO HEAD-TO-HEAD IN A SPEED RECALL CHALLENGE, PLACING THEM ON A MAP AS FAST AS POSSIBLE.

We both make YouTube content, always chasing that next viral hit. I create memory videos. Trevor . . . well, it is hard to explain. The best way to understand him is to watch him work.

I glanced over from my editing to see him recording himself, deadpan. "You can't find my flight in fifteen minutes," he said, quoting a comment from one of his videos—a challenge, accompanied by a random photo from an airplane window. Then, straight-faced, he responded, "You're right. It took me five."

And he wasn't bluffing. For the past five minutes, he'd been locked in, dissecting this single, seemingly useless photo. No clear landmarks, no major clues—just a random aerial shot. But in that time, he'd figured it out. The country. The time of year. The airline. The exact flight number. Even the seat number. He basically reconstructed the person's entire itinerary from a single image.

It was like watching Sherlock Holmes, but instead of solving crimes, he was pinpointing locations on Earth with almost supernatural precision. Trevor's talent is part razor-sharp deduction, part encyclopedic world knowledge, and part uncanny ability to spot and interpret details most people wouldn't even notice. And the wildest part is that it all stemmed from him training on a quirky online game called GeoGuessr, where you're given a random Google Street View image and have to figure out where you are on a map, using nothing but the clues in the image.

I shook my head. "Dude, how do you do that?"

He faced me and shrugged. "It's easier than it looks. Just practice and knowing what to look for. Wanna see it in action?" he asked.

He turned back to his computer and loaded up GeoGuessr.

The first image popped up—a tree-lined road. That's all I saw.

"See this bollard?" he asked, pointing to a tiny, seemingly insignificant pole in the ground, off to the side of the road.

I nodded.

"They only have these cigarette-shaped ones in France."

He moved his cursor to a world map and clicked somewhere in eastern France.

His guess was within *ten* kilometers of the actual spot.

Incredible. How on earth did he figure that out? I thought to myself as he pulled up the next image.

"You see this Google car image quality? It's Gen-4."

I nodded again, pretending to follow.

"This version was only used in Norway when these photos were taken."

I stared at the screen. Trees. A road. Sky.

"Angle of the sun, camera quality, tree types, road lines—it all adds up. Has to be northern Norway."

He clicked. The actual spot was a mere three kilometers away.

"That's better."

Round after round, he nailed them. Always within a few kilometers.

Then the last one loaded. He paused. A dirt road. Reddish sand. Blue sky. Blazing sun. No signs, no structures. Nothing.

I'd have guessed Africa. Maybe a desert. But what did I know?

"That's western-Brazil red dirt," he muttered.

I blinked. "You know the *color* of western Brazilian dirt?"

"Yeah, of course. Everyone knows that." He said this like he was pointing out water is wet.

I stared at the screen. I saw *sand*. He saw *Brazil*. He clicked.

His guess was just 150 meters from the *actual* spot.

I leaned in. "Trevor. That. Was. Insane."

He shrugged. "Anyone can do it."

I rolled my eyes.

"I'll show you."

In that instant, I realized I was about to spend a week with a different kind of genius—the kind who can solve problems and make sharp deductions from the tiniest, most obscure details.

This trip was about to get a whole lot more interesting.

Let's talk about the kind of problem-solving that makes you feel like a genius. The kind that takes raw information, a sharp mind, and a little creative magic to crack something wide open.

If you've never heard of Trevor, he's basically a superhero when it comes to GeoGuessr.

How? Trevor doesn't rely on just one piece of information. He stacks clues, focusing on details most people wouldn't even notice. The color of the dirt. The type of road paint. The shape of the power lines in the background. Even the way the sunlight hit the ground, revealing the hemisphere. He is a master class in breaking a problem down, analyzing its elements, and using logic and creativity to reach an impossible-seeming answer. He's trained his brain to intuitively think about insanely specific details that most others wouldn't even think of noticing.

This kind of thinking isn't limited to experts in obscure geography-based games. It's the same process that underlies genius-level problem-solving in any field. Whether you're tackling a difficult riddle, trying to debug a tricky piece of code, or pushing through a mental block on a creative project, the ability to break a problem down into pieces, extract the right clues, and think flexibly is what separates great thinkers from everyone else.

In this chapter, we're going to break down problem-solving as a skill. We'll explore puzzles and riddles that force you to stretch your brain in new ways. We'll also talk about how to push through frustrating moments when inspiration dries up and nothing seems to work; how to inspire creativity.

Oh, and remember how I promised earlier in the book that we'd talk about one of Einstein's famous proofs? This is where we'll break down one of his key insights into special relativity—not just as a physics lesson, but as an example of deep, creative problem-solving at its finest.

Because in the end, problem-solving isn't necessarily about knowing all the answers, it's about knowing how to find them.

Let me show you what I mean with one of my favorite examples from history—way before GPS, satellites, or even globes.

Picture this: It's more than two thousand years ago, and a Greek mathematician named Eratosthenes is sitting in a library in Alexandria. He learns that in a town south of him—Syene—the sun shines directly overhead at noon on the summer solstice. No shadows. But on that same day and time in Alexandria, there *are* shadows.

Now, here's the part that makes Eratosthenes a genius.

He doesn't just find this interesting and move on. He asks, *Why?* Why would the sun behave differently in two places at the same time? He knew the Earth was curved (that was already understood at the time), but he realized this observation could tell him *how curved*. He could measure the size of the Earth itself.*

So, what does he do? He plants a stick in the ground in Alexandria and measures the angle of the shadow on that same day. Then he calculates the distance between the two cities. Using basic geometry, he figures out the Earth's circumference—with insane accuracy—just from comparing two shadows and asking the right questions.

---

* Sorry, flat-Earthers.

No telescope. No travel. No advanced tech. Just logic, observation, and a bit of imagination.

That's what this chapter is about. Not just solving problems but training your brain to *see problems differently.* To look at the metaphoric shadows and think, "What does this *really* mean?" To notice details the average person would miss—and stack those details like puzzle pieces until something bigger clicks into place.

That's exactly what Trevor does. It's what Einstein did. And it's what you can train yourself to do too.

Let's dig in.

EINSTEIN'S PROOF

One of history's greatest problem-solving feats was Albert Einstein's discovery of time dilation—the phenomenon showing that time moves slower for an observer in motion relative to one at rest. But how did Einstein derive the equation that describes this? I briefly hinted at it back at the start of this book, so now let's break it down step-by-step.

This genius breakthrough started as most do, with a thought experiment. All Einstein was doing was playing with an idea, stretching his mind into impossible scenarios. Creative, playful, though. And then, in a flash of insight, he saw it.

He imagined a beam of light bouncing between two mirrors inside a moving train. Simple enough. But then, critically, he viewed the same event from two different perspectives.

1. **INSIDE THE TRAIN—If you're sitting on the train, from your perspective, the light moves in a straight vertical line, up and down between the mirrors.**
2. **OUTSIDE THE TRAIN (standing on a platform)—To a bystander watching the moving train, the light doesn't just go straight up and down—it travels diagonally, forming a longer path because the train itself is moving.**

That's where the paradox kicked in. The speed of light (c) is constant*—it doesn't matter if you're moving or standing still; it stays the same.

* Genius fact: The speed of light c is 299,792,458 meters per second. That's about 3.00×10^8 m/s when rounded for simplicity. That's also about 671 million miles per hour (in case you were wondering).

INSIDE

OUTSIDE

But the problem is that from the bystander's perspective, the light must travel a longer diagonal path, yet it still moves at speed *c*.

That means only one thing: The time experienced must be different in each frame of reference.

The key was looking at both frames of reference and applying basic physics:

1. Einstein probably started by drawing out both frames of reference. The frame of reference inside the moving train, R', and the frame of reference on the embankment *outside* of the train R. This would have been done to get a visual down on the paper, noting any information given about the situation. For example, we would assume to know the speed of the train, *v*. We surely know the speed of light, *c*. And the height of the train, *h*. There presumably is some time, *t*, elapsing as well.
2. Then, he probably remembered one of the most basic physics equations that relates distance, speed, and time: $d = v \cdot t$ (distance traveled = velocity × time)
3. Next, he most likely worked on each frame of reference to derive any equations he could.

- In frame of reference R':
    - Nothing is moving from the R' perspective, except the light directly up and back down.
    - For the light moving up and down, we have $d = vt'$ (t' being the time elapsed for the light to travel at a certain speed *v*, and covering a distance *d*).

- The distance *d* here is just 2 times the height (since it goes up and then back down). The speed *v*, is just *c*, since it's the speed of light.
- Plug those in and you get $2 \cdot h = c \cdot t'$
- Or rewritten as $h = c \cdot t' / 2$

4. On to frame of reference R:

- Both the train *and* the light are moving from this perspective.
- So, we have two equations in the mix:
  - $d = v \cdot t$ where *v* is the speed of the train, *d* the distance the train moved in time *t* as it sped on by.
  - $d = c \cdot t$ where *d* is the distance the light traveled in the same time *t*
  - Instead of the light traveling up and down, it's traveling at a diagonal up, then a diagonal down (see the diagram below).
  - Pythagorean theorem for right triangles says $a^2 + b^2 = c^2$. (Remember that one from grade school?)*
  - Looking at the diagram below, you can see there are two right triangles. We know one side of the triangle—the height *h* of the train. The bottom part of the triangle is half the distance the train has moved in time *t*. So, $a = v \cdot t / 2$ and $b = h$.

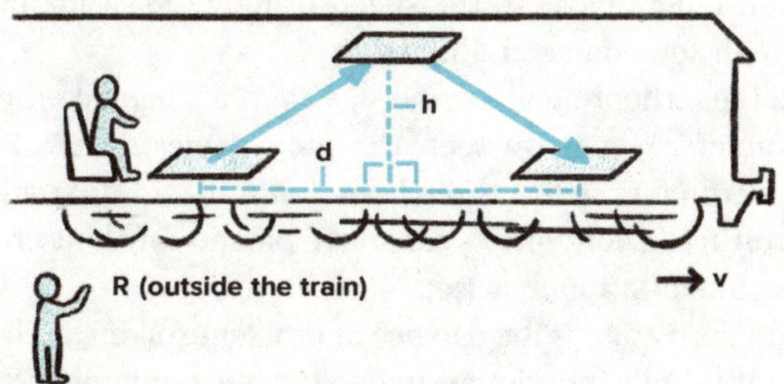

  - Plugging those into Pythagoras's theorem, and remembering that we solved $h = c \cdot t' / 2$ in our other frame of reference (we can now plug that in too), we get:

* c here is not c, the speed of light, but the length of the diagonal side of a right triangle. Let's call it s instead to reduce confusion.

$$s = \sqrt{a^2 + b^2} \longrightarrow s = \sqrt{\left(\frac{vt}{2}\right)^2 + \left(\frac{ct'}{2}\right)^2}$$

- **We now have the sloping diagonal of the triangle. Since the light goes up that and then down the same distance, the full distance it travels is twice that. So, if we plug all that in for d in d = c • t (since d is the distance the light has traveled in the R frame of reference), we get:**

$$2 \cdot \sqrt{\left(\frac{vt}{2}\right)^2 + \left(\frac{ct'}{2}\right)^2} = ct$$

Finally, he just simplified his algebra and moved t to one side of the equation, keeping t' all on the other:

$$t = \frac{t'}{\sqrt{1 - \left(\frac{v}{c}\right)^2}}$$

If you skipped all the math and just looked at this equation for what it is, it would probably look a bit strange to you. The equation *should* simply be t = t'. But it isn't, and that's what makes this such a monumental discovery. The equation shows something wildly counterintuitive: that time is not absolute. It actually can vary depending on how fast you're moving.

For centuries, people assumed time was the same for everyone. If you and I synchronized watches and went about our day, we'd expect them to stay in sync. But Einstein's equation proved that's not true at high speeds. If one person moves close to the speed of light, less time passes for them compared with someone standing still.

This isn't just theoretical anymore, either. It's been confirmed by countless experiments. Have you seen the movie *Interstellar*? There's a scene where the astronauts spend three hours on a planet near a black hole, but when they return, twenty-five years have passed for their crewmate on the ship. That's time dilation in action.*

Einstein's derivation is the essence of problem-solving at the highest level: breaking reality down into simple, understandable components, following logical steps, and arriving at insights that revolutionize the way we see the world.

Also—round of applause—you now know how to derive this Einsteinian formula on the back of a napkin like a true genius.

---

* Though in that case, it's caused by the intense gravity of the black hole rather than speed alone.

HOW TO PROBLEM-SOLVE LIKE A GENIUS

Let's be honest: Most of us aren't living day-to-day thinking like Einstein. But the strategies that made him such a brilliant problem-solver (and the ones in the previous example) can absolutely be borrowed. Here's how to apply them.

1. DEFINE THE PROBLEM CLEARLY.

Big problems often feel intimidating, but that's usually because they're not clearly defined. Before trying to solve anything, take a beat to figure out what's actually being asked. What are you trying to solve? What's known? What's missing? What are the limits you're working within? Just getting clear on the question can often point you halfway toward the answer. Jotting this down on paper (not required, but helpful) gives your brain the structure it needs to dig in.

Let's say there's a trained chef, and she's given the task of creating the most delicious meal possible using a specific set of ingredients. Then there's a basic recipe follower given the same task. The recipe follower might dive in without fully reading the instructions. The chef, though, pauses, takes stock of what she's working with, and understands what needs to happen, before even touching a pan. This is what a great problem-solver does before tackling any problem.

2. USE FIRST-PRINCIPLES THINKING.

Once the problem is clear, it's time to challenge how you're thinking about it. This is where first-principles thinking comes in.* It's a method that involves stripping a complex problem down to its most basic, undeniable truths, and then building your reasoning up from there, instead of leaning on assumptions, shortcuts, or borrowed ideas.

Ask: *What do I know for sure? What am I assuming without realizing it?* Peel away the "givens" and rebuild from the ground up. Breakthroughs often come from realizing you've been solving the wrong version of the problem or accepting a rule that doesn't actually apply.

Back to the kitchen. The recipe follower sticks to the instructions, even when they don't make sense. The chef, however, understands *why* the recipe says what it does. If something's off, she improvises with confidence because she knows the fundamentals, the first principles of cooking.

3. LOOK FOR PATTERNS AND MAKE ANALOGIES.

Genius-level problem-solvers are great at spotting familiar structures in unfamiliar territory. Most problems are just variations of ones you've

---

* A first principle is a foundational proposition or assumption that stands alone. A first principle can't be deduced from any other proposition or assumption.

seen before. If you can recognize a pattern—or relate it to something you already understand—you're halfway there.

Analogies, in particular, are one of the brain's favorite tools for understanding things and figuring them out. As cognitive scientist Douglas Hofstadter puts it, "Analogy is the core of all thinking." It's how we make sense of the unfamiliar: by mapping it onto something we already know (this is also, in general, how we learn). A new concept becomes clearer when you can say, "Oh, it's kind of like that other thing I know." The best solutions often come from these connections between seemingly unrelated ideas.

In the kitchen, the recipe follower might make one dish really well. The chef, who understands the underlying techniques, can adapt those methods to new ingredients or create something entirely original. She's not following anything. Instead, she's mapping flavor, structure, and outcome across dishes, comparing and making analogies to the hundreds of dishes she already knows.

4. EXPERIMENT AND ITERATE.

You won't know whether something works until you try it. Testing an idea, even a rough one, gives you feedback you can't get from just thinking about it. Refine, rework, and retest. Trial and error is crucial here.

When I teach coding to first-year university students, this is exactly what I tell them. You write your code, compile it, inevitably hit an error, try to fix it, and run it again. Over and over again. Each cycle gets you one step closer. Most of the time coders spend on a problem is actually debugging. As you break and fix, break and fix, again and again, you begin to understand the problem on a deeper level. That process *is* the path to the solution.

The chef tweaks as she goes. Taste, adjust. Add heat. Reduce. Start over if needed. The recipe follower may get frustrated when the outcome isn't perfect and might not know what to do next. The chef sees every attempt as a test run that gets her closer to the final masterpiece.

5. THINK BEYOND THE OBVIOUS. STAY FLEXIBLE. STAY CURIOUS.

Don't get stuck in one approach. Flip the problem on its head. Map it out. Visualize it. Change your perspective. Sometimes the breakthrough only shows up when you come at the problem sideways.

Also, stay curious. The best problem-solvers are relentless. They *want* to know the answer. They *want* to figure it out. And they don't want to give up when it's unclear or when they hit a snag. They lean in, ask better questions, and treat the challenge like a puzzle waiting to be cracked.

This is what separates the chef from the recipe follower: curiosity. The chef experiments because she wants to understand what happens. She follows her instincts. She explores. She solves "errors" with flavor

> **adjustments and technique. The recipe follower knows only what's in front of him, and that's all they've got.**

Let's see if you can tackle this next problem using some of these strategies.

THE MOST FAMOUS TECHNICAL INTERVIEW QUESTION

This is an infamous interview question,* and one almost everyone gets wrong. That being said, there are many creative answers out there but one simple one. Here's the setup:

> **You are shrunk to the height of a nickel and thrown into a blender. Your mass is reduced so that your density is the same as usual. The blades start moving in 60 seconds. What do you do?**

This is a classic problem designed to test problem-solving skills and creative thinking. Pause here for a moment and see if you can come up with the solution on your own.

The key detail is that while you are shrunk down to the height of a nickel, your density remains the same, meaning your muscle strength–to–body weight ratio has significantly increased.

The answer is pure physics. As your size shrinks, your weight drops exponentially, but your muscle strength doesn't shrink nearly as fast. That means pound for pound, you're now insanely strong.

Ever seen a flea jump hundreds of times its body height? That's exactly what's happening here. You've just been given superhuman jumping ability. A standard kitchen blender is only a few inches tall, easily within your new jump range.

So, as you might have guessed by now, the answer is . . . to *jump out*!

* There are many variations of the problem, but it's generally something like this.

The trick to this question is realizing that being tiny actually gives you a physical advantage rather than putting you in a helpless position.

That said, most interviewers aren't necessarily looking for the "correct" answer. Heck, you may not even have known the physics behind the correct answer. But it doesn't actually matter. They just want to see how you think. Maybe you assume the blender is voice-activated and start negotiating with it. Maybe you signal for help using reflections off the glass. Whether it's humor, improvisation, or out-of-the-box logic, creative thinking under pressure is what really will stand out to the interviewer.

Here's another great question:

There's a tennis tournament with 127 players. You've got 126 people paired off in 63 matches, plus 1 unpaired player who gets a bye. In the next round, there are 64 players and 32 matches. How many matches, total, does it take to determine a winner?

This is one of these problems that has such an elegant solution that doesn't require hard calculations. The genius of this problem is that it looks complex but has a ridiculously simple solution if you think about it the right way. Instead of tracking rounds and counting matches, flip the perspective: Every match eliminates exactly one player. Since there are 127 players and only one winner, that means 126 players must be eliminated, requiring exactly 126 matches. No need for calculations, just pattern recognition. Top problem-solvers are great at that; they can step back, spot the shortcut, and realize when a problem is way easier than it looks.

Here's another good one (and one you might recognize from *Die Hard 3* or Netflix's *The Mole*):

You have a 3-gallon bucket, a 5-gallon bucket, and an infinite supply of water. How can you measure out exactly 4 gallons?

The beauty of this problem is that you already have everything you need: two buckets with fixed capacities. So now, to find the solution, you just need to manipulate what's in front of you.

To do that, a great approach would be to mentally simulate each step, tracking how the water moves. It might seem tricky at first, but if you take it one step at a time, it should click into place.

Here's the solution:

Start by filling the 5-gallon jug completely. Pour water from the 5-gallon jug into the 3-gallon jug until the 3-gallon jug is full. Empty the 3-gallon jug. Next, pour the remaining water from the 5-gallon jug into the 3-gallon jug. Now fill the 5-gallon jug again. Finally, pour water from

GENIUS PROFILE:
MARIE CURIE

In 1898, Marie Curie and her husband, Pierre, discovered a new element—polonium—after processing tons of pitchblende ore. But that was just the beginning. To isolate another, even more radioactive element, radium, Marie spent the next four years stirring and boiling several tons of ore by hand in a makeshift shed, often in freezing temperatures. With no formal lab and limited funding, she worked tirelessly, driven by an unshakable belief in her results. Eventually, she isolated one-tenth of a gram of pure radium chloride—a scientific breakthrough that helped launch the field of nuclear physics. She went on to become the first person ever to win two Nobel Prizes, in two different sciences: physics and chemistry. A master class in grit, vision, and scientific thinking.

the 5-gallon jug into the 3-gallon jug until the 3-gallon jug is full, leaving exactly 4 gallons in the 5-gallon jug.

Yippee ki yay, mother lover. You did it!

HOW TO MAKE BETTER DECISIONS

Every day, we make hundreds—if not thousands—of decisions. Most of them feel small: what to eat, what to wear, whether to respond to that text now or later. But over time, even small decisions stack up and shape the trajectory of our lives. Then there are the big ones—the career moves, the investments, the risks we take or don't take. And while some people seem naturally wired to make the right calls at the right time, the truth is that great decision-making is a skill. And like any skill, it can be improved.

At its core, great decision-making isn't about guessing or relying on instinct alone. It's about having a process; one that allows you to weigh options effectively, see potential pitfalls, and avoid making emotional or biased choices. The best decision-makers use a mix of logic, experience, and sometimes even a little game theory to increase their odds of success.

That said, intuition matters too—a lot, actually. Gut feelings can be powerful guides, though they're hard to train and explain (we'll explore this more in chapter 9). The challenge is that relying on them alone risks overlooking important facts hiding in plain sight.

Still, there are moments when a gut decision feels right, and *is* right. As Derek Sivers suggests in his "Hell yeah or no" framework: If a decision doesn't spark a clear "Hell yeah!," then it's a no. This filter helps you avoid drawn-out deliberations and stay focused on what truly excites you.

But when a decision isn't obvious, and when the stakes are high or the outcome is unclear, a logical framework becomes essential. It doesn't replace instinct. But it gives your instincts something solid to work with, especially if you feel a situation deserves a little more thought and consideration.

In terms of that logical framework, these are the key steps I've found to be the most effective in decision-making:

HAVE AWARENESS

This is the first step to making better decisions. Most bad choices come from rushing, acting on impulse, or making assumptions without questioning them. Slowing down creates space to evaluate what's actually happening instead of reacting mindlessly. Before deciding anything important, ask yourself: What's influencing me right now? Am I making this choice out of fear, excitement, impatience? Emotions aren't bad, but when they dominate decision-making, they can lead to costly mistakes.

RECOGNIZE THAT GOOD DECISIONS ARE BUILT ON GOOD INFORMATION

The more you know, the better you can assess risks and rewards. This doesn't mean endlessly researching every small choice, but it does mean gathering enough data to see the full picture. When in doubt, follow the rule of three: Seek out at least three solid sources, three perspectives, or three different possible outcomes before committing. Too often, people base their choices on a single data point—one article, one person's opinion, one assumption about how things will play out. Expanding your inputs reduces blind spots.

CONSIDER THE SHORT-TERM AND LONG-TERM CONSEQUENCES

The best choice isn't always the most comfortable in the moment. Eating junk food feels good now, but how does it impact you in a year? Avoiding a tough conversation keeps things peaceful today, but does it lead to resentment later? Zooming out and seeing the long game separates impulsive decisions from strategic ones.

COMMIT

Even with perspective, uncertainty is unavoidable. No one has a crystal ball, and every decision has risks. But the best decision-makers don't get stuck in analysis paralysis. They gather enough information, weigh the options, and then commit.

Here's something worth considering: In many cases, you already know your decision. Think about when someone asks a friend, "Should I wear the white shoes or the blue shoes?" More often than not, they've already made up their mind—they're just seeking validation. And they'll probably go with their original choice anyway. The same thing happens with bigger decisions. You may be consciously aware of what you want, or it might be sitting there subconsciously. Either way, it's worth pausing to ask yourself honestly: Do I already know my decision? Recognizing this can speed up the process and help you commit faster.

Overthinking often comes from a fear of making the wrong choice. But in most cases, the worst decision isn't choosing wrong, it's failing to decide at all while opportunities pass you by.

A powerful way to improve decision-making is to reverse engineer it. Instead of asking, "What should I do?" ask, "What would future me wish I had done?" Think of yourself six months, a year, five years from now. Which choice leads to the version of you that you actually want to be? This reframing helps cut through momentary distractions and focus on what really matters.

LEARN FROM THE PAST

Finally, great decision-makers learn from past choices. They analyze what worked, what didn't, and why. They spot patterns in their thinking and adjust. If something keeps leading to a bad outcome, they don't repeat it hoping for a different result. Instead, they refine their approach, getting sharper with every decision they make.

Better decisions lead to better outcomes. And great decision-making is about creating the life you want. The more you train yourself to think strategically, gather the right information, and balance logic with intuition, the more confident and effective your choices will be. That's when you stop reacting to life and start *acting on it* instead—building momentum, aligning your goals, and moving things in your favor not by accident, but by intention.

WARREN BUFFETT'S 5/25 RULE

Warren Buffett has a ridiculously simple but brutally effective method for making decisions and figuring out what actually matters in life. It's called the 5/25 Rule, and I use it all the time. Using it correctly will change how you make decisions forever.

According to the story, Buffett once asked his longtime pilot, Mike Flint, to list his top twenty-five career goals. Flint thought about it, wrote them all down, and handed the list over.

Buffett then told him, "Now circle the five most important ones."

Easy enough. Flint picked his five biggest goals—the ones that meant the most. Then he assumed the next logical step: focus on those top five *first* and work on the other twenty whenever he had extra time.

Buffett stopped him cold.

"No," he said. "The other twenty aren't just lower priority. They're your *Avoid at All Costs* list."

Let that sink in. The biggest obstacles to success aren't the bad choices; they're the harmless, *pretty good* ones, the projects that *seem* important. The goals that *kind of* matter. Anything that isn't your top priority is, in fact, a distraction. Buffett's rule forces a brutal truth: most people don't fail because they lack talent or ambition, but rather because they spread themselves too thin. They chase too many things at once, never fully committing to the ones that would actually change their life.

So, here's how you use the 5/25 Rule in real life:

1. **Write down twenty-five things you want to accomplish—career goals, personal projects, whatever.**
2. **Circle the top five. The nonnegotiables. The things that, if achieved, would make everything else feel secondary.**
3. **Look at the other twenty and accept that they're *the enemy.* These are the distractions in disguise. The things that feel productive but are actually pulling you away from what truly matters.**
4. **Ruthlessly cut them out. Don't dabble. Don't try to "fit them in." You focus on your top five, and that's it.**

The hardest part isn't knowing what to focus on; it's having the discipline to *let go* of the rest. The people who actually make progress aren't

GENIUS PROFILE: LEWIS CARROLL

While most know Lewis Carroll as the author of *Alice's Adventures in Wonderland*, few realize he was also a mathematician and logician of serious caliber. At Oxford, under his real name, Charles Lutwidge Dodgson, he taught mathematics and published works on symbolic logic, including *Symbolic Logic* (1896) and *The Game of Logic* (1887). One of his contributions was a visual method of logic diagrams—using subdivided rectangles to solve syllogisms—though this approach came *after* John Venn's more famous diagrams in 1880.

Carroll was also obsessed with puzzles and riddles, often crafting intricate logic problems that still stump people today. He even invented a word game called Doublets (now known as Word Ladders), where you transform one word into another by changing a single letter at a time—turning HEAD into TAIL, for instance, through a chain of valid words. The puzzles became so popular that *Vanity Fair* magazine published them regularly.

Beyond logic, he created his own mnemonic number system for remembering dates and numbers, remarkably similar to the modern Major System mentioned earlier in this book. Just another example of how Carroll's creative mind constantly sought bridges between structure and imagination.

always the smartest or most talented. They're just the ones who get crystal clear on what they want and stay locked in on it.

CREATIVITY AND BREAKING THROUGH BLOCKS

Where does creativity come from?

It's a big question, and maybe a little beyond the scope of this book. But what I can tell you is how to stir it up when it's gone quiet. Creativity isn't just something that strikes like lightning. Sure, sometimes it does. But most of the time, it's something you have to summon. You have to make it show up.

The best creative minds don't sit around waiting for inspiration. They've got tools, tricks, systems. I live in a world where creativity is part of my job (even my memory work runs on it). So if you're feeling stuck, here are a few of my favorite ways to get the ideas flowing again.

DO SOMETHING BORING

Seriously. It's counterintuitive, but when your mind is overstimulated, it struggles to make creative leaps. Mundane tasks such as washing dishes, showering, and folding laundry give your subconscious opportunities to wander and connect ideas in unexpected ways. So put your phone away and *get* bored. You'll see how quickly your mind will start to entertain itself!

MOVE YOUR BODY

Physical movement jump-starts mental movement. Movement increases blood flow to the brain, making you more alert and creative. Go for a run, take a walk, do some push-ups. Many of the world's greatest thinkers, from Einstein to Steve Jobs, swore by walking when they needed fresh ideas. There's even an ancient Latin phrase for it: *solvitur ambulando*—"it is solved by walking." Research backs this up: Walking, especially outdoors, can boost creative output by up to 60 percent. Same goes for me. Whenever I need a spark of inspiration or to flesh out an idea, I go for a run. Inevitably, on that run, I come back loaded up with fresh ideas and solutions. The rhythm of movement and change of scenery help your mind make new connections.

FLIP THE PROBLEM UPSIDE DOWN

If you're stuck on a problem, ask: *What's the opposite of what I'm trying to do?* If you're designing something, what would the worst version look like? If you're writing, how would you approach it in a completely different genre? Thinking in extremes forces your brain to look at things from a fresh angle.

STEAL LIKE AN ARTIST

Great ideas don't come from a vacuum. If you're stuck, immerse yourself in others' work. Read a book; watch a documentary; explore a completely unrelated field. Creativity is about connecting dots—go gather more dots!

SET A TIMER AND JUST START

Perfectionism kills creativity. If you're stuck, set a ten-minute timer and *force yourself* to create something—anything. Write nonsense, doodle randomly, speak your ideas out loud. Often, just starting is enough to get unstuck.

SLEEP ON IT

Your brain keeps working on problems even when you're not. If you're frustrated, stop. Walk away. Sleep on it. It's not wasted time—your subconscious is still processing; your memory is consolidating, and often, the answer will come when you least expect it.

STREAM-OF-CONSCIOUSNESS WRITING

Try writing whatever comes to mind—no filter, no overthinking—even if it's messy nonsense (remember that "Brain Dump" exercise from chapter 3? THAT). The point is to get your brain moving. You'll be surprised how often a buried idea surfaces from the noise. Set a timer, start writing, and don't lift your pen off the page until the time is up. Whatever comes out, comes out.

READ SOMETHING UNFAMILIAR

If you consume only the same kinds of books, articles, or media, your brain keeps recycling the same ideas. Read (or watch or listen to) something wildly outside your comfort zone—a history of ancient shipwrecks, a book on fungi, or a deep dive into Japanese game design. If you can't decide what to read, go to Wikipedia, hit "Random Article," and you'll be led to something most likely new and interesting. Creativity thrives on unexpected inputs.*

DRAW, DOODLE, COLOR—EVEN IF YOU SUCK AT IT

Your brain processes information differently when you engage visually. Sketch out a problem. Doodle random shapes. Color in a coloring book if you have to. Engaging your visual brain can shake ideas loose in ways words can't. Remember mind maps from chapter 4? Those can also serve as a way to boost creativity and generate ideas.

---

* I personally believe that reading more *in general* can cause an uptick in creativity.

THE "WRONG ANSWER" CHALLENGE

If you can't come up with a great idea, brainstorm the worst ones possible. Trying to start a business? What's the absolute *dumbest* business you could launch? Worst marketing slogan? Most useless invention? Creativity lives in extremes. Sometimes bad ideas have a spark of brilliance hiding in them. Another way to frame it is to ask yourself, "What's the second right answer?" We often assume there's only one solution and get stuck chasing it. But if you force yourself to imagine a second right answer, you'll open up fresh possibilities. More often than not, that second answer is the breakthrough, or at least the doorway to one.

USE THE "HALF-FINISHED" TRICK

Start something, then stop halfway through and walk away. Your brain *hates* unfinished business—it will keep mentally working on the problem in the background (this is called the Zeigarnik Effect*). When you come back, you'll often have an insight you didn't see before.

GET GROUNDED IN NATURE

When you're really stuck, get outside and disconnect. Step onto grass; sit under a tree; find water. Nature resets your nervous system and quiets mental noise. Studies show that even twenty minutes in a natural setting significantly boosts creative problem-solving. The Japanese call it shinrin-yoku (forest bathing)—giving your overstimulated brain a break from screens and constant decisions while your subconscious processes in the background.

CHANGE THE WAY YOU WRITE

If you type everything, write by hand. If you write by hand, type in an unusual font (Comic Sans, Old English, something weird). The simple act of changing your physical interaction with words rewires how you think.

PLAY

Play is one of the most underrated creativity hacks. When you give yourself permission to mess around, to experiment without pressure or judgment, you stumble into connections you'd never find if you were being "serious." Play lowers the stakes, loosens the rules, and creates space for wild, silly ideas, the exact kind that often sparks real breakthroughs.

---

* We mentioned it briefly back on page 75.

REMEMBER THE EARLY CHAPTERS

Don't forget a lot of the tips I suggested in the earlier chapters of this book. Many of the techniques we used to remember things had to do with creativity stimulation. In general, remember that novelty sparks new connections in the brain, making it easier to think differently (and remember more!).

Creativity isn't magic. It's a muscle. The more you train it and stimulate it, the better it will perform. And when it stalls, shake things up, step away, and trust that the ideas will come back, because they usually do.

Disrupt the loop. Force your mind to connect dots in ways it normally wouldn't.

PUZZLES AND RIDDLES

My comedian-magician friend Wes Barker happens to be a *phenomenal* riddle solver. I didn't realize this until we were on a mountain climb together. We'd fill our downtime with questions, puzzles, and brainteasers—things I always love to keep stocked in my mental bag of tricks. Every time I threw one out, Wes would solve it almost instantly.

How, though? I was completely fascinated by his ability to find answers quickly and almost without ever giving up or asking for the solution.

His answer? "Oh, man, I've just solved so many riddles and their variations that I know all the tricks. I've seen them all before."

And *that* is the real insight. He doesn't have a superhuman brain capable of insane calculations, he's just trained in pattern recognition (similar to my GeoGuessr genius friend, Trevor). Because he's built up a mental database of problem structures, when he hears a new one, he instinctively matches it to a familiar pattern and attacks it from the right angle. And if the pattern isn't familiar, he reaches into a mental Swiss Army knife of tactics and finds another way in.

Wes's advice was basically this: If you want to get better at solving problems, solve more problems!

This advice isn't just for riddles but for any kind of problem-solving. The more you practice, the more familiar the patterns become. You stop reinventing the wheel and start spotting shortcuts; structures, clues, strategies you've seen before. Each new challenge becomes less about figuring everything out from scratch, and more about recognizing what kind of problem it is. You break it down, apply first principles, draw on analogies—just as we've been doing—and, piece by piece, the answer comes into view.

Do that enough times, and you'll start to think like Wes: calm, prepared, and ready for whatever problem lands in front of you.

GENIUS PROFILE: RAYMOND SMULLYAN

Smullyan was a brilliant mathematician, logician, and self-taught magician known for blending deep logic with playful creativity.

Smullyan loved telling stories that bent the rules of reason, often with a cheeky wink. One of his favorites was the story of how he supposedly met his wife. On their first date, he asked her whether she would agree to the following: He was going to make a statement. If the statement was true, she would give him her autograph. She agreed. Then he continued: "But if my statement is false, you have to agree NOT to give me your autograph!" She agreed again, not seeing any harm in it. (So, remember, a true statement gets him an autograph, and a false statement does not—that's very important!) The statement was the following: "You will give me neither your autograph nor a kiss."

If the statement was true, she would have to give him her autograph as agreed, but doing so would make it false that she gave him neither her autograph nor a kiss, which is a contradiction, and as the statement can't be true, it must be false. Since it's false that she gave him neither, then she must have given him either and thus must give him either her autograph or a kiss. But the rule was that she can't give him her autograph for a false statement, so . . . Well, let's just say logic demanded she gave him a kiss, and the rest is history.

To wrap up this chapter, I thought it would be fun to include some of my favorite puzzles, great for tossing out in conversation or testing your friends. Puzzles make for clever icebreakers and also have a way of saying, *Hey, I'm smart.*

We'll also take a look at the solutions. As you've seen by now, the more puzzles you tackle, the sharper your problem-solving skills become.

Let's start with a few classics by Raymond Smullyan.

To first get a little taste of his way of thinking, here's a fun little logical conundrum he once wrote:

> **"Which is better, eternal happiness or a ham sandwich? Most people would say eternal happiness, but this can't be true, as the following syllogism proves: Nothing is better than eternal happiness. A ham sandwich is better than nothing. Therefore, a ham sandwich is better than eternal happiness."***

Now for some of his better-known puzzles:

> **A man was looking at a portrait. Someone asked him, "Whose picture are you looking at?" He replied: "Brothers and sisters have I none, but this man's father is my father's son."**
>
> **Whose picture was the man looking at?**

Solution: The man's son.

This problem is purely a play on words. When there are problems with confusing wordings like this, it's helpful to focus on details and making sure you understand those before tackling the whole.

For me, I first had to understand what "my father's son" was first.

Okay, well, *my son*, would be the son I had. *My father's son*, would be . . . well, me! Wouldn't it? So, I could replace that sentence as "But this man's father is me" and now suddenly it's clear, I'm the father, and the man shown in the portrait is my son.

> **A man held in his hand two American coins that added up to 30 cents, yet one of them was not a nickel. How was this possible?**

Solution: He held a quarter and a nickel. One of them—the quarter—was not a nickel.

In this example, the answer is so simple once you realize the trick. The lesson learned here is to make sure you read the problem! Only *one* coin is not a nickel, but there are two coins! Make sure you process the language and avoid assumptions. By doing so, you overlook the solution.

---

* I *almost* agree. Just replace the ham with some French saucisson, thank you very much!

There was a convention of one hundred scientists; each was either a physicist or a chemist. One physicist noted that given any two of the members, at least one of them was a chemist. From this observation, can it be determined how many of them were chemists and how many were physicists?

Solution: To say that given any two of them at least one is a chemist, is just another way of saying that no two are both physicists. Thus, there is only one physicist; the other ninety-nine are chemists.

The key to a problem like this is in the wording. Being able to read the problem carefully, and making note of what the main statement means, is key.

A certain street contains one hundred buildings. A sign maker is called to number the houses from 1 to 100. He has to order numerals to do the job. Without using pencil and paper, can you figure out in your head how many 9s he will need?

Solution: 20

This is one of those kinds of puzzle problems where it's just a matter of mentally visualizing and counting out the answers carefully. You'd guess that since it *sounds* simple, there is a catch to it that is often overlooked. Obviously, there are all the numbers that end in 9: 9, 19, 29 . . . 99. Aha, but that last one has two 9s, so that's 11 so far. And then the thing you might have overlooked: all the other 90s: 90, 91, 92, 93, etc. There are 9 there (since we already took care of the 99). So, 20.

There is an island where certain inhabitants called "knights" always tell the truth, and others called "knaves" always lie.

There are three people—A, B, and C—standing together in a garden. A stranger passed by and asked A, "Are you a knight or a knave?" A answered, but rather indistinctly, so the stranger could not make out what he said. The stranger then asked B, "What did A say?" B replied, "A said that he is a knave." At this point the third man, C, said, "Don't believe B; he is lying!"

The question is, what are B and C?

Solution: It is impossible for either a knight or a knave to say, "I'm a knave," because a knight wouldn't make the false statement that he is a knave, and a knave wouldn't make the true statement that he is a knave. Therefore, A never did say that he was a knave. So, B lied when saying that A said that he was a knave. Hence B is a knave. Since C said that B was lying and B was indeed lying, then C spoke the truth, hence is a knight. Thus, B is a knave and C is a knight. It's impossible to know what A is, by the way.

There are hundreds of logic puzzles like this that deal with liars and truth tellers and how to tell who is whom. Smullyan was well known for creating many variations. But solving them is just a matter of systematically working through each option and considering the case if it were to be true. For example, I might start by saying, okay, what if B were a knave, and then follow that hypothesis. If I hit a contradiction, then I have some more information. B must be a knight! And then the answer typically falls into place.

There are so many other classic logic puzzles and riddles to share, but these are some of my favorites:

On the ground floor of a house there are three electric switches—two of them are false and one of them is genuine. The genuine one turns a bulb on the second floor on or off. At the moment, the bulb has been off for quite a while. You are allowed to do anything you want with the switches, and then go upstairs to observe the bulb. You are then to determine which of the three switches is the genuine one.

Solution: Use heat!

First, turn on one switch (Switch A) and leave it on for a couple of minutes. This will give the bulb time to heat up if it's the real switch.

After a few minutes, turn off Switch A and quickly turn on another switch (Switch B). Leave Switch B on.

*Now go upstairs and check the bulb. If the bulb is **ON**, then Switch B is the genuine switch. If the bulb is **OFF** but warm to the touch, then Switch A is the real one (since it was on long enough to heat up but was turned off before you went up). If the bulb is **OFF** and cold, then Switch C is the genuine switch, because the other two didn't activate it.*

It's such a satisfying answer! And a prime example of a puzzle that requires you to think outside of the box. The answer might not be immediately obvious, but through some mental trial and error, you might realize what information you have and/or can get.

Using 3 cuts, how can you divide a birthday cake into 8 equal slices (the birthday cake is round)?

Solution: There are two ways to do this. First is to cut the cake in half (slice 1). Then cut it perpendicularly (slice 2) to make 4 slices. Then for the third slice you could cut all four slices horizontally (but who cuts cake that way, you psychopath!), but my preferred third slice is to stack all four slices on top of each other and make one tall dividing cut through all 4 slices to make the 8.

A problem that requires just a minimal amount of creative thought, thinking outside the box.

Ten red socks and ten blue socks are all mixed up in a dresser drawer. The twenty socks are exactly alike except for their color. The room is pitch dark and you want two matching socks. What is the smallest number of socks you must take out of the drawer in order to be certain you have a pair that match?

Solution: 3 socks

For this problem, it's helpful to think about the worst-case scenario:

- **The first sock you pull out could be red.**
- **The second sock you pull out could be blue.**

At this point, you still wouldn't have a matching pair. But the third sock, no matter what color it is, must match one of the first two. So, no matter how unlucky you are, once you pull out three socks, at least two of them will be the same color, guaranteeing a matching pair.

Imagine that you have three boxes, one containing two black marbles, one containing two white marbles, and the third, one black marble and one white. The boxes are labeled for their contents—BB, WW, and BW—but someone has switched the labels so that every box is now incorrectly labeled. You are allowed to take one marble at a time out of any box, without looking, and by this process of sampling you're to determine the contents of all three boxes. What is the smallest number of drawings needed?

Solution: Just one marble needs to be drawn. The key to the solution is knowing that the labels on all three boxes are incorrect. You must draw a marble from the box labeled BW. Assume the marble drawn is black. You know then that the other marble in this box must be black also; otherwise the label would be correct. Since you have now identified the box containing two black marbles, you can at once tell the contents of the box marked WW: You know it cannot contain two white marbles, because its label has to be wrong; it can't contain two black marbles either, for you have identified that box already; therefore, it must contain one black and one white marble. The third box, of course, must then be the one holding two white marbles. You can solve the puzzle by the same reasoning if the marble you draw from the BW box happens to be white instead of black.

This is another one where you figure it out by trying out solutions and see if the logic stands. If it breaks, then you're on the wrong track.

Here is one of my favorite number sequence puzzles.

Find the next number in the sequence:
1, 11, 21, 1211, 111221, . . .

Solution: Read the numbers as their digits. They literally represent the presented digits for the previous number in the sequence. One, One 1, Two one, One 2 one 1, one 1 one 2 two 1. So, the next number would be 312211.

EXERCISES AND RESOURCES

- In a very similar way to how we derived the time dilation equations, you can also derive equations that show how length contracts as the speed of an object approaches the speed of light. (Yes, this is a real phenomenon.) See if you can figure it out! Find the solution here: www.everydaygeniusacademy.com/book/einstein.
- Spend an afternoon trying some of the techniques I shared to spark creativity. Have the goal of creating *something* and see what comes out. Oftentimes the hardest part of being creative is sitting down and allowing yourself the opportunity to do so. This tip right here is your encouragement to go and do that *right now.*
- If you want to try what is considered by some to be the world's hardest riddle, try "Einstein's Riddle." According to the legend, Einstein himself came up with this riddle . . . as a child! No tricks, just one answer. And this one is pure logic. That's all you need (and a bit of patience): www.everydaygeniusacademy.com/book/riddles.

Here are a number of my favorite books that will help you work on honing your problem-solving abilities:

- *The Art and Craft of Problem Solving* by Paul Zeitz—A beautifully written guide to creative thinking and mathematical problem-solving.
- *Thinking, Fast and Slow* by Daniel Kahneman—A powerful look into how our brains process information and make decisions.
- *What Is the Name of This Book?* by Raymond Smullyan—A logic puzzle classic packed with paradoxes and clever twists.
- *The Colossal Book of Short Puzzles and Problems* by Martin Gardner—A treasure trove of bite-sized puzzles and challenges for all levels.
- *Are You Smart Enough to Work at Google?* by William Poundstone—All the interview questions you'll ever see and how to answer them.
- *A Whack on the Side of the Head* by Roger von Oech—A beautifully fun and whimsical book about creativity, jam-packed with tips on how to spark it.
- *Gödel, Escher, Bach* by Douglas Hofstadter—A mind-bending deep dive into patterns, recursion, and thought itself. And (fun fact) my favorite book of all time.

CHAPTER 7

STRATEGIC THINKING

"LIFE IS NOT ALWAYS A MATTER OF HOLDING GOOD CARDS, BUT SOMETIMES, PLAYING A POOR HAND WELL."
—JACK LONDON

VEGAS, BABY. THE NEON HEARTBEAT OF THE DESERT, WHERE FORTUNES FLIP ON THE TURN OF A CARD AND THE HOUSE ALWAYS WINS (EXCEPT WHEN YOU KNOW WHAT YOU'RE DOING).

THIS WAS MY FIRST REAL TRIP AS A CARD COUNTER. WE WERE TECHNICALLY STILL IN TRAINING, BUT THIS WAS OUR FIRST OUTING AS A TEAM TO IRON OUT THE KINKS AND GET REAL HOURS IN. AND I WAS ITCHING FOR ACTION. NOT JUST TO PLAY, BUT TO WIN. TO PROVE I COULD DO IT. THAT ALL THE HOURS OF DRILLING INDEX NUMBERS, RUNNING SIMULATIONS, AND COUNTING DOWN MULTIPLE DECKS AT MY KITCHEN TABLE HADN'T BEEN FOR NOTHING.

IT WAS JUST ABOUT 11 P.M.—GAME TIME. MANDALAY BAY WAS OUR FIRST STOP. I HAD $3,000 IN MY POCKET, MY FIRST REAL WORKING CASH (THE AMOUNT WE WERE ENTRUSTED WITH BY OUR INVESTORS ON OUR FIRST FORAY). IT WAS HEAVY IN MY POCKET, AND EVERY DOLLAR MATTERED MORE WHEN IT WAS YOURS TO LOSE.

We were part of a card-counting team—not criminals, not cheaters, just advantage players using math and memory to flip the odds in our favor. Card counting isn't illegal; it's simply an application of a strategy with a well-trained mind. The goal for me was to create a profitable side hustle, offer our investors a solid return, and walk away with some memorable stories.

I wasn't in it to get rich. Not at all.

I was in it to grow, to push myself and challenge my mind. Okay, and yeah . . . to beat the house.

At my first table, I started counting. Fifteen minutes of hovering, waiting, scanning the tables like a predator stalking the weakest in the herd. Then, my buddy Patrick gave the signal from across the pit—arms crossed. That meant the shoe (the box that holds multiple decks of cards, used by the dealer) at his table was starting to get hot.

Time to move.

I walked closer, pretending I didn't know him, didn't see him. He scratched his nose, which was a signal for me to get into the game.

I swooped in, sliding into a seat next to him. "You're not sitting here, are you?" I muttered, just loud enough. The goal was to act like a stranger while coaxing him to speak so he could relay the running count.

Patrick stood, stretching as if he was just killing time. "Nah, I think I'm gonna go. I'm *really cold*."

Really cold. That was code for a running count of 27. The word "cold" on its own was just a seven. Add "really," and that number becomes *twenty-seven*. That was a high count. And the higher the count (and the fewer the cards left in the shoe), the more it meant that it was time to start betting big.

I bought in for $500. Three and a half decks left in the shoe.

Perfect.

I kept my hands steady, my bets calculated—two hands of $110 to start. The count climbed; my bets followed. I kept winning.

The count called for two hands of $205.

My stomach tightened. I was still nervous, still getting the hang of counting cards out in the wild instead of the hot, sweaty basement where I had been practicing for months prior.

But it didn't matter. I won. And then I kept winning, hand after hand. Every move, every calculation, lined up. The dealer moved like molasses, which played right into my hands. The slower the better, because I had more time to track, to make the perfect plays. I was *running* the table.

Jared, our team manager, strolled by just as I slammed down another winning hand. He gave me a subtle nod of approval.

By nearly the end of the shoe, I was up $4,800. On one of my recent hands, I had even lost a grand, but I barely felt it. It didn't matter. I was still up by so much. This was the rush I had been seeking—the moment when skill and luck crash into each other and, for once, *you* come out on top.

Then, the dealer slid me an 8. Then another.

Sixteen. Two 8s. Always split 8s.

The dealer was showing a 10.

I could feel the heat from the pit bosses behind me, their eyes drilling into my stack. Every instinct screamed to play it safe.

I didn't. I stuck to the book, and split.

First new card—another 8. Split again.

Now I had three hands in front of me. One 8 stood alone, waiting. The other two had new cards coming.

First hand—dealer tossed me a 3. Eleven.

Time to double down.

I shoved in more chips. Next card—a face.

Twenty-one. No better hand.

Second hand. Another 3. Another eleven.

Another double down. More chips in.

Next card—King. Twenty-one again.

Are you kidding me? my mind was screaming.

Last, the dealer turned to the last hand: an 8, waiting.

He dropped a 10 on it. Eighteen. I stood.

Three hands. Two double downs. Every move textbook. Every move loud. My adrenaline surging.

I locked eyes with the dealer. His face gave nothing away, but I knew. This was it.

He flipped the card hiding under his visible 10.

It was a 6. Totaling 16.

He drew again.

The card floated in the air for a second too long before slamming into the felt.

Bust.

All my hands won. What a rush! I'd just stacked another $2,400 in one fell swoop.

Then my phone buzzed. I peeked at it under the table: WAY TOO MUCH HEAT, the text read.

I didn't hesitate. Cashed out. Walked out as cool as I could, but inside, I was buzzing.

Outside, I met up with the team, still riding the high of my first big session. Patrick and Jared filled me in. The pit boss had been making *multiple* phone calls about me, and security was already in the loop.

I hadn't even noticed their eyes on me, careless in my rush of adrenaline. The high of winning had consumed me (as it should have—the count was sky-high), but I'd forgotten the rule: Always keep a low profile.

Still so much to learn. But this was my first real taste of what was to come.

I wasn't just some random player anymore. I was a *threat*.

And it wasn't because I was lucky, No. It was because my mind was sharp. To casinos, my mind was now a weapon.

Back in 2012, moments after having just secured my second USA Memory Championship win, I was drowning in post-victory chaos. Interviews, photos, handshakes; it was relentless. But as the crowd finally thinned, one man remained.

He was dressed way too sharply for a memory competition: three-piece suit, perfectly shined shoes, the whole deal. He definitely wasn't a journalist. He wasn't a fan either. He was *waiting*. Watching.

When he finally approached, he slipped me his card. No small talk. Just a quiet offer—he was putting together a blackjack card-counting team and looking for people with elite mental skills. I'd always been fascinated by the legendary MIT card-counting teams of the early 2000s. I'd read the books, watched the movie *21*, but I'd never actually *done* it. And here was a guy inviting me to the real thing.

Except, this wasn't just standard card counting. His team was working with another technique—one that required memory. Most people assume card counting is about memorizing every card in the deck. It's not. It's literally just *counting*. Card counting doesn't require memory at all. But what this team was doing did.*

Fast-forward a few years, I had ended up training with that man's team. They were working with John Chang, one of the original MIT team members. That alone made it legit. I learned a ton, but it never really turned into anything beyond kick-starting my interest in blackjack. Eventually, I got other memory athletes training too. While I moved on to other projects, *they* kept going, built a real team, secured a sizable bankroll.

By 2018, blackjack had long since faded from my radar. Then, out of nowhere, I got the call.

---

* For those curious, they were using a strategy known as "ace sequencing" where, in addition to counting the cards, you also memorize sequences of cards that come out before all the played aces.

GENIUS PROFILE:
ED THORP

Often credited as the inventor of card counting, Edward Thorp was a mathematics professor who realized blackjack had a vulnerability: Unlike other casino games, the odds shifted depending on which cards had already been played. Using probability theory and early computers at MIT in the late 1950s, he ran simulations that proved keeping a simple count of high and low cards could give the player a statistical edge over the house.

To prove it wasn't just theory, Thorp headed to Reno with $10,000 in backing from financier Claude Shannon (yes, the father of information theory). At the tables, he used his Ten Count method and started stacking up wins. The casinos, convinced he must have been cheating, changed dealers on him, shuffled early, and even sent "observers" to hover at his table. At one point, a pit boss instructed the dealer to shuffle after every hand just to kill his edge. But Thorp still walked away with thousands in winnings.

In 1966, he published *Beat the Dealer*, which introduced the first card-counting system to the world. It proved, with math, that blackjack could be beaten.

Fast-forward to today, and I still play, and I still count cards when I have time. Semi-professionally, sure, but mostly for the *mental challenge*. There's something about the strategy, the precision, the *edge* that keeps me coming back. Of course, the exhilaration of being in Vegas, sticking it to the big casinos and taking their money, is a large draw as well.

But let me make one thing clear: I'm *not* promoting gambling. Really, this all goes back to mental training. Counting cards is one of the best brain exercises out there. It sharpens focus, pattern recognition, and decision-making skills. And while it sounds cool as heck to say you know how to count cards, some of those card-counting skills translate into real-life situations in unexpected ways.

We've tackled puzzles and problem-solving in general, and now in this chapter, we'll be diving into the *art* of beating games.

So, strap in, and as they say, *winner winner, chicken dinner.*

HOW TO COUNT CARDS LIKE A GENIUS

Card counting may seem mysterious. Thanks to Hollywood, people picture a genius sitting at a blackjack table, glancing at the cards, nodding cryptically, and then *bam*—placing the perfect bet at the perfect moment, walking away with stacks of cash while the casino scrambles to figure out what just happened.

But the truth is, card counting isn't some ultra-advanced memory skill. It's just basic math. You don't need to be a memory champion. You don't need to memorize every single card in the deck. If you can count, you can card count.

Let me show you how.*

STEP 0: MASTER BASIC STRATEGY

Before anything else, you need to learn basic strategy. And not just learn it but *master* it; it needs to be engrained in you.

If card counting is the *advanced* way to beat blackjack, basic strategy is the *foundation*—the mathematically optimal way to play every single hand. These have been calculated; all you need to do is learn them and play each scenario as it comes into play, strict and without deviation. If you're going to count cards, you can't play the game with *gut feelings* or *lucky guesses*. It's about cold, hard probability.

---

* For this section, I'm assuming you know the basic rules of blackjack, how the game works, and some of the nomenclature of the actions in the game. If you don't know anything about blackjack, querying your favorite AI tool (or just a simple Google search) should do the trick.

Casinos set the rules so that, long-term, they always win. But with basic strategy, you reduce the house edge to nearly zero (it's actually 0.5 percent, which may not sound like much, but in the long run, it means they will still win).

Play it perfectly, and you're making the best possible decision in every situation.

Here is the chart you need to memorize. You can find this anywhere online. It's no secret. You're even allowed to carry this cheat sheet with you at the casino tables. Ask the dealer what to do "by the book" in a certain situation, and they will most likely help you.

BASIC STRATEGY CHART*

4-8 Decks, Dealer Stands on Soft 17

Player / Dealer's card

hard	2	3	4	5	6	7	8	9	10	A
4-8	H	H	H	H	H	H	H	H	H	H
9	H	Dh	Dh	Dh	Dh	H	H	H	H	H
10	Dh	Dh	Dh	Dh	Dh	Dh	Dh	Dh	H	H
11	Dh	Dh	Dh	Dh	Dh	Dh	Dh	Dh	Dh	H
12	H	H	S	S	S	H	H	H	H	H
13	S	S	S	S	S	H	H	H	H	H
14	S	S	S	S	S	H	H	H	H	H
15	S	S	S	S	S	H	H	H	Rh	H
16	S	S	S	S	S	H	H	Rh	Rh	Rh
17+	S	S	S	S	S	S	S	S	S	S

soft	2	3	4	5	6	7	8	9	10	A
13	H	H	H	Dh	Dh	H	H	H	H	H
14	H	H	H	Dh	Dh	H	H	H	H	H
15	H	H	Dh	Dh	Dh	H	H	H	H	H
16	H	H	Dh	Dh	Dh	H	H	H	H	H
17	H	Dh	Dh	Dh	Dh	H	H	H	H	H
18	S	Ds	Ds	Ds	Ds	S	S	H	H	H
19+	S	S	S	S	S	S	S	S	S	S

splits	2	3	4	5	6	7	8	9	10	A
2,2	Ph	Ph	P	P	P	P	H	H	H	H
3,3	Ph	Ph	P	P	P	P	H	H	H	H
4,4	H	H	H	Ph	Ph	H	H	H	H	H
6,6	Ph	P	P	P	P	H	H	H	H	H
7,7	P	P	P	P	P	P	H	H	H	H
8,8	P	P	P	P	P	P	P	P	P	P
9,9	P	P	P	P	P	S	P	P	S	S
A,A	P	P	P	P	P	P	P	P	P	P

- H — Hit
- S — Stand
- Dh — Double if allowed, otherwise hit
- Ds — Double if allowed, otherwise stand
- P — Split
- Ph — Split if double after split is allowed, otherwise hit
- Rh — Surrender if allowed, otherwise hit

4-8 Decks, Dealer Hits on Soft 17

Player / Dealer's card

hard	2	3	4	5	6	7	8	9	10	A
4-8	H	H	H	H	H	H	H	H	H	H
9	H	Dh	Dh	Dh	Dh	H	H	H	H	H
10	Dh	Dh	Dh	Dh	Dh	Dh	Dh	Dh	H	H
11	Dh	Dh	Dh	Dh	Dh	Dh	Dh	Dh	Dh	Dh
12	H	H	S	S	S	H	H	H	H	H
13	S	S	S	S	S	H	H	H	H	H
14	S	S	S	S	S	H	H	H	H	H
15	S	S	S	S	S	H	H	H	Rh	Rh
16	S	S	S	S	S	H	H	Rh	Rh	Rh
17	S	S	S	S	S	S	S	S	S	Rs
18+	S	S	S	S	S	S	S	S	S	S

soft	2	3	4	5	6	7	8	9	10	A
13	H	H	H	Dh	Dh	H	H	H	H	H
14	H	H	H	Dh	Dh	H	H	H	H	H
15	H	H	Dh	Dh	Dh	H	H	H	H	H
16	H	H	Dh	Dh	Dh	H	H	H	H	H
17	H	Dh	Dh	Dh	Dh	H	H	H	H	H
18	Ds	Ds	Ds	Ds	Ds	S	S	H	H	H
19	S	S	S	S	Ds	S	S	S	S	S
20+	S	S	S	S	S	S	S	S	S	S

splits	2	3	4	5	6	7	8	9	10	A
2,2	Ph	Ph	P	P	P	P	H	H	H	H
3,3	Ph	Ph	P	P	P	P	H	H	H	H
4,4	H	H	H	Ph	Ph	H	H	H	H	H
6,6	Ph	P	P	P	P	H	H	H	H	H
7,7	P	P	P	P	P	P	H	H	H	H
8,8	P	P	P	P	P	P	P	P	P	Rp
9,9	P	P	P	P	P	S	P	P	S	S
A,A	P	P	P	P	P	P	P	P	P	P

- H — Hit
- S — Stand
- Dh — Double if allowed, otherwise hit
- Ds — Double if allowed, otherwise stand
- P — Split
- Ph — Split if double after split is allowed, otherwise hit
- Rh — Surrender if allowed, otherwise hit
- Rs — Surrender if allowed, otherwise stand
- Rp — Surrender if allowed, otherwise split

* The chart slightly varies based on the game, but I have included the one for four to six deck shoes, which is what you'll mostly find at casinos. Double-deck or single-deck games are also popular but have slightly different charts.

A helpful tip if you're new to this is to remember that each hand you want to go through four possible actions. This little rhyme helps: *Surrender, Split, Double, Hit.* Always run through the actions in that order to make sense of what your move should be.*

Don't even think about going to the next steps unless you can play basic strategy *perfectly*, without hesitation. Once you can do this without thinking, you're ready to count.

STEP 1: THE RUNNING COUNT

Card counting is all about keeping track of the ratio of high cards (10s, face cards, aces) to low cards (2s, 3s, 4s, etc.) left in the deck. Why? Because high cards are good for *you* (they help make blackjacks and bust the dealer), and low cards are good for the *casino* (they keep the dealer in the game).

So, we assign values to the cards:

2, 3, 4, 5, 6	+1
7, 8, 9	0
10, J, Q, K, A	–1

The more positive your count is, the more it means that mostly small cards have been played and that there are lots of larger cards waiting in the remaining shoe. Larger cards equal more chance of getting a value close to twenty-one or even a blackjack.

This system is what's known as the Hi-Lo counting system. There are many other systems, and each has its own pros and cons, but this one is easy enough to learn and can deliver great results.

* "Surrender" means you fold your hand in exchange for half of your bet back. "Split" means you split your two duplicate cards into two new hands. "Double" means you double your bet in exchange for one more card. "Hit" means you ask for another card.

Now, as cards are dealt, you just keep a simple running tally in your head. That's it. No photographic memory. No crazy calculations. Just simple addition and subtraction.

Let's practice. Say this is the first round of a shoe:

Running Count = +1

That's all you're doing: counting up or down as cards hit the table.

This *is* simple. But, when playing in a casino, while doing a bunch of other mental tasks, keeping a simple number in your head while playing perfect basic strategy and doing other side calculations, is tricky (not to mention, you also have to act cool and as if you're doing anything but card counting).

My recommendation? Start by taking a single deck of cards, shuffle it, and remove two cards. Then time yourself as you count through it. By the end, whatever count you have, the two removed cards' count should total the opposite of what your count is for the rest of the deck (a full deck will always count to zero, because it is balanced). To be a realistic card counter, you need to be able to do this in under twenty-five seconds (ideally under twenty). You should also be able to count four consecutive shuffled decks in under two minutes.

STEP 2: THE TRUE COUNT

The Running Count (RC) alone isn't enough. You need to adjust for how many decks are left in the shoe—this gives you the True Count (TC), which is what actually determines your bets. Imagine you *just* started a new six-deck shoe and only half a deck has been played, but the count is high. There's so much of the shoe still to play that a high running count isn't really a true indication of how hot* the deck is. Now, if instead you had a single deck remaining (five decks have already been played) and the RC is high? Well, damn, you know that remaining deck is going to be very, very hot!

To get the TC:

* In blackjack, a "hot" shoe refers to a deck (or shoe) that is rich in high cards—10s, face cards, and aces—that haven't yet been played. This favors the player, increasing the chances of hitting blackjacks, winning double downs, and the dealer busting.

1. ESTIMATE HOW MANY DECKS ARE LEFT IN THE SHOE.

This takes practice. You should be able to glance at the discard tray (the tower where played cards have been discarded) and make an accurate guess as to how many decks are left in the shoe. For example, if you see about two decks in the discard tray, you know there are four left to play (assuming it's a six-deck shoe). To get good at this, you need to be very familiar with the size of decks and half decks (being able to estimate this to a half deck accuracy is more than enough).

2. DIVIDE THE RC BY THE NUMBER OF DECKS REMAINING.

This also takes practice. Some divisions will be trickier than others. See if you can come up with your own tricks (you have some of the mental math know-how from chapter 5, pages 129–136, right?).

EXAMPLE:

- **RC = +12**
- **About three decks left in the shoe**
- **12 ÷ 3 = TC of +4**

A TC of +4 means the remainder of the deck is heavily loaded with high cards. To give you an idea, our threshold for a hot deck was when the TC got to +3. That's when we would start signaling to our teammates to jump in and start playing at the table. Otherwise, we wouldn't bother because the deck was "cold" and less likely to be profitable.*

Also, the TC is what would indicate our bet size. Most players will have a betting unit. It is good practice, if you are playing for real, with real money, to figure out what your unit size and spread would be (i.e., the range between your minimum and maximum bets). This should be based on how big your bankroll is and a calculation of your risk of ruin.†

Let's say your unit was $100. And let's say the TC was +7, but your max bet you make is 5 units. Then you would bet $500. In some cases (and on some teams I played on), we had no max bet unit. So, if the TC was +7, I would have played $700. We also try to play two hands at the same time, so I would have put two hands of $700. Big money!

---

* We usually rely on a tactic called "back-counting": standing by a table, quietly keeping track of the count without playing. If the shoe turns hot, we jump in or signal a teammate to take a seat. If it doesn't, we move on or wait for the next shoe. That way we're not burning through our bankroll on dead games.

† I'm not going to go into all this here, because you're not playing with real money, now, are you? No sirree, no. Because I don't promote gambling, remember?

STEP 3: USE YOUR INDEX NUMBERS

There is another chart you need to memorize (sorry!)—a map of index numbers that indicate when a player should deviate from basic strategy to maximize their edge, depending on the TC and what hand you have versus the dealer's.

A great example is a hand of 16 versus a 10. Basic strategy says to always hit. To many players who have no idea what they're doing, this situation is one where they might go with their gut and "stand" (the term used in blackjack to stop accepting any more cards) because they feel like they might bust (i.e., go over twenty-one). Nope. Always hit. No matter what. The probabilities say to.

That is, *unless* the TC is positive. The index number for this situation is 0. Meaning, if you have a TC of 0 or higher (any positive count), then you stand in that situation. If the index number on the chart is your TC in play, don't do the basic strategy move that typically applies, do the opposite.

Some serious players memorize a crazy amount of index numbers, but I don't believe that's necessary. All you need to learn are the famous *illustrious 18*—eighteen index numbers that account for the largest majority of plays that will give you the most edge.

INDEX PLAYS: THE ILLUSTRIOUS 18

Players Hand vs. Dealer's Up- Card	True Count
Insurance	+3 or Higher Take Insurance
16 vs. 10	0 or Higher Stand
15 vs. 10	+4 or Higher Stand
10, 10 vs. 5	+5 or Higher Split
10, 10 vs. 6	+4 or Higher Split
10 vs. 10	+4 or Higher Double
12 vs. 3	+2 or Higher Stand
12 vs. 2	+3 or Higher Stand
11 vs. Ace	+1 or Higher Double
9 vs. 2	+1 or Higher Double
10 vs. Ace	+4 or Higher Double
9 vs. 7	+3 or Higher Double
16 vs. 9	+5 or Higher Stand
13 vs. 2	–1 or Lower* Hit
12 vs. 4	0 or Lower Hit
12 vs. 5	–2 or Lower Hit
12 vs. 6	–1 or Lower Hit
13 vs. 3	–2 or Lower Hit

*Lower = more negative, like –2, –3, –4, etc.

STEP 4: NOT GETTING CAUGHT

The biggest misconception about card counting is that it's illegal. It's *not*. Casinos just don't like it because it gives *you* an edge. And when you have an edge in a casino, they don't exactly roll out the red carpet. They show you the door.

So, one of the most important parts of being a successful card counter is staying undetected. That means you need to be able to play super smoothly while not looking as if you're doing a bunch of mental calculations. On top of that, card counters will often build *cover plays* into their routine—plays that veer off from basic strategy from time to time to throw off the monitoring security and pit bosses who are specifically looking for card counters. Nowadays, it's fairly easy to spot a card counter's techniques. But play with a few wild, nonsensical plays from time to time, and security won't have any idea if you're a card counter or just a regular, idiot player.

The *real* way to win is longevity. The best card counters aren't the ones who crush a casino in one night—they're the ones who make steady, calculated profits while staying under the radar. Casinos actively track suspected counters, and if they catch you—or even just *think* you're counting—they can restrict your play, ask you to leave, or even ban you from the property.

And that's card counting. It's not some secret, mystical ability. It's just basic counting, with a little math, a little deception, and whole lot of practice ("ass-time," as my good friend Brad says—the time you spend sitting on your ass honing your craft).

But hey, it works.

If you stick to the system, card counting flips the game slightly in your favor, turning blackjack into one of the *only* casino games where you can actually beat the house in the long run.

On top of that, learning how to count cards sharpens your focus, boosts your memory, and teaches you how to stay calm under pressure. And it's a skill that casinos *don't want you to have.*

Which is exactly why you should learn it (insert devil emoji here).

HOW TO MEMORIZE A DECK OF CARDS

The basic approach to memorizing a deck of cards is relatively simple. To do so, we need to turn each card into a mental picture and then store it in a Memory Palace. The Memory Palace will be the tool we use to remember the order of the cards.

But how do we turn a card into a picture? Just as we did with numbers in chapter 1 (page 37), we will use a system to translate the card value and suit into letters and words to memorize them better.

PERSON-ACTION-OBJECT

While you could use a similar system as the Major System, a better one for cards is the Person-Action-Object method, or PAO.

First, we translate the value into a letter, then the suit. Together, that makes a pair of initials that we can map onto a person—a friend or family member, an athlete, celebrity, whomever! Each person you map to a card will also have an associated action and object.

The phonetic code for the values is as such:*

A	2	3	4	5	6	7	8	9	10
A	B	C	D	E	S	G	H	N	O

Easy enough to remember, right? Each number basically translates to the letter at that position in the alphabet (except for 6, which is *S* because it's a very *s*-sounding number; 9, which is *N* for similar reasons; and 10, which has the zero in it, hence it maps to *O*).

The phonetic codes for the suits are:

Diamonds: D
Clubs: C
Hearts: H
Spades: S

(It's just the first letter of the word.)

So, if I had the ace of spades, that would translate to an A.S. For me, that's Arnold Schwarzenegger. That means, whenever I see that ace of spades, I don't see that suit and value; I see the muscular Governator.

For face cards—jack, queen, and king—I recommend coming up with a person that feels intuitive to the card. For example, maybe the jack of hearts could be someone you love (the hearts) whose name starts with "J." You can also make each suit a category. For example, hearts could be friends and loved ones, clubs could be athletes, diamonds—rich people, and

* This phonetic system is also known as the Dominic System, invented by eight-time world memory champion Dominic O'Brien.

spades—famous musicians. And then for each of the face cards, just think of someone in that category who is the king (a leading male figure), a queen (a leading female), and a jack (a strong supporting character—male or female). For example, king of spades could be the king himself, Elvis Presley. Maybe the queen of clubs is Serena Williams. King of diamonds—Bill Gates.

What about the action and object? For each person you come up with, you'll want to create a unique, associated action and object. For Arnold, the ace of spades, his action might be *weightlifting* and his object, a *barbell*. For Serena, the queen of clubs, her action might be *swinging* and her object, a *tennis racket*.

Once you have all these selected (I recommend creating a spreadsheet to keep track) and memorized, you can start applying these images to a real deck.

Here's how it works: As you go through a shuffled deck, group cards in threes. For each triplet, the first card is the PERSON, the second card the ACTION, and the third card the OBJECT. Place that PERSON-ACTION-OBJECT image in the next location in your Memory Palace. Repeat until the deck is done. You'll have seventeen images total, and one card left over (just memorize that final card by looking at it).

For example, if your sequence of three is ace of spades, queen of clubs, king of diamonds . . . the ace of spades (since it's in the PERSON slot) would be *Arnold, swinging* (the ACTION of the second card), a *window* (the OBJECT associated with Bill Gates. Microsoft Windows, get it?). To memorize that three-card sequence, you'd have the bizarre, but utterly memorable image of Arnold swinging a window. The only thing left to do is place that image in a location in a Memory Palace and then move on to the next set of three cards.

As you attempt to master doing this, start with just a single suit. Shuffle it and see if you can memorize the thirteen cards (you'll have a single card left over after grouping them by three, but that last card can just be a lone PERSON). Then move on to a half deck (here, you'll have two leftover cards, so just pair those as a PERSON-ACTION). When you're ready, try the full deck. It may take you twenty to thirty minutes. But with practice, you can cut down on that time significantly.

Building this system is a project, no doubt. But once you've done it, you've got it for life. And once you have it down, you'll have a dedicated formula for memorizing cards in chunks of three at a time. With some dedicated practice, you can potentially get your card memorization time down to under 60 seconds.*

By the way, you can take these fifty-two images and expand them into a full two-digit number system. Back in chapter 1 (page 37), we covered the Major System—a solid method for turning numbers into images. But there's another approach: creating a PAO system for every number pair from 00 to 99.†

HOW TO MEMORIZE THE COLORS OF A DECK OF CARDS

Maybe you don't care to memorize the *whole* deck, suits and values and all. If you want something quicker to learn and easier to master, memorizing just the order of the colors is a fun little trick. This approach can also be applied to any binary sequence: a sequence of heads or tails coins, a sequence of male or female humans in a line or audience, heck, even a sequence of straight up binary digits (1s and 0s).

To do it, we will again group cards in threes. Since there are two options for each card (red or black), the number of possible configurations is 2^3, or 8. If we come up with letter sounds for each of these triplets, we can construct words (like the Major System) for each of those eight groupings. Then, with those words, we can just create a little story to memorize the whole deck (we can also use a Memory Palace to store each image, whatever is fastest for you).

First, I think it's helpful to think of the red and black colors as a light switch—on or off (1 or 0). If the light is on (red), it's a 1; if the light is

---

* The world record for memorizing an entire deck of cards is 12.74 seconds, achieved by Shijir-Erdene Bat-Enkh.

† More on that in my other book, *Remember It!*, if you're interested.

off (black), it's a zero. You can reverse it if you prefer, as long as you're consistent.

Looking at all eight possible combinations of red and black (or now, 1s and 0s), I associate a letter sound with each based on what it looks like (just to keep things quick and simple to remember):

000	None (no 1s)	N
111	All (all 1s)	A
101	Sides (1s on the sides)	S
010	Middle (1 in the middle)	M
100	Left (1 on the left)	L
001	Right (1 on the right)	R
110	Back (two 1s on the back end)	B
011	Front (two 1s on the front end)	F

Now you can stick with the letters above and just create words as you memorize, or you can come up with a preset image for each letter. Maybe an actual *thing* that starts with the letter (to make it easier to visualize). *N* could be a narwhal or a nose, perhaps. *A* could be an apple. *S*, a shoe, etc. Whatever you want! Categorize them if that helps you (maybe you make them all animal names, or foods). In the end, it doesn't truly matter what your system is for converting the cards, as long as you commit to it and learn it!

Example: Let's say you started memorizing and first saw the cards RED, RED, RED, RED, BLACK, RED.

That would be (111, 101) = A + S.

If I had decided *A* was for "apple" and *S* was for "shoe," my image to remember that sequence would be an apple shoe—a shoe made entirely of apples.

And just like that, "apple shoe" represents six cards! To memorize the whole deck, continue on, creating images from the remaining cards and placing them in your Memory Palace. As I did in the above example, I'd recommend pairing images together (it saves space). Pretty cool, right?

HOW TO BEAT ANY GAME

Most people play games *one move at a time*, reacting to whatever happens in front of them. They make decisions based on instinct, gut feelings, or whatever seems right in the moment. And that's exactly why they lose.

Geniuses tend to think many moves ahead—not just about what's happening *now* but about what will happen *next* and how to control it. While game theory might seem as if it's all about winning, it's actually not. It's about *forcing* your opponent into situations where their best option is still worse than yours.

Take poker. The average player sees a strong hand and bets big. But a game theory master bets not just based on their cards, but on what their opponent thinks they have. They know that being unpredictable is more powerful than simply playing well. If people can't read you, they can't outplay you.

It's the same in chess. Most people make moves that look strong in the moment, like threatening or taking a piece. But a smarter player knows that the real battle is happening *several moves in the future*. Every move should limit their opponent's options, forcing them down a path where they're playing defense while you're executing a plan they never saw coming.

This is the key to all strategy games: Control the choices, and you control the game. If you can take away your opponent's best moves before they even realize what's happening, you're already winning.

So, stop playing like everyone else. If you want to win more—at cards, board games, negotiations, or even life—you need to stop playing the game *as it is* and start playing *the people who are playing it*. Every game has patterns, and every player has weaknesses. The trick is recognizing them before they recognize you.

Here are the key strategies to keep in mind for *any* game:

- ***ALWAYS ASSUME YOUR OPPONENT KNOWS WHAT THEY'RE DOING.***
  If you're counting on them making a mistake, you're setting yourself up for failure. Play as if they'll always make the best possible move, then plan accordingly.
- ***PREDICTABILITY IS A WEAKNESS.***
  If your opponent can read you, they can beat you. Mix up your strategy, make unexpected plays, and control what they *think* you're going to do.
- ***LET THEM THINK THEY'RE WINNING . . . UNTIL IT'S TOO LATE.***
  The biggest power move is patience. Let others take the spotlight while you stay under the radar and set yourself up for the real win.
- ***KNOW WHEN TO TRUST AND WHEN TO BETRAY.***
  Cooperation is a weapon if you know when to use it. Long-term alliances beat short-term greed, but knowing when to break that trust is the difference between winning and just surviving.
- ***THE BEST MOVE IS SOMETIMES NO MOVE AT ALL.***
  Let your opponents make the first mistake. In strategy games, in poker, in negotiations—whoever panics first typically loses.

- **NEVER LET EMOTIONS CONTROL YOUR DECISIONS.**
  Anger, frustration, impatience aren't strategies. The moment you let emotions dictate your play, you've stopped thinking logically. That's when you risk losing.
- **THINK FIVE MOVES AHEAD, NOT JUST ONE.**
  Winning is about making sure you're in the strongest position *when it actually matters*, not necessarily about being in the best position *right now*.
- **YOU'RE PLAYING PEOPLE.**
  Rules and strategies can be learned by anyone, but a big part of the game is understanding the people sitting across from you.

Let's take a look at some specific games and some simple strategies to employ to gain an edge, or to flat-out win!

ROCK-PAPER-SCISSORS: READ YOUR OPPONENT

Most people assume rock-paper-scissors is random. It's not. Humans are bad at being random and follow subconscious patterns.

- Rock is the most commonly played first move. If you're up against a beginner, start with paper.
- Losers tend to switch moves. If your opponent just lost with rock, they're less likely to throw it again.
- Winners tend to repeat. If they just won with scissors, they'll likely throw it again.

How to win: If you lose a round, assume your opponent will change their move, and counter accordingly. If you win, expect them to predict your repeat move, and switch ahead of them.

THE MONTY HALL PROBLEM: ALWAYS SWITCH

The famous Monty Hall Problem works like this: You're on a game show with three doors—one hides a car, two hide goats. You pick a door. The host (who knows what's behind them) opens another door to reveal a goat. Now you get to switch or stick with your original choice.

Most people assume it's a 50/50 shot at this point. It's not.

Mathematically, switching gives you a 2/3 chance of winning. Staying with your first choice is only 1/3. Your initial choice had a 1/3 chance of choosing the car, and the other two doors combined had a 2/3 chance.

When the host eliminates one door, that 2/3 probability shifts to the remaining unopened door.

Lesson: When faced with a situation where new information changes the odds, always recalculate. Your first instinct is usually wrong.

COIN FLIPS AREN'T 50/50

A fair coin flip? Not quite.

Studies show that a coin is slightly more likely to land on the same side it started on (about 51 percent of the time).* It's a tiny edge, but over hundreds of flips, it adds up.

The move: If you're calling a flip in the air, pick the side that's facing up before the toss.

TIC-TAC-TOE: NEVER LOSE AGAIN

Tic-tac-toe is a *solved* game. If both players play perfectly, it will always end in a draw. But most casual players don't play perfectly.

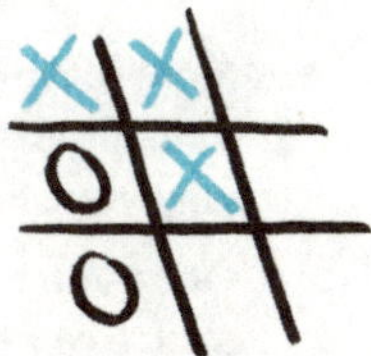

Winning strategies: If you go first, always start in the center. This gives you the most control. If your opponent goes first and picks a corner, take the center. You can also force a fork (a situation where you create two ways to win at the same time), forcing your opponent into an unwinnable situation.

MONOPOLY: PLAY FOR HOUSES, NOT HOTELS

Most people play Monopoly wrong. They focus on buying properties and upgrading to hotels as fast as possible. That's a mistake.

The best strategy:

- **Focus on three-house sets. Houses are *way* more cost-effective than hotels. The moment you put up a fourth house, you're wasting money.**
- **Orange and red properties are the best investments. Statistically, they get landed on the most.**
- **Bankrupt players strategically. If an opponent is struggling, don't just crush them. Offer trades that keep them in the game *while* giving you key advantages.**

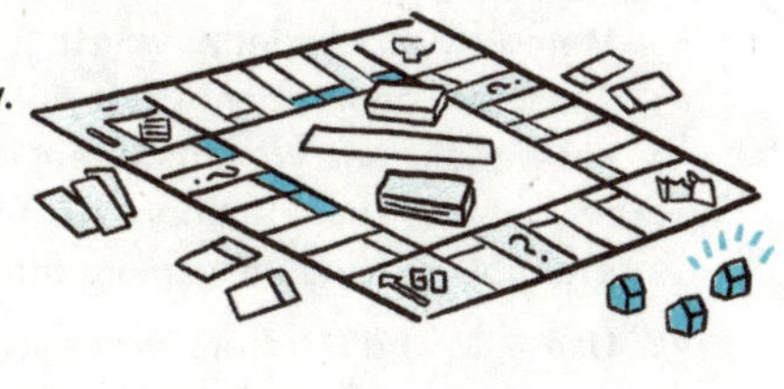

* František Bartoš et al., "Fair Coins Tend to Land on the Same Side They Started: Evidence from 350,757 Flips," *Journal of the American Statistical Association* (August 2025): 1–10.

CONNECT FOUR: THE FIRST MOVE WINS

Always go first. Always start in the center.

- **If you play perfectly and start in the middle, you can't lose.**
- **The key is to force your opponent into a losing position by stacking your pieces in a way that creates a double win condition (two ways to win at once).**
- **If you don't go first, take the column directly next to the center—it's your best shot at disrupting your opponent's strategy.**

BATTLESHIP: TARGET THE CORNERS FIRST

People don't place ships randomly.

- **Most players avoid the edges and corners, thinking they're too obvious. That's exactly why you should check them early.**
- **Once you hit a ship, don't just fire randomly; stick to a pattern to sink it quickly.**
- **The optimal targeting strategy is the "checkerboard" method: Attack every other square to maximize efficiency.**

SCRABBLE: PLAY DEFENSE, NOT JUST BIG WORDS

Control the board, not just the score.

- **Don't go for the longest words, go for words that block your opponent from bonus squares.**
- **Memorize all two-letter words (like "QI" and "JO"). These are game changers in tight spaces. If you know these and your opponent doesn't, it's a *huge* advantage. There are only 107 to memorize, and you probably already know more than a third of them.***
- **Use *S*, *R*, and *D* letters strategically, placing them to create multiple words at once.**

---

* Using our memory skills from chapter 1, this shouldn't be a problem.

CHECKERS: CONTROL THE CENTER, NOT THE SIDES

Never take the first jump your opponent offers.

- The middle is the strongest position. Don't hug the edges too early.
- Set traps by offering a jump that looks good but actually leads your opponent into a position where you can double-jump or control the board.
- Always trade pieces when you're ahead; reducing the number of pieces helps the winning player.

DOMINOES: CONTROL THE BOARD EARLY

- Play your doubles (tiles with the same number on both ends, like 6-6) early. They give you more control over the board, because they create branching points and can limit your opponent's options.
- Watch which numbers your opponent avoids or delays playing. It can reveal what tiles they don't have, helping you plan your plays and set up blocks.
- Force them to draw by blocking their number options.

SUDOKU: ELIMINATE OPTIONS FASTER

These strategies eliminate options faster and speed up the game.

- Naked Pairs:
  If two squares in a row, column, or box can only be the same two numbers (e.g., 3 and 7), no other squares in that unit can be those numbers. This quickly eliminates options.
- Hidden Singles:
  If a number can only go in one square of a row, column, or box, that's its spot (even if other candidates are penciled in).

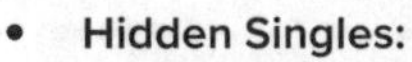

- Pointing Pairs:
  If two candidates for a number in a box fall in the same row or column, that number can't appear elsewhere in that row or column.
- Box-Line Reduction:
  If all candidates for a number in a row or column are inside one box, you can eliminate that number from the rest of the box.

- X-Wing:
  If a candidate appears in exactly two squares across two rows (and those squares line up in the same columns), you can eliminate that number from all other squares in those columns (or vice versa for columns/rows).

HANGMAN: PICK THE MOST COMMON LETTERS

The most common letters in English are your best bet.

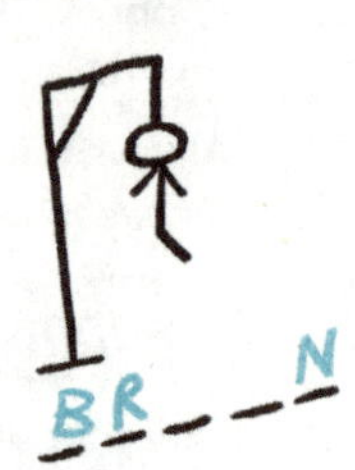

- If you're guessing, start with vowels (E, A, O) and then move to S, T, R, L, N.
- If you're the one choosing the word, pick short words with tricky letters (J, Q, X, Z, V, K) to make it harder to guess.

HOW TO BE A GENIUS AT CHESS

I'll be the first to admit, chess is *insanely* complex. People devote their entire lives to mastering it. I'm still very much a beginner compared with serious players. But as I've studied and practiced, I've picked up strategies that make a *huge* difference, even if you're not aiming to be the next grandmaster.

CONTROL THE CENTER, OR LOSE FAST

The first few moves decide a *lot*. If you're not fighting for the center, you're already behind. The key squares are e4, d4, e5, d5. Control them, and you control the board. Simple rules:

- Push your pawn to e4 or d4 (as White), and respond to White's center moves as Black (often by mirroring, or with moves like c5 or e6).
- Develop knights and bishops toward the center, not the edges.
- Castle early. Get your king safe before launching attacks.*

You don't need to memorize openings to play well early. Just follow this principle, and you'll start off stronger than most casual players.

---

* Castling is a special move that lets you tuck your king behind a wall of pawns while bringing your rook into play. It's the only move in chess where you move two pieces at once—and it's one of the best ways to protect your king early in the game.

DON'T JUST THINK ABOUT YOUR MOVE. THINK ABOUT THEIRS.

Most beginners focus only on what they want to do. Stronger players think about what their opponent is planning. Before every move, ask:

1. **What does their last move threaten?**
2. **What happens if I ignore it?**
3. **How can I improve my position *while* stopping them?**

This single habit alone will stop most beginner's blunders.

TACTICS WIN GAMES. LEARN THESE THREE FIRST.

Tactics are small, forcing move sequences that win material (i.e., pieces) or checkmate. If you learn *just three*, you'll start beating people who don't know them.

1. **Forks—One piece attacks two at the same time.**
2. **Pins—A piece can't move without exposing something behind it.**
3. **Skewers—Like a pin, but reversed. The more valuable piece is in front, and when it moves, you take the one behind it.**

STOP MAKING ONE-MOVE THREATS

Bad players attack in bursts; they threaten a piece, hope for a mistake, then scramble when it doesn't work. Genius players build up pressure over multiple moves.

- **Improve your position first, then attack.**
- **Make threats part of a bigger plan, not just random shots.**
- **Before you move, always ask: What happens after this? If the answer is "nothing," find a better move.**

ENDGAMES WIN GAMES

Most people study openings, but games are actually decided in the endgame. If you know just a *few* endgame principles, you'll crush players who don't.

- **King activity is everything. Bring your king toward the center. It's a weapon, not a liability.**
- **In pawn endgames, get opposition: Face your opponent's king with one square between you, forcing them to move and give ground.**

- **Rooks belong behind passed pawns. Always put your rook *behind* your advancing pawn, not in front.**

Mastering just these three endgame principles will win you games against people who haven't studied them.

THINK IN PLANS, NOT JUST MOVES

If you're just moving pieces randomly, hoping something works, you're already losing. Strong players play plans; they don't play moves.

Every few moves, ask yourself:

- **What's my goal for the next five moves?**
- **What's my opponent's weakest point?**
- **Can I improve my worst-placed piece?**

If you do this consistently, your game will improve dramatically.

PLAY FOR THE LONG GAME

Most players obsess over winning material (taking pieces). Genius players focus on winning positions (controlling key squares, preparing for the endgame).

The difference?

- **A beginner sees a free piece.**
- **An advanced player sees a tactic.**
- **A genius player sees a future winning position—five moves ahead.**

The moment you stop thinking move-to-move and start thinking positionally, you'll start playing *like a genius*.

HOW TO MEMORIZE CHESS MOVES LIKE A GENIUS

Every chess move has two key elements: the piece that moves and the square it moves to. If you can convert both into images, memorizing entire games or openings becomes easy.

Here's how to do it.

The chessboard is already a grid of numbers and letters, perfect for converting into mnemonics. If you're familiar with chess notation, you know that:

- **Files (vertical columns) are labeled a to h (left to right from White's perspective).**
- **Ranks (horizontal rows) are numbered 1 to 8 (starting from White's side). So every square is a letter-number pair (e4, d5, f6, etc.).**

A simple way to turn those coordinates into images is by using the Dominic System we used for cards earlier (see page 199). The only adjustment you would need to make is that file f would be converted to an S letter, since that's in line with our original Dominic System.

Then we assign images to moves. Let's take e4 as an example.

- **E4 → "E" and "D" (since 4 = D in the Dominic System).**
- **If you've built out your PAO system, maybe E.D. is Ed the Talking Horse (from the old TV show).**
- **Ed has an action (riding a horse) and an object (a toy horse).**

Since a chess move has only two components, we need only the person and action. The person will be the piece; the action will be the coordinate. So every move in a chess game becomes a person doing an action.*

Next, store each move at a location inside a Memory Palace, and continue this process until you're done placing the entire sequence.

EXAMPLE: MEMORIZING THE ITALIAN GAME OPENING

If you're serious about chess, the first opening you should memorize is the Italian Game.† It's simple and powerful and sets you up for solid, tactical play without getting lost in endless theory. Here's what the move sequence looks like (I'm assuming you know chess notation):

1. **E4—Take control of the center.**
2. **E5—Black fights back for the center.**
3. **NF3—Attack the e5 pawn and develop your knight.**
4. **NC6—Black defends and develops.**
5. **BC4—The bishop lines up on c4, eyeing the weak f7 square.**

* Quick note: Pawn moves are written as just the square (e.g., "e4"). Other pieces include their letter first (e.g., "Nf3" for knight, "Qd5" for queen).

† Genius fact: You can also learn the Scholar's Mate. It's a classic four-move checkmate that destroys unprepared beginners. As White: e4, Bc4, Qh5, then if Black plays carelessly (like g6 or Nc6), strike with Qxf7# for checkmate. Most experienced players are well prepared to defend against this "trick," but it's a quick and devastating way to beat a beginner in just a few moves.

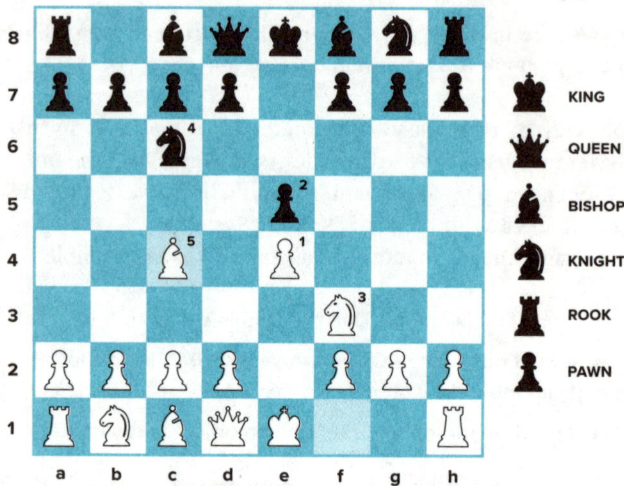

It's one of the classics. It teaches development and how to center control, and it works at every level of play.

Next, let's assign an image to each piece, so they're easier to visualize:

- Pawn (no letter designation)—a shrimp (or prawn, sounds like "pawn")
- Bishop (B)—a pope-looking guy (that's what I think of for a bishop)
- Knight (N)—an actual knight in armor
- Rook (R)—a castle (the rook looks like one)
- Queen (Q)—the Queen of England
- King (K)—LeBron James (since he's known as "King James")

Now here's how I would memorize it, placing these images in a memory palace:

1. ***E4***—Pawn to e4 → shrimp riding a horse (E.D.)
2. ***E5***—Pawn to e5 → shrimp writing a poem (e5 = E.E. → E. E. Cummings action is writing a poem)
3. ***NF3***—Knight to f3 → A knight sitting at a desk (f3 = S.C. → Stephen Colbert's action is sitting at a desk)
4. ***NC6***—Knight to c6 → A knight coding on a computer (c6 = C.S. → Computer Scientist's action is coding)
5. ***BC4***—Bishop to c4 → A pope dunking (c4 = C.D. or 34, which is Shaquille O' Neal's jersey number; his action is dunking)

Once you master the encoding and can translate easily between chess square and image, as well as piece image to piece, memorizing sequences like this will be a breeze!* With this method, you can learn multiple openings *fast* and recall them under pressure.

You can also use this approach to memorize *entire* games. While there's no substitute for having a strong understanding of chess and its moves, using memory techniques to encode and store moves will allow you to analyze moves thoroughly.

GENIUS PROFILE:
JUDIT POLGÁR

At just fifteen years old, Judit Polgár became the youngest grandmaster in history, breaking Bobby Fischer's record. But it wasn't just her age that made headlines; it was who she beat. Throughout her career, Judit defeated eleven world champions, including Garry Kasparov, Viswanathan Anand, and Magnus Carlsen. One of her most famous games was against Kasparov in 2002, where she capitalized on a slight misstep and outplayed him with clinical precision, becoming the first woman to beat him in a classical match.

Trained from childhood in a radical homeschool experiment by her father, Judit shattered the norms, proving that brilliance in chess had nothing to do with gender and everything to do with mindset, training, and raw cognitive firepower.

* If you want to take chess memorization seriously, I highly recommend writing down and learning all your person-actions for all possible chess positions. That way, you'll always have an image at the ready for whatever chess sequence you want to memorize.

HOW TO SOLVE THE KNIGHT'S TOUR

The Knight's Tour is a classic chess puzzle where a knight must visit every square on the board exactly once using only legal knight moves. It looks impossible at first, but there's a system behind it. Once you understand the method, you can pull off this genius-seeming chess flex anytime. You can also pre-memorize a sequence of moves, but that's not as cool as solving it on the fly.

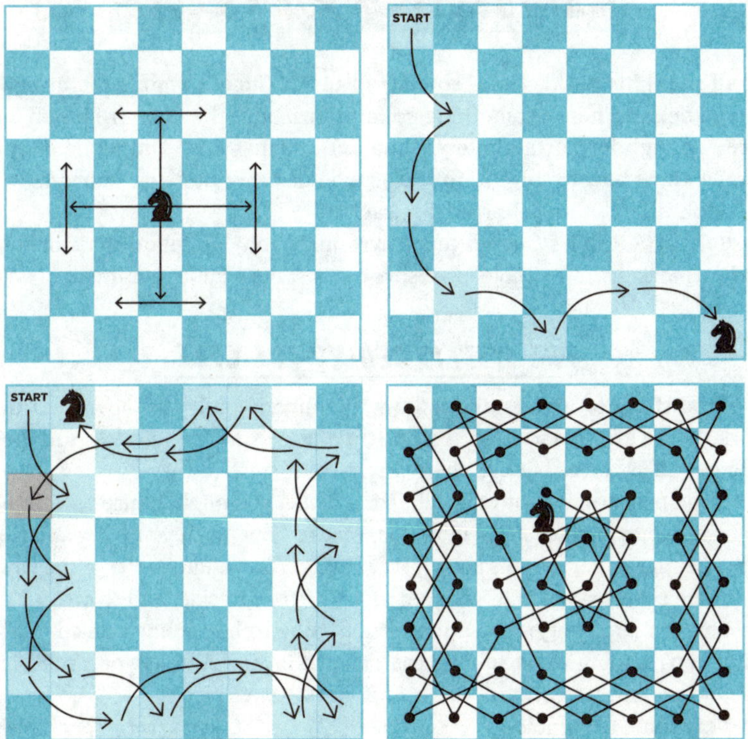

First, let's make sure you understand how the knight moves. A knight moves in an L-shape: two squares in one direction, then one square perpendicular; or one square in one direction, then two squares perpendicular.

This unique movement lets the knight jump over pieces and reach squares that would be inaccessible with normal sliding moves.

Let's tackle the simplest way to do a knight's tour, which is by having the knight start at any one of the corners on the board. Stick to the outermost available square that you can. Always keep moving in the same direction (either clockwise or counterclockwise).

That's it! Stick to those rules and you'll be able to solve this complicated puzzle!

Once you get the hang of it by completing it a few times, you'll be able to complete the Knight's Tour on demand, making it look effortless. And nothing says "chess genius" like casually solving a legendary puzzle in front of others.*

HOW TO SOLVE A RUBIK'S CUBE

Of all the skills in this book, solving a Rubik's Cube is among the ultimate genius flexes. There's something so familiar about the cube from pop culture and eighties nostalgia; everyone knows what it is. And while a lot of people know how to solve it, for those who don't, witnessing someone who can looks like nothing short of a miracle.

Solving a Rubik's Cube is just a system. If you can follow a set of steps and memorize a few simple moves, you can solve a cube in minutes.

THE SYSTEM BEHIND THE CUBE

The first thing to understand is how the cube is built and how the turns work. There are six faces, each made up of nine smaller squares. Your goal is to get all six faces back to their single-color state (duh!).

If you play around with the cube for a while, you might notice something: that the center squares *never* move. No matter how much you twist and turn the cube, the center squares always stay in place. So: White center = the white side; blue center = the blue side; red center = the red side; and so on.

This is important because you're not going to be solving one color at a time; you're going to be solving the cube in layers. And as you rotate any face, you're rotating around these stationary center pieces.

Now some terminology.

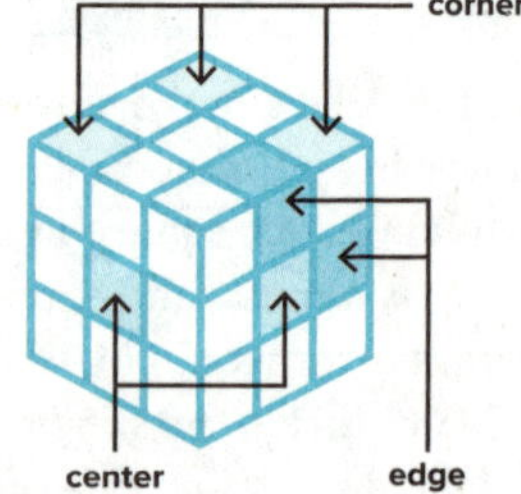

There are three kinds of pieces on the cube:

- **Center pieces—With only *one* sticker, and as we just established, they don't move.**
- **Corner pieces—These are in the corners**

---

* If you want to tackle situations where the knight starts on *any* piece, not just the corners, check out my full video tutorial on YouTube: "The Knight's Tour (chess puzzle) – Tutorial" (https://www.youtube.com/watch?v=O1ZtjLDog7M).

of the cube and have *three* stickers on them. There are eight total (as an exercise see if you can inspect the cube and locate them all).

- Edge pieces—These are on the edge of each face and in between corners. The have *two* stickers on them. There are eight of them (see if you can locate them all as well).

To learn how to turn the cube correctly to solve it, we will refer to each face as follows (all with respect to you holding the cube in front of yourself):

- F—the front face, facing you
- B—the back face, facing away from you
- L—the left face, facing left
- R—the right face, facing right
- U—the upper face, facing up
- D—the down face, facing down

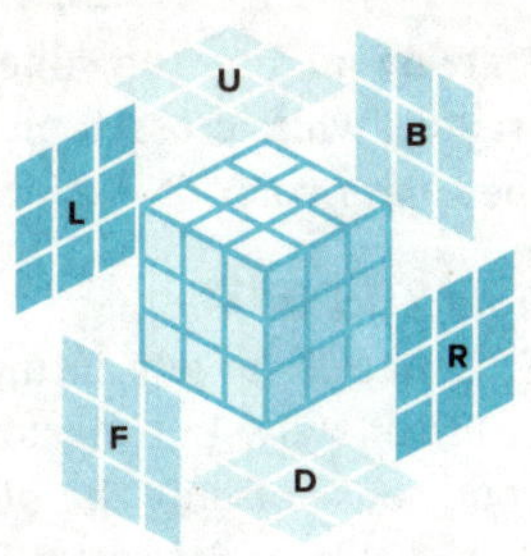

If you read an algorithm (fancy word for "sequence of face turns") that has a sequence of these letters, it means you need to turn each one in the order of the sequence. If just the letter, turn that face a single turn in the clockwise direction;* if there is a little apostrophe next to the letter, turn that face counterclockwise. If you see a 2 next to a letter, it means to turn the face twice (either direction is fine).

EXAMPLE:

A sequence like R U R' U2 means:

1. Turn the right face once clockwise.
2. Turn the upper face once clockwise.
3. Turn the right face once counterclockwise.
4. Turn the upper face twice (in either direction).

Congratulations! You just completed your first algorithm!

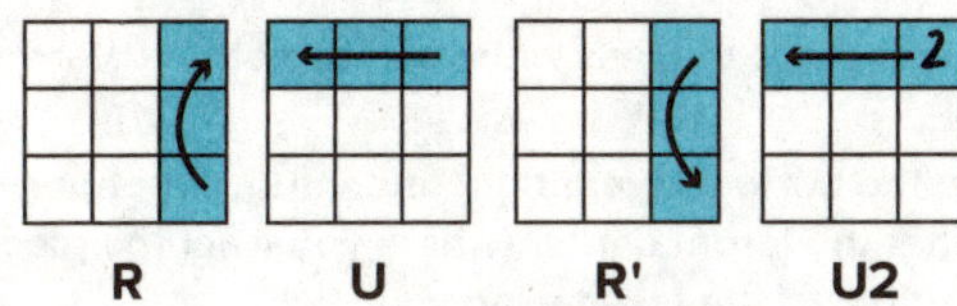

* It might be confusing to think which way is clockwise based on how you're holding the cube, but just remember: If you imagine having the face in question right in front of you, whatever the clockwise direction would be in that frame of reference, that's what is considered the clockwise direction.

Next, let's learn how to solve the cube. The following is often referred to as the Layer-by-Layer (LBL) Method. To me, it's the easiest method, because it breaks it down into solving one layer at a time.

There are other, more advanced systems, but I'll leave that to you to explore later if you want. Just so you know, though, world record holders in the sport of speed-cubing have methods to solve cubes in *under five seconds*!

STEP 1: SOLVE THE WHITE CROSS

Start by holding the cube with the white center facing up. Your goal is to create a white cross: a plus sign (+) on top, with each edge piece matching the center color of the face it touches.

HOW TO DO IT:

This step is largely intuitive; there are no algorithms, unfortunately. But mastering this step will give you a good sense of how the pieces move on the cube as you turn different faces. So I would spend some time just trying to play around figuring out this step.

I suggest first locating a white edge piece (because these are the pieces you need to make the cross; no corners yet). Once you locate it, look at the other color sticker on that piece. That needs to be touching the matching color center, while also having the white sticker on top.

Another general tip is to think of the bottom layer as a conveyer belt of sorts. If you can get a piece down to the bottom layer, you can rotate it around and get that piece to travel to any side of the cube without messing up the cross you're building on the top.

There are some trickier situations, but once you get familiar with them, it all should be mostly intuitive.

Do this for all four edges, and you'll have a white cross.

STEP 2: SOLVE THE WHITE CORNERS

Now you need to place the white corner pieces to complete the white face.

1. **Find a corner piece that has white and two other colors (e.g., white-red-blue).**
2. **Move it to the bottom layer,* right under its correct position. Hold the cube so that the target corner (where you want the piece to end up) is at the top-right of the face facing you.**
3. **Use this algorithm until it snaps into place:**

* It might already be on the bottom layer. If it isn't, apply the same algorithm in #3 and it will move there.

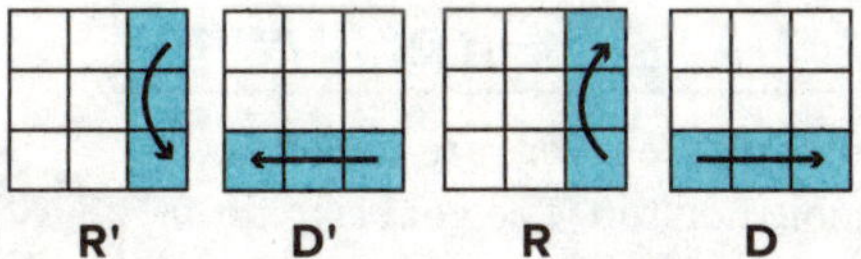

Repeat until the corner moves into the right spot. Do this for all corners, and you'll have a completed first layer.

STEP 3: SOLVE THE SECOND LAYER

Now that the entire white face is solved, we move to the second layer—the edges between the middle and top layers. Since the center stickers (also in the second layer) don't move, they are already solved, and we don't need to worry about those.

To solve the rest of the cube, let's flip the cube over so our completed first layer is now our bottom layer.

1. **Find a non-yellow edge piece in the top layer.**
2. **Rotate the top layer until the front color of the piece matches its center color and that sticker is directly facing you.**
3. **Depending on whether it needs to move left or right, use one of these algorithms:**

LEFT MOVE:

RIGHT MOVE:

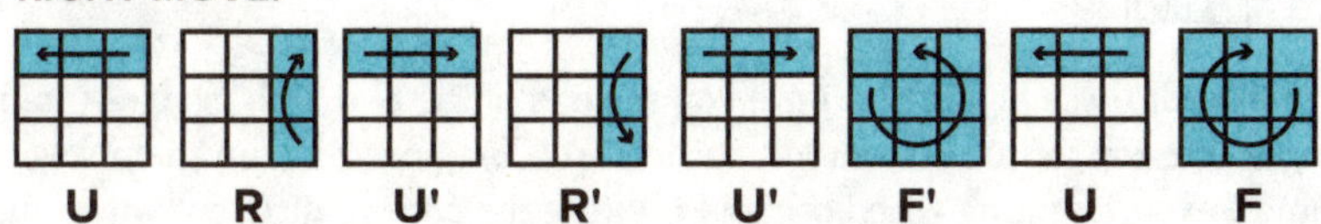

Repeat this for all four middle-layer edges until the second layer is fully solved.*

* If an edge piece is in its correct spot, but flipped, simply do either one of the algorithms above to get the piece out into the top layer. Same, if there is an incorrect edge piece in a slot. Then continue with 2.

STEP 4: MAKE A YELLOW CROSS ON TOP

At this point, the bottom and middle layers are solved, and the yellow pieces are scrambled on top. The goal is to form a yellow cross first.

Keep the yellow face up and position the cube based on whichever pattern of yellow stickers you see (center dot only = any orientation; backwards L = top-left; line = horizontal). Then use this algorithm until you see a yellow cross form:

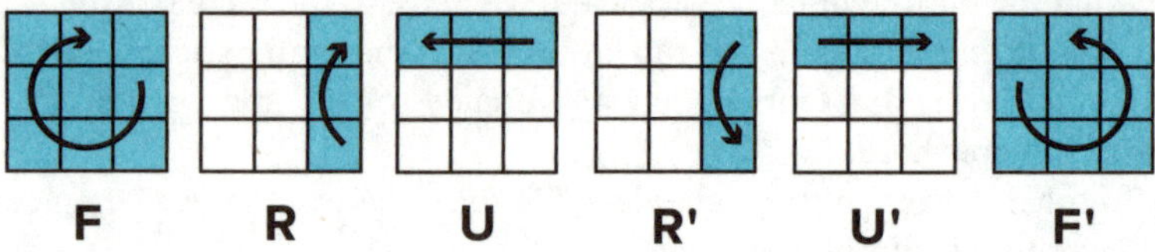

You might have to do it a few times, depending on what shape you start with (a dot, L-shape, or straight line).*

STEP 5: SOLVE THE YELLOW FACE

Now we want to turn all the yellow pieces on top to orient their face up. The edges are already there from the last step, so we solve the yellow corners using these two algorithms:

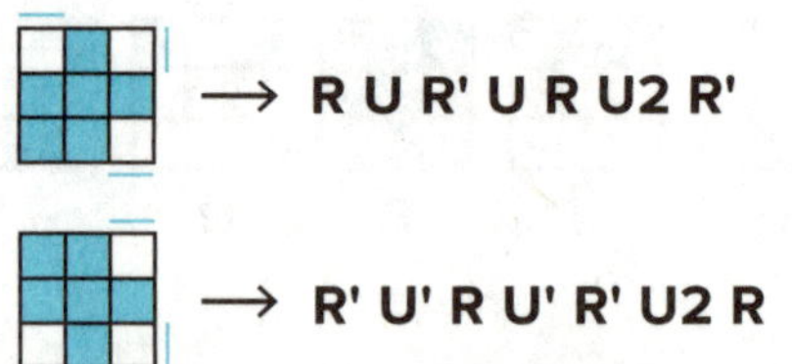

Repeat these algorithms until you see one of the two "fish" shapes (pointing to the top left or bottom left corner). You may need to run them several times, experimenting with both and rotating the cube in different ways—but always keep yellow on top. Once a fish shape appears, orient it as shown in the picture and perform the associated algorithm one last time to complete the yellow face. Don't worry if the sides don't match yet—we'll fix that next.

---

* Sometimes a step will advance you farther than expected. For instance, aiming for a yellow cross might complete the whole yellow face. If that happens, just skip the next step and keep going.

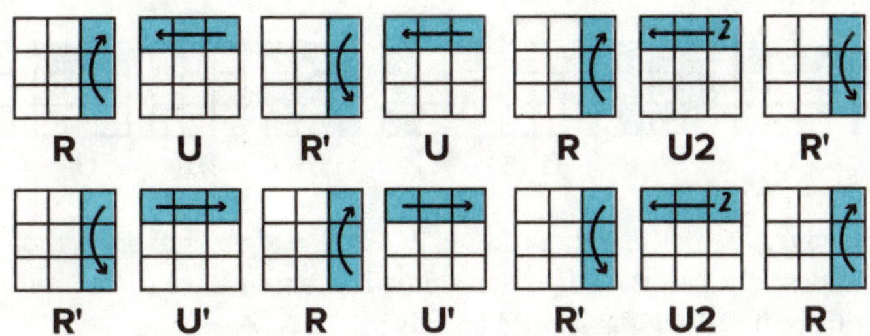

STEP 6: POSITION THE YELLOW CORNERS CORRECTLY

Now that all the yellow pieces are facing up, we need to move them into the right position. Find two corners that need to be swapped and rotate the top layer so that they're both on the top right side. Then use this algorithm:

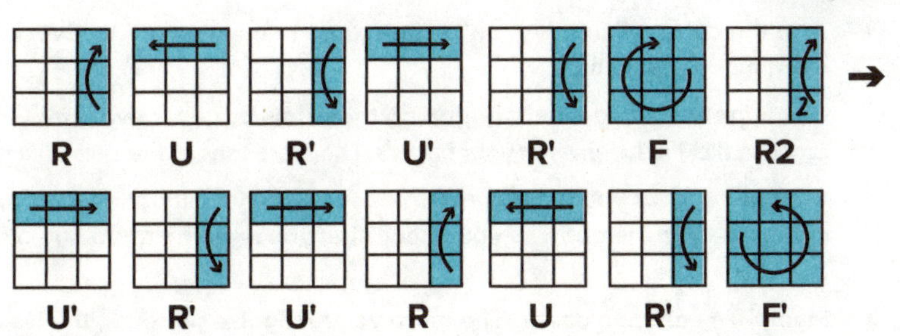

This will swap the two top right corners. Repeat until all the corners are correctly positioned.

STEP 7: SWAP THE YELLOW EDGES TO SOLVE THE CUBE

The last step is to position the last four edge pieces correctly. This is where the magic happens—your final few moves will bring the cube together!

1. **Find an edge that is already in the right place.**
2. **Hold the cube with that solved edge on your left, and use this algorithm:**

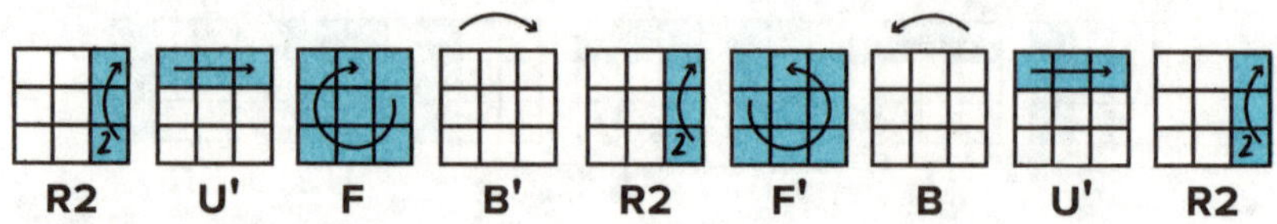

If no edges are in the right position, just do the algorithm once, then check again. Repeat until all the edges are aligned. You may have to do it twice.

At this point, the cube should be solved!

HOW TO GET FASTER

Now that you can solve a cube, the next step is speed. The fastest speed-cubers use the CFOP method (Cross, F2L, OLL, PLL), which replaces the beginner method with faster pattern recognition and fewer moves. But even without learning advanced techniques, there are a few tricks to instantly improve your time:

- **Turn the cube efficiently. Don't rotate more than you need to. Every extra move adds time!**
- **Use finger tricks. Instead of gripping the whole cube for every move, practice flicking layers with your fingers. There are tons of tutorials online.**
- **Start looking for your white cross pieces *before* you start solving the cube. Analyze the cube so you know what you're going to do straight out of the gate.**
- **Memorize common cases. The more you recognize patterns, the less you'll need to think about what to do next.**
- **Learn more algorithms for more scenarios. Top speed-cubers often have hundreds of them memorized.**

HOW TO MEMORIZE ALGORITHMS

Memory techniques will surely help you memorize more algorithms. You could potentially come up with an image for each face letter and just create a story that helps you remember the sequence. But your end goal here is to be able to do these algorithms without thinking, using muscle memory (remember procedural memory?). It's often better to just drill them until they stick.

I know, I know. Not the best advice from a memory champion. But you can still use some strategies to do this anyways.

- **Look at the algorithm and see if you notice any symmetries or groupings. For example, FRUR'U'F' is really just FRU and then the same three moves reversed RUF (but with apostrophes).**

- **Break the algorithm into smaller segments and physically repeat those chunks on the cube until it feels familiar in your hands.**
- **Name some of the smaller moves. Give them weird names so that when you encounter them again, you recognize them, and they'll be easier to memorize. For example, R U R' U' is famously known as the "sexy move."**
- **Pay attention to how each part of an algorithm affects the cube. The last few moves often just return pieces back to their original places. If you watch closely, you'll notice that these moves tend to "clean up" the cube—restoring parts that were already solved before the algorithm started.**

If you followed these steps correctly, you've just solved a Rubik's Cube. Congrats! That alone puts you ahead of most people. But the cooler flex is being able to solve it effortlessly, in under a minute, while casually talking to someone. With the system above, that's possible. It just takes a bit of practice.*

Solving a Rubik's Cube is satisfying. It takes logic, pattern recognition, and a trusted system. In a weird way, that same mindset is exactly what I brought to the blackjack table.

I walked out of Mandalay Bay that night feeling as if I had unlocked a cheat code to reality. Not just because I had won big (though yeah, that felt incredible), but because, for the first time, I *knew* the game was beatable.

There I was, just a random guy, who had worked hard at something and followed a system that allowed me to beat a game that usually beats *you*. It was an amazing feeling.

That's the difference between an average player and someone who actually *wins*.

When you start thinking like that—when you stop playing like everyone else and start playing like someone who expects to win—everything shifts. The board game nights, the card tables, the bets with friends, the random challenges life throws at you. Suddenly, you're the one in control; the one always winning. Suddenly, you're the genius.

* For reference, I once taught my friend Alvaro all these same steps in one morning. He practiced all day, and that evening he was able to solve the cube on his own in under ten minutes. Fun fact: we were climbing the tallest peak in South America, and he practiced all day as we hiked from base camp to Camp 1 and 2 (up to eighteen thousand feet)!

EXERCISES AND RESOURCES

- For blackjack, learn the Hi-Lo system, basic strategy, deck estimation, true count conversions, and index plays. Practice routinely every day, either with a live setup at home or by using one of the following card-counting tools: Casino Verite (www.qfit.com) or Blackjack Apprenticeship (www.blackjackapprenticeship.com).
- For chess, use chess.com or lichess.org for tactics training, endgame puzzles, and casual games.
- Take some time and come up with your PAO for all fifty-two cards in a deck. Once you have this in place, you'll be able to start memorizing decks of cards. You could even use it to memorize the Mnemonica Stack I mention in the next chapter (page 249).
- If you want to take Rubik's Cube solving to the next level, may I suggest attempting to learn how to solve it *blindfolded*? Yes, *blindfolded*. It's actually easier than it sounds. I have a whole tutorial on my YouTube channel. Once you've mastered the cube with your eyes open, give it a shot: "LEARN TO SOLVE A 3x3 RUBIK'S CUBE BLINDFOLDED (OP METHOD)" (www.youtube.com/watch?v=huVVIwD2nbs).
- You can also pre-memorize some really cool patterns for the Rubik's Cube. So whenever you see a solved cube lying around, bust out with one of these and leave the cube behind and you'll earn some instant genius points:*
    - Checkerboard pattern: **U2 D2 F2 B2 L2 R2**
    - Single spot each face: **U D' R L' F B' U D'**
    - Cube in a cube in a cube: **U' L' U' F' R2 B' R F U B2 U B' L U' F U R F'**
    - Snake pattern: **F2 R' B' U R' L F' L F' B D' R B L2**
    - The Superflip: **U R2 F B R B2 R U2 L B2 R U' D' R2 F R' L B2 U2 F2**

Here are some useful books:

- *Beat the Dealer* by Edward Thorp—The book that invented modern card counting.
- *Bringing Down the House* by Ben Mezrich—A dramatic retelling of real-life card counters taking on Vegas.

---

* Repeat the pattern once (or a few times) to end up back at the solved Rubik's Cube.

- *Bobby Fischer Teaches Chess*—A surprisingly accessible classic for building chess fundamentals.
- *Rock Breaks Scissors* by William Poundstone—A collection of strategies to beat many popular games.
- *The Mathematics of Games and Gambling* by Edward Packel—Understand the odds and the edge.

CHAPTER 8

SOCIAL SKILLS MASTERY

"WHEN DEALING WITH PEOPLE,
REMEMBER YOU ARE NOT DEALING WITH CREATURES
OF LOGIC, BUT CREATURES OF EMOTION."
—DALE CARNEGIE

CHRIS HANDED ME THE SHUFFLED DECK AND NODDED TOWARD MY HANDS. "PUT THEM BEHIND YOUR BACK."

AFTER I DID THAT, HE INSTRUCTED: "CUT THE DECK ANYWHERE YOU LIKE."

I COULDN'T SEE THE CARDS, BUT I COULD FEEL THEM—THE FAMILIAR WEIGHT, THE CRISP EDGES SLIDING AGAINST MY FINGERTIPS. I CUT SOMEWHERE IN THE MIDDLE, GUESSING BLINDLY.

"AGAIN, IF YOU WANT. AND ONCE YOU'RE DONE, TAKE THE TOP CARD AND HOLD IT TO YOUR CHEST. DO NOT LOOK AT IT."

I FOLLOWED ALONG, MY CURIOSITY PIQUED.

Chris leaned back and watched as if he was three steps ahead. "Now, at this point, neither of us knows your card," he said. "Which is interesting . . . because I'm going to have *you* guess it."

I paused. *Me? How?*

That was not the direction I expected this to go. I'd seen plenty of magic tricks—sleight of hand, misdirection, forces—but this? This was different. *How would I even know what the card is?*

Chris snapped his fingers. "Red or black?"

"Black," I said before even thinking.

"Clubs or spades?"

"Spades."

"Give me a number between zero and thirteen."

I hesitated. There was no way I'd get this right. But the way he said it, so at ease, was as if he'd planted an idea in my head without my realizing it, as if I wasn't guessing at all.

"Nine," I replied, still doubting this could be anything more than a wild guess.

Chris grinned, slow and knowing. "Have a look."

I slowly peeled the card from my chest and flipped it over.

My stomach dropped.

It was the *9 of spades*!

I had known of Chris Ramsay for a while—his name had popped up here and there. One day, I saw a DM from him. *Wait, Chris Ramsay, the magician and puzzle YouTuber with millions of followers? Why on earth is he messaging me?*

I clicked on his message. *We should collab,* it read.

My YouTube channel wasn't exactly massive at the time. It was growing, sure, but I had only been at it for three years. It had started as a passion project—something creative, something that felt missing in the memory world. Most memory content online was dry, lifeless, just a person talking into a camera. I wanted to change that.

Chris asked me to fly up to Montreal to film some memory content with him. Specifically, to teach him how to memorize a deck of cards. It felt surreal. I had never collaborated with another YouTuber before, let alone someone with millions of subscribers. But I wasn't about to pass up the opportunity.

I'd met magicians before, but only in passing. I had definitely never spent an entire day with one. The moment Chris picked me up from the airport, I could tell why he was so successful. He was effortlessly charming, completely at ease, and had this way of making you feel as if you were the most interesting person in the room. It wasn't an accident—I knew he was using subtle tricks, tiny psychological nudges, ways to win people over without their even realizing. I had dabbled in that space myself. But Chris was a master.

Now, don't get me wrong, Chris is a *genuinely* great guy. He's curious and thoughtful, and actually cares about the people around him. But there's something about being a magician, about performing for a living, that forces you to deeply understand people—how they think, react, what makes them tick. Magicians don't only fool people; they guide them toward a reality they didn't even know they were choosing. They control attention, direct focus, and subtly steer people.

Chris is now one of my closest friends. Spending time with someone like Chris, paired with all the work I've put in to combat social anxiety and project confidence, made me hyperaware of how social interactions actually function: People don't label you a genius just because of what you know, but also because of how you make them feel.

That card trick Chris performed on me during our first meeting embodied everything I want to cover in this chapter.* Simple, yet powerful techniques that help you build connections, make people feel comfortable, and subtly guide interactions in your favor. Whether you want to be more likable, more persuasive, or just less awkward, this chapter is packed with tools to help make you an everyday social genius.

Some geniuses are intimidating, detached, socially challenged savant types who seem untouchable. Then there are those who just seem to know things and are quick, sharp, insightful, yet outgoing and relatable. If you're too cocky, a know-it-all, people tune you out. But if you can come across as smart, approachable, and genuinely interested in others? That's the sweet spot.

Is social intelligence the most important part of unlocking your inner genius? Not necessarily. But it's a huge piece of the puzzle. You could be the smartest person in the room, but if no one likes talking to you, it won't matter. Mastering social skills is about rounding out your genius, making sure your ideas and insights actually reach people.

I'm not going to pretend I can cover psychology, behavioral science, and body language expertise in one chapter—people have been studying this stuff for centuries. I also don't have all the answers, and honestly, I still consider myself plenty awkward in many social settings (it's always a work in progress). But because none of this came naturally to me, I had to learn

---

* You can actually watch the whole video of my collaboration with Chris here: "Magician BREAKS IN to My Mind Palace!!" (https://youtu.be/FYU-oqyKWMU?si=Wu_bwKN22SXNduXo)—the trick starts about seven minutes into the video.

and experiment my way into being someone who can navigate social interactions smoothly and confidently. And along the way, I picked up plenty of tricks and strategies to help me win people over.

This chapter is a compilation of those things. Some may work for you. Some might not. But I'm laying them all out here so you can pick and choose what fits. Or, at the very least, so you can see how someone who wasn't naturally social figured out ways to be.

FIRST ENCOUNTERS

They say you only get to make your first impression once. Whether it's meeting someone for business, making a new friend, or just leaving a positive mark on a random encounter, how you interact in those first few moments sets the tone for everything that follows.

The following are rules and principles I do my best to live by in most encounters. Some of these principles were drilled into me as a kid, others I learned the hard way through experience, and plenty more I've picked up from people far wiser than me. But what I know for sure is that these simple, intentional behaviors lead to reciprocated positivity, warmth, and openness.

- **ALWAYS STAND UP WHEN MEETING SOMEONE NEW.**
  No exceptions. It shows respect and immediately makes you more engaged. If you're already standing, turn toward them fully—no half-turned, distracted energy.
- **A FIRM HANDSHAKE. ALWAYS.** Weak handshakes feel unsteady; overcompensating ones feel as if you're trying too hard. The sweet spot is a confident, controlled, and natural handshake. There's something so off-putting about a limp-fish handshake. Don't be that limp fish.
- **LOOK PEOPLE IN THE EYE.** This communicates confidence, presence, and warmth. Too much eye contact is intimidating; too little shows disinterest. Look *at* them, not through them.
- **BE GENUINELY INTERESTED AND PRESENT.** Act as if the person you're talking to is the most important in the room. No looking over their shoulder, glancing at your phone, or distracted half listening. Engage fully. Nod, react, and respond in a way that shows you're actually processing what they're saying. If possible, put your phone away. And I don't mean face down on a table—put the dang thing in your pocket. Whenever you can, summarize or paraphrase what they said back to them to reaffirm that you're paying attention.

- ***PEOPLE LOVE TO TALK ABOUT THEMSELVES. LET THEM.*** Ask about their interests, background, what excites them. And go deeper than the usual small talk. Instead of "How was your weekend?" ask, "What was the best part of your weekend?" Open-ended, less-common questions lead to better conversations. Also, let them fully finish their thoughts before responding.
- ***SMILE.*** Simple, but ridiculously effective. A genuine, warm smile instantly makes you more likable. Even if you feel nervous, smiling relaxes both you and the person you're talking to.
- ***ASK FOR THEIR NAME, REMEMBER IT, AND USE IT.*** You've got the skills to do this now! (See chapter 1, page 34.) Dale Carnegie said it best: "Remember that a person's name is to that person the sweetest and most important sound in any language." Use it casually in conversation and that little effort will make people feel seen and valued. Bonus points for using it to greet them the next time. Showing them you remembered will make their day.
- ***AVOID CRITICISM, CONDESCENSION, OR NEGATIVITY.*** First encounters are not the time to debate or nitpick, especially if you want to leave a lasting positive impression. Lean into appreciation instead of correction. Compliment sincerely, find something to admire, and make people feel good about themselves. Let them know how amazing they are!
- ***DON'T ONE-UP. EVER.*** If they just got back from Italy, resist the urge to tell them about how *you* went to Italy twice. If your achievements come up, downplay and shift the spotlight back to them as best you can.
- ***MAKE PEOPLE FEEL IMPORTANT, BUT DO IT SINCERELY.*** A well-placed compliment can elevate an entire interaction. The key is specificity. "You seem like someone who's great under pressure—what's your secret?" is infinitely more powerful than "You're smart." Also, empathize whenever you can (but don't overdo it, and be genuine). When someone shares something challenging, exciting, or deeply personal, acknowledge it in a way that validates their experience without making it about you. Avoid saying "Oh, I know exactly how you feel!" unless you truly do—because most of the time, experiences aren't identical, and assuming this can be dismissive or presumptuous. Instead, try saying, "I can only imagine what that must have been like for you . . ." Responses like this keep the focus on them while showing that you're engaged and genuinely care. This is empathy in action.

People often remember how you made them feel more than what you said. That feeling is shaped largely by body language. While the old idea that "93% of communication is nonverbal" has been debunked,* recent research confirms that posture, gestures, and expressions play a powerful role in shaping first impressions. Confident, open body language makes you instantly more likable and trustworthy, while closed-off or defensive signals can create distance, even if your words are friendly. The key is aligning your body language with the warmth and engagement you want to project.

- **NEVER CROSS YOUR ARMS.** This makes you look closed off, even if you aren't.
- **USE CASUAL, APPROPRIATE TOUCH.** A light touch on the arm or shoulder can instantly build connection.
- **MIRROR THEIR ENERGY.** Subtly matching someone's tone, speed, and posture makes them feel more comfortable.
- **FACE THE PERSON DIRECTLY.** Angling your body away, even slightly, can subconsciously signal disinterest or discomfort. Always position yourself fully face on. It shows you're engaged and present in conversation.

Sometimes, little details make the biggest difference. The following are some often-overlooked actions that transform an interaction from good to unforgettable. They demonstrate thoughtfulness, effort, and an extra level of attention that makes people appreciate and remember you.

- If texting, text emotively. Digital conversations lack tone, so add energy. Use exclamation marks, "hahas," and "lols," and break long messages into short, punchy bursts instead of giant walls of text. It makes the exchange feel more like real-life conversation.
- Be polite and courteous. For example, if the situation calls for either of these: Allow them to order first or pick something first, offer the better seat or position, or offer to hold the door, step aside for them to go first. These are small gestures that convey respect and thoughtfulness.
- Always say thank you. No matter how small the gesture. Whether someone gives you a compliment, buys you a coffee, or even just shares their time, express gratitude. Also, say "please" when requesting something, and "you're welcome" (or "my pleasure") when thanked. Good lord, your mother would be proud!†

---

* See Miles L. Patterson, Alan J. Fridlund, and Carlos Crivelli, "Four Misconceptions About Nonverbal Communication," *Perspectives on Psychological Science* 18, no. 6 (2023): 1388–411, https://doi.org/10.1177/17456916221148142.

† And mind your table manners too, if food or drinks are involved. Don't talk with your mouth full. Chew with your mouth closed. Elbows off the table. Okay, now I sound like my dad!

- **End every interaction on a high note. Be emphatic in your goodbye. "It was awesome meeting you, Alice—hope we cross paths again soon!" This leaves them with a final burst of positivity.**

If you use these tips consistently, not only will you start having better, more meaningful interactions, but people will remember you for it. I promise you'll notice a difference in how people respond to you.

MEANINGFUL CONVERSATIONS

So you've moved past the first impression. You know this person now, at least a little. Maybe it's someone you work with, a gym buddy, a casual friend, or even someone you're dating. What now?

First, don't stop doing the things that made a great first impression—consistency matters. But now you can go deeper, shift past surface-level conversation, and start having meaningful conversations that create real connection.

Personally, I like to keep a mental inventory of interesting, thought-provoking questions and icebreakers. These kinds of questions get people to reflect, share stories that they wouldn't otherwise, and tap into their memories (that's where real connection happens). Nostalgia is especially powerful. If you can get someone reminiscing about their past, you're immediately inside their world, building trust and rapport.

Here are some of my favorite go-to conversation deepeners:

- **What are the three happiest moments of your life?**
- **What age would you like to be forever? Why?**
- **What would you do if you were immortal?**
- **If you could bring anyone back for a day, who would it be and why?**
- **Do you remember your first day of school? Tell me about it.**
- **What was your favorite childhood book?**
- **If you had to live for one thousand years or in ten separate one-hundred-year lifetimes, which would you choose?**
- **What's the sweetest thing you've ever done for someone?**

Would-you-rather questions might seem silly, but they're good at sneakily revealing personality. Sprinkled into a conversation, they can break the ice and sometimes lead to surprisingly deep discussions.

GENIUS PROFILE:
DALE CARNEGIE

Dale Carnegie understood people. He knew how to make them *like* you, *trust* you, and follow your lead. He was a self-made master of human connection who figured out something most people never do: Social success is about how you make people feel, not necessarily about what you say.

Born in 1888 in rural Missouri, Carnegie struggled through sales jobs before finding his calling as a public-speaking instructor. His breakthrough came on a train ride when he struck up a conversation with a botanist. Carnegie barely spoke—he just asked questions and listened. Hours later, the botanist called him "one of the most interesting conversationalists" he'd ever met. Carnegie realized: You become fascinating by being fascinated. He could read people, connect instantly, and turn strangers into allies by understanding what they needed and genuinely caring about it.

This insight led to his legendary book *How to Win Friends and Influence People*, which became the social skills bible for business leaders, public speakers, and anyone who wanted to master influence.

Here are some fun ones:

- **Would you rather have your face and body but the brain of a chimpanzee or be a chimpanzee but have your human brain?**
- **Would you rather wake up and find your teeth have fallen out or your hair has fallen out?**
- **Would you rather have all your food too salty or too sweet?**
- **Would you rather have arms that don't bend or one leg considerably longer than the other?**
- **Would you rather live without music or without sex?**
- **Would you rather be able to converse with (nonhuman) animals, or have lifelong fluency in every (human) language?**
- **Would you rather be able to read minds or instantly absorb any book by touching it?**
- **Would you rather have an obsessive, insane person love you or hate you?**

Used in the right context, these can ignite some of the best conversations (or at least get people laughing).

Beyond questions, I also like to collect weird, mind-blowing facts, paradoxes, logical conundrums, and conspiracies*—stuff that naturally sparks interest for me.

For example, did you know the Southern Hemisphere has a more spectacular night sky? The galactic center of the Milky Way—the dense, star-packed core—appears in the constellation Sagittarius, which is best viewed from southern latitudes. That's why the Milky Way appears so vivid and rich from places like Australia or South America, with that dense band of stars stretching across the sky. Northern observers can still see the Milky Way, but they're looking more toward the galactic edge—beautiful, but less dramatically bright.

That kind of thought blows my mind every time.

And even if the person I'm talking to has zero interest in astronomy, my excitement for it makes it infectious.†

The key is, whatever you bring up, make sure you're genuinely into it. Witnessing someone's passion for something is magnetic.

---

* I've included a few of my favorites at the end of the chapter (page 263) in case you want to investigate any of them!

† Plus, you can use your newfound memory skills to memorize a ton of them.

THE CUBE: A MIND GAME THAT NEVER FAILS

The Cube is one of my *absolute* favorite ways to take a conversation deeper. It's an icebreaker, a personality analysis tool, and a low-key magic trick all in one. People always love it, without fail, and it instantly bonds you to the other person. Try answering the following questions as you read through it, to experience it yourself. Here is how it goes. (You don't have to stick to my exact version of the script, but try to follow the main beats. The full, original routine is available in the book *The Cube: Keep the Secret*, by Annie Gottlieb.)

Imagine you're in a room. And there's a cube in the room.

Where is the cube positioned? Describe the cube, its size, material, color, anything you want to say about the cube.

Is it on the ground or floating? Do you see it three-dimensionally or straight on?

Okay, next, I want you to picture a ladder. Where is the ladder?

Describe this ladder? How high is it? Is it sturdy? What material is it made out of?

If you were to climb it, do you think you could reach the top? Safely? With trepidation?

Next, picture flowers in the room.

Where are the flowers? How many are there? What kind and what color?

When you look at these flowers, what do they make you feel?

Next, picture a horse.

Where is the horse? Describe it in detail. Is it bridled or free? How does it interact with the other contents of the room? If you had to describe the personality of this horse with three words, what would they be?

Finally, picture a storm.

Where is the storm? Describe the storm.

Is it powerful or is it calm? How does it affect the contents of the room? How does the storm make you feel when you look at it?

That's it!

At this point during the routine, the other person will be so curious as to what it all means (as I'm sure you are!). It's up to you to decode. Each item represents how they see . . .

- **The cube = themselves**
- **The ladder = their career ambitions**

- **The flowers = their friends and family**
- **The horse = their ideal partner**
- **The storm = their view of life's challenges**

You can read more in Gottlieb's book, but there are some general analysis points that apply. Also, you want this to be a positive experience. If something comes across kind of negative, twist it so it sounds more positive.

For example, a huge cube usually implies self-centeredness or a big ego, but you could try reframing that by saying something like, "Oh wow, you have a big personality and have a large presence."

Some answers can even be turned into Barnum statements: statements that are general enough that anyone can agree with them (we'll talk more about them later). Here's a little more on each one:

- **A large cube means they have a big personality or strong sense of self. A small cube? More reserved, introverted.**
- **A ladder leaning on the cube suggests their career is central to their identity. A tall, sturdy ladder? Big aspirations.**
- **A wild, untamed horse? They want a free-spirited, independent partner. A gentle, saddled horse? They prefer stability.**
- **If the storm is distant, they see problems as manageable. If it's right on top of them, they feel overwhelmed by life's struggles.**

- **Comment on the size, the coloring, the placement and location of the items in the room in relation to each other. They all mean something!**
- **Their answers largely speak for themselves, and you can always improvise, but for a deeper dive into the full range of responses and their meanings, be sure to check out Gottlieb's book.**

The beauty of the Cube is that regardless of accuracy (though it can be eerily accurate!) it sparks amazing conversations. It blends psychology, storytelling, and mind tricks. There are so many possible interpretations. If you keep them mostly positive and have fun, the game will serve its purpose, which is to build a deeper connection. At the very least, it makes for an unforgettable interaction.*

Ultimately, great conversations aren't about talking more, they're about talking better. When you know how to ask the right questions, tell the right stories, and create moments of intrigue, you leave a lasting impression.

People don't just remember what you said, they remember how you made them feel. If you can make them feel engaged, curious, and genuinely valued, *that's* how you win people over, time and time again.

DEEPER CONNECTIONS

I've deepened my connections with the people closest to me through the powerful experience of sharing vulnerable and emotional moments.

I've had my share of major screwups. Regrets. Moments I'd rather forget. And contrary to what you might think, being open about those things doesn't drive people away, it often pulls them in closer. Your first instinct might be, *They'll think I'm an idiot. They'll judge me. Why would I tell them this?* And yeah, some people might. You never truly know. But often, if you share with honesty, humility, and self-awareness, people don't push you away, they lean in. Because vulnerability is relatable. It creates trust. And it invites them to be open with you in return.

One of the most fascinating studies on this idea was published in 2015 by *The New York Times*, based on psychologist Arthur Aron's research on deepening emotional connections. It's known as the "36 Questions to Fall in Love" experiment.† Now, you're probably not looking to fall in love with every per-

---

* I'll include some other resources for similar psychoanalytic games at the end of the chapter, page 263. They are just too much fun!

† Here is the article, "The 36 Questions That Lead to Love." Grab a bottle of wine and find someone to do this with! It's such an experience: https://www.nytimes.com/2015/01/09/style/no-37-big-wedding-or-small.html.

son you want to form a deep connection with, but these questions dig deep and create space for real conversations, not just surface-level chatter.

The idea is simple: Two people sit down and ask each other a specific set of thirty-six progressively deeper questions. Each question requires more vulnerability than the last. By the end, you feel as if you truly know the other person.

A word of warning, though: The final part of the experiment involves staring into each other's eyes for four minutes straight. If that sounds simple and easy, trust me, it's not.

At first, it's awkward. You'll probably laugh. Most people do because we usually laugh when we feel uncomfortable; when we feel exposed. But after the second minute, you realize there's nowhere else to go except *into* the other person. And by the last minute, it's almost impossible not to feel something deeply—about them, about yourself, about connection in general.

It's *such* a powerful experience. There is so much truth in the saying that "the eyes are the window to the soul." And at the end of the day, that is one of the most important things to recognize: that deep connection is more than knowing facts about someone; it's knowing their *soul.*

HOW TO READ ANYONE

Learning how to read someone is an incredibly powerful tool. While it isn't an exact science, there are cues you can analyze to make some often-right generalizations that can help you navigate social situations. You can use someone's body language, their handwriting, or being in tune with their emotions and responses to your advantage.

BODY LANGUAGE BASICS

1. THE FEET NEVER LIE

Most people are great at controlling facial expressions, but their feet often reveal their true feelings. Feet pointed toward you show interest, while pointing away suggests disengagement. Bouncing feet or shifting weight indicates excitement or impatience, while tightly crossed legs signal nervousness. If someone's torso faces you but their feet aim at the door, they're likely eager to leave.

2. WATCH FOR PACIFYING BEHAVIORS

When people feel anxious, they instinctively self-soothe with small repetitive gestures. Rubbing the neck, playing with jewelry, and adjusting

clothing are common pacifying behaviors. If someone rubs their neck while answering a question, they may be uncertain or uncomfortable with their response.

3. THE FACE CAN BE DECEPTIVE—FOCUS ON MICROEXPRESSIONS

Microexpressions are fleeting facial cues that reveal true emotions before someone masks them. A genuine smile creates crow's feet, while a one-sided smirk signals contempt. A nose wrinkle often indicates disgust, and wide eyes with raised brows suggest fear or surprise. If someone says they're happy for you but flashes a quick smirk, they may actually feel jealous.

4. THE POWER OF EYE CONTACT

Eye contact conveys engagement and confidence in many Western contexts. Steady but natural eye contact typically shows interest, while avoiding eye contact can suggest discomfort, shyness, or—in some cultures—respect. Dilated pupils can indicate excitement or attraction (though lighting matters too). Excessive blinking often signals stress or anxiety, but be careful: no single cue reliably indicates deception. People look away when thinking or uncomfortable, not just when lying.

5. CROSSED ARMS AND LEGS—NOT ALWAYS DEFENSIVE

Crossing arms or legs is often seen as defensive, but context matters. Tightly crossed arms may indicate resistance, while holding an object across the chest creates a subconscious barrier. However, if someone is smiling and relaxed, crossed arms might just be a comfort habit.

6. SUDDEN CHANGES IN BEHAVIOR

People have a baseline behavior when they're comfortable. Sudden shifts—like stopping gestures, stiffening up, or crossing their legs tightly—can signal an emotional reaction to something they just heard. If a candidate in an interview fidgets after a tough question, they may be hiding something.

7. THE HANDS REVEAL CONFIDENCE OR ANXIETY

Open gestures and upward-facing palms suggest honesty, while steepled fingers indicate authority. Rubbing hands together, hiding them in pockets, or clenching fists can be signs of anxiety or stress.

8. MIRRORING—A SIGN OF CONNECTION

We've touched on this earlier, but people naturally mirror each other's body language when they feel connected. If someone subtly matches your posture or gestures, it's a strong sign of engagement. If they lean back or remain stiff, they may be disinterested or uncomfortable.

9. TENSION VS. RELAXATION

Tension in the body—like raised shoulders, a clenched jaw, or stiff movements—signals stress or anxiety. Relaxed shoulders, controlled breathing, and fluid gestures indicate ease and confidence. If someone starts a meeting tense but gradually relaxes, they're becoming more comfortable.

Reading body language is about understanding people's unspoken feelings and responding appropriately. The key is to observe clusters of behaviors rather than relying on a single gesture. For example, crossed arms alone don't mean someone is defensive, but if they're also avoiding eye contact, tapping their foot, and angling their body away, it's likely they're uncomfortable.

That said, some people are just hard to read. These tips aren't foolproof and might sometimes lead you to the wrong conclusion. You could be way off. So don't treat them as facts; think of them as general guidelines to help you better interpret what might be going on. They'll help you become more perceptive in conversations, negotiations, and everyday interactions.

HANDWRITING ANALYSIS

Handwriting analysis, or *graphology*, is the study of handwriting to infer personality traits, emotions, and even cognitive tendencies. While it's not a perfect science, graphology often aligns with psychological and body-language reading concepts.*

1. SIZE OF HANDWRITING: BIG VS. SMALL

The size of someone's handwriting can indicate how they see themselves and interact with the world.

- **Large handwriting (big letters, takes up space) → Extroverted, confident, seeks attention**

  - **These people are often outgoing, expressive, and love being the center of attention.**
  - **Very large writing can indicate a need for validation or a dramatic personality.**
- **Small handwriting (tiny, compact) → Introverted, detail-oriented, focused**

small handwriting

* The following tips draw from well-established principles in the field. I'll recommend a book or two at the end of the chapter (page 264) if you'd like to dive deeper.

    - People with small handwriting are usually introspective and reserved.
    - They may also be meticulous, academic, and prefer working behind the scenes.
- Medium handwriting → Balanced personality

  medium handwriting

    - Neither too loud nor too withdrawn. Someone who adapts well socially but doesn't necessarily seek attention.

2. SLANT: RIGHT, LEFT, OR NO SLANT?

The slant of someone's writing can indicate how they process emotions and engage with people.

- Right slant → Emotional, social, expressive

  right slant

    - These people are open with their feelings and enjoy interactions.
    - A strong right slant suggests a passionate, impulsive personality.
- Left slant → Reserved, introspective, independent

  left slant

    - Often seen in people who keep their emotions private.
    - May indicate someone who thinks deeply before acting or struggles with trust.
- No slant → Logical, practical, emotionally controlled

  no slant

    - These people make decisions based on reason rather than feelings.
    - Often seen in scientists, analysts, or people who value structure.

3. SPACING BETWEEN WORDS: CLOSENESS VS. GAPS

The way someone spaces their words can show how they interact in relationships.

- Wide spacing between words → Likes personal space, independent

  wide spacing

    - These people need emotional distance and prefer to work alone.
    - May have a strong sense of individuality and dislike clinginess.
- Narrow spacing (words close together) → Social, dislikes being alone

  narrow spacing

    - Often seen in those who thrive in groups and love deep connections.
    - Can indicate a fear of being alone or needing constant interaction.

4. PRESSURE: LIGHT VS. HEAVY WRITING

The pressure applied while writing can indicate emotional intensity and energy levels.

- Heavy pressure (deep marks on paper) → Determined, intense, emotional depth

  heavy pressure

  - These people experience emotions strongly and are often persistent.
  - If the pressure is too heavy, it can indicate stress, anger, or stubbornness.

- Light pressure (faint, barely pressing on paper) → Easygoing, sensitive, lacks energy

  light pressure

  - These people are often flexible, but they may also lack motivation or confidence.
  - If too faint, this might indicate someone who avoids conflict or struggles with assertiveness.

5. LETTER CONNECTION: CURSIVE VS. PRINT

The way letters connect can reveal thought patterns and social tendencies.

- Connected letters (cursive, fluid writing) → Logical, systematic thinker

  connected letters

  - These people like order and often process information sequentially.
  - They may be methodical in decision-making and good at problem-solving.

- Separated letters (print, broken handwriting) → Creative, independent thinker

  separated letters

  - These people think outside the box and prefer individual expression.
  - They may be more intuitive than logical.

6. LOOPS IN LETTERS (E.G., L, Y, G, D)

Loops in handwriting reveal subconscious emotions and thought patterns.

- Big, open loops → Imaginative, expressive, free-spirited

  big open loops

  - Found in artists, dreamers, and those with a playful side.

- Tight or no loops → Restrained, disciplined, private
    - Seen in serious, practical individuals who keep emotions in check.

tight / no loops

There's meaning in each letter, too! A big loop in *y* or *g* suggests a desire for adventure and spontaneity. A tight loop in *l* or *d* might indicate emotional restraint or perfectionism.

7. THE SIGNATURE: PUBLIC VS. PRIVATE PERSONA

A signature represents how a person presents themselves to the world.

- Clear, legible signature → Transparent, confident, no hidden agendas
- Messy, unreadable signature → Private, secretive, or rushed thinker
- Big, bold, exaggerated signature → High self-esteem, attention-seeking
- Small, delicate signature → Humble, introverted, modest

Nelson Dellis

Nelson Dellis

Nelson Dellis

Nelson Dellis

If someone's signature is huge and flamboyant, they likely have a strong need to be noticed. If it's tiny and compact, they might prefer to keep a low profile.

8. SPEED OF WRITING: QUICK VS. SLOW

The pace of someone's handwriting can reflect how they think and act.

- Fast writing → Impatient, high energy, quick thinker
    - Often seen in ambitious, spontaneous people who like efficiency.
    - Can indicate someone who talks fast or processes ideas quickly.
- Slow writing → Careful, methodical, deep thinker
    - Indicates someone who takes their time and pays attention to detail.
    - Can suggest a thoughtful, deliberate nature.

fast writing

slow writing

Handwriting analysis is about spotting patterns that align with personality traits. The key is looking at multiple elements together rather than relying on just one feature.

Want to spot an extrovert? Look for large, right-slanted, fast handwriting with connected letters.

Looking for a perfectionist? Small, upright handwriting with tight loops and precise strokes.

Curious about emotional intensity? Heavy pressure, deep loops, and dramatic strokes can indicate deep feelings.

COLD READING

Cold reading is a skill that makes you seem incredibly perceptive, even though it's based on educated guesses, subtle observations, and psychological principles (much like analyzing the results from the Cube exercise). With these tricks you'll seem like you can really read someone and *know* them. Here are some of the best tips to master the art of cold reading:

1. START WITH BROAD STATEMENTS (BARNUM STATEMENTS)

Barnum statements, as I mentioned earlier, make people believe you "know" something about them. In reality, they're just general truths, and are vague but feel deeply personal because of how they apply to almost everyone.

Start with broad, safe guesses to build credibility. Once they confirm something, refine your approach based on their responses.

EXAMPLES:

- "You're the type of person who enjoys being around others but also needs time alone to recharge." (Applies to most people.)
- "You sometimes feel like you haven't lived up to your full potential." (Who doesn't?)
- "You can be outgoing, but deep down, you sometimes feel misunderstood."

2. USE THE FORKING TECHNIQUE (COVER ALL OUTCOMES)

This technique ensures that no matter what, you sound correct, by phrasing your statements so they work in multiple ways.

EXAMPLES:

- "You're a private person, but when you trust someone, you really open up." (If they agree, great. If they start to disagree and say they're actually very open, you say, "Yes, I sensed you're an exception. Very open, but only to the right people.")
- "You've had a big change recently . . . or maybe you're feeling like you're ready for one." (Covers both recent changes and anticipation of one.)

Whatever their response, adjust accordingly. If they confirm, act as if you knew all along. If they deny, pivot: "Interesting. That means you're the type of person who keeps things stable when needed."

3. OBSERVE AND MAKE QUICK DEDUCTIONS

Cold reading starts before you even speak. Look for clues in a person's appearance, body language, and speech. Be observant of the following:

- Clothing and accessories
  - A well-dressed person → Might value status, professionalism.
  - Worn-out shoes → Might be practical, hardworking, or thrifty.
  - Jewelry, tattoos, or unique accessories → Might be expressive, sentimental.
- Hands and nails
  - Calloused hands → Likely does physical work or hobbies like climbing, carpentry, or weightlifting.
  - Well-manicured nails → Might work in a profession where appearance matters, or they prioritize self-care.
- Speech patterns
  - Fast talker → Likely energetic, confident, or anxious.
  - Slow, measured talker → Might be thoughtful, reserved, or careful with words.

If someone has calloused hands, you might say, "You strike me as someone who works with your hands. Carpentry, lifting, or something similar?" If they confirm, act like you knew. If they deny, pivot: "Ah, I see. You just have a strong grip; must be an active lifestyle."

4. USE CONFIRMATION BIAS TO YOUR ADVANTAGE

People tend to remember the hits and forget the misses. If you make five guesses and only one is correct, they'll focus on the one you got right.

- If you say, "You have a strong connection to an older male in your life," and they don't, say, "Ah, but I sense the absence of one has had a big impact on you."
- If they say you're wrong, brush it off with, "Interesting. Sometimes these things manifest in ways we don't immediately recognize."

5. LET THEM FILL IN THE GAPS

People naturally want to make sense of things. If you give them just enough information, they'll connect the dots themselves. Keep statements slightly vague and let them do the work of making it personal.

EXAMPLE:

- Instead of saying, "I know you lost someone recently," say, "I'm sensing there's someone who was important to you, but there's some distance or loss there."

- If they confirm, say, "Yes, I felt there was an emotional weight there."
- If they deny, say, "It could be a symbolic loss; someone who drifted away, not necessarily passed on."

6. BUILD ON SMALL WINS

If you make a correct guess, double down on it and elaborate.

EXAMPLE:

- If you guess they have a creative streak and they confirm, say, "I thought so! You probably get lost in your work, right? It's something that helps you escape and feel totally in your element."
- If you guess they've recently traveled and they confirm, say, "That makes sense! I bet you're the type of person who thrives on new experiences."

7. BE CONFIDENT AND SPEAK WITH AUTHORITY

Even if you're making an educated guess, deliver it as if you're completely certain. Confidence makes people believe you.

EXAMPLE:

- Instead of "Maybe you're the type of person who likes helping others?" say, "You're the kind of person who gets a lot of satisfaction from helping others. It's something that really drives you."

8. KNOW WHEN TO PIVOT

If you make a wrong guess, don't dwell on it; pivot immediately.

EXAMPLE:

- If you say something like "You're very independent," and they say, "Not really," follow with "That's interesting. I actually get the sense that you value deep connections but don't let just anyone in. Does that sound more accurate?" If they still disagree, move on: "It's fascinating—sometimes we don't even recognize certain patterns in ourselves until later."

THE MAGIC OF MAGIC

I opened this chapter with a magic trick—one that left me stunned, questioning everything I thought I knew in that moment. Magic has that effect. It disarms people, breaks tension, and creates a shared experience of wonder. People love to be amazed. They love experiencing something they can't quite explain. And if you can be the person who creates that moment—someone who seems to know something others don't—you instantly elevate your presence.

I know this isn't a magic book, so I won't go deep into sleight-of-hand techniques or misdirection principles, but I do think it's worth learning a few simple tricks. The key isn't in mastering difficult sleight of hand but in presenting the trick with confidence and personality, which is a throughline for all of the conversational skills we've been talking about.*

GENIUS PROFILE:
HARRY HOUDINI

In 1904, the *London Daily Mirror* challenged Harry Houdini to escape from a pair of custom handcuffs said to be unpickable, crafted by a locksmith who took five years to make them. Before a crowd of four thousand spectators and a team of journalists, Houdini struggled for more than an hour, even disappearing behind a screen at one point, emerging drenched in sweat. Finally, after ninety minutes, he freed himself. What the audience didn't know was that Houdini had studied lock design obsessively, had exceptional flexibility and body control to escape tighter binds, and had likely inspected the cuffs ahead of time—possibly even having a duplicate set made. Either way, Harry Houdini was the greatest escape artist of all time. Not only that, but he was also a master showman; he knew exactly how to build tension, play to the crowd, and turn every escape into a moment of unforgettable drama.

---

* I've included a bunch of suggestions for learning some really killer magic tricks at the end of this chapter (page 263). There are so many videos and books that explain them way better than I ever will.

A well-placed trick at a party, over dinner, or even during a casual conversation can completely shift the dynamic of an interaction. It turns you into the center of attention, not in a show-off way, but in a way that makes people intrigued by you.

So let's break down the trick that Chris performed at the beginning of the chapter—the one that made me question reality for a moment. And, more importantly, let's talk about why it worked so well.

BREAKING DOWN THE TRICK, OR HOW CHRIS MADE ME GUESS MY OWN CARD

Chris is going to kill me for revealing this, but here's the truth: He knew my card the moment I placed it on my chest. The rest of the trick was all about subtly guiding me toward "guessing" the right answer myself.

Now, you might be thinking, *But he shuffled the deck before handing it to you! Then you shuffled it too!* Did he? Did I?

As an experienced magician, Chris knows all sorts of *false shuffles*—shuffles that look random but actually preserve the deck's order. And actually, if you watch the video carefully (see page 265 for the link), you'll notice that he does only a few cuts, not a thorough shuffle. That's because he already had the deck memorized before we even started.

This is a classic magician's move. Some use a Mnemonica Stack—a specific, pre-memorized order of cards (see the card order on page 264). Initially learning this ordered deck can take a regular magician a long time, but with the memory techniques you've already picked up earlier (and the card memorization method I taught you in the last chapter, page 198), you'll be able to do this in minutes.

Even though we cut the cards, the order of cards never actually changes, just their starting point. So, when I took a card from the top and handed the deck back, Chris simply peeked at the bottom card and immediately knew what my card had to be; it would have been the next one in the stack sequence, which I had conveniently cut to the top and placed on my chest.

Knowing my card wasn't enough, though—Chris had to make me say it. That's where subtle persuasion came in.

- ***THE RED OR BLACK CHOICE:*** **He asked, "Red or black?" but stressed "black" ever so slightly. Maybe he said it a little louder, held on to the word just a beat longer, or even said it second so it stuck freshly in my mind. You may have noticed he raised his hand slightly for the second choice (and even snapped his fingers on it). Subconsciously, I'm nudged toward "black."**

- ***CLUBS OR SPADES:*** **Same trick here. Without realizing it, I "chose" spades.**
- ***THE NUMBER:*** **Now this part gets trickier. The range (1–13) isn't a 50/50 choice, but human psychology gave him an edge. If you ask someone to pick a random number between 1 and 10, most people say 7. Chris uses this to his advantage. When he said, "Pick a number between one and thirteen," he slightly stressed the higher number with his voice. I was unlikely to say 13, and I didn't want to be too obvious by picking dead center. Nine felt just right. He also used subtle hand gestures again while asking for my number—starting low when he said 1 and gradually raising his hand when he jumped up to 13. That upward motion could have subconsciously nudged me to choose a higher number, simply based on where his hand stopped.**

Of course, there was no guarantee I'd land on 9. If I had picked something different, what would he have done? I have to assume Chris had a backup plan. All great magicians do. I suspect he would've smoothly adjusted the trick, maybe having me place my card back in the deck (without looking at it) and then swapping it for the one I guessed. Not as impressive as making me guess my own card, but still a solid trick.*

You and I aren't magicians like Chris, so where does that leave us if we'd like to try this trick? Well, you could go for broke and see if you can land the same amazing effect Chris did. If they don't quite say what you want them to say, it's an opportunity for fun banter and play to see if you can morph the trick to still be effective. You could also just keep it simple and have fun pretending to guess the card yourself (since you know the card already). Ultimately, the more theatrical you make the trick, the more memorable it becomes. That's what we're truly after here anyway. A fun engagement that creates connection.

PREDICTION GENIUS

Here is an easy mind-reading trick that can be done anywhere.

Have another person think of a number between 1 and 10 in their head. Go ahead and think of a number yourself, and go through each step that follows as you read to get a sense of how this works.

Ask them to multiply it by 9. If the result is a two-digit number (like 63),

---

* Chris will be the first to admit there was some luck and synchronicity in this trick; in that moment—and that can't be ignored. On any other day, I might have given different answers. But he'll also tell you that moments of real magic and coincidence like this happen surprisingly often in performance, especially when a magician is riding a high, fully in the zone, late into the night. Interesting . . .

they add those two digits together to create a totally new number (6 + 3 = 9).

Instruct them to subtract 5 from this number (9 – 5 = 4) and then take the result and think of the letter associated with it. For example, "1" is "A," "2" is "B," "3" is "C," and so on.

Once they've confirmed they have a letter, tell them to quickly think of a country that starts with that letter. They should then think of the second letter in that country and think of an animal that starts with that letter. Tell them to create a really vivid image of this animal in their head, including its color.

For a bonus effect, you can ask them to think of another animal that starts with the last letter of the nation they chose, and then a fruit that begins with the last letter of the animal from the previous step.

Despite the fact that no one has said anything out loud, you somehow can read their minds and know they're all thinking of a gray elephant in Denmark (and kangaroo and orange).*

Those are a few of the common answers people will think of in that situation. Here are a bunch of others, according to practicing mentalists. Answers can always vary, but there is always a common answer that *most* people will choose if they answer quickly (there are also other likely answers when people *are* given a few moments to think). Use the following in conversation or in a routine to get an effect that makes you seem like you can read minds!

- **A number between 1 and 5: 3.**
- **A number between 1 and 10: 7 (By far the most commonly chosen, because it feels unique—not even, not a multiple of 5, not right in the middle, and appears often in culture, like "lucky 7.")**
- **Two-digit number: 37. (A strangely common choice, likely because it's a prime number and seems "random.")**
- **Color: Red or blue. (Red is the most common if given no time to think, and blue would be the second most common, chosen more often if the person is allowed more time to think.)†**
- **Vegetable: Carrot, primarily. Broccoli, chosen with more thought.**
- **Fruit: Apple. (The most iconic fruit thanks to media, branding, and education.)**

---

* This trick works because any single digit multiplied by 9, if you add up the result's digits, will add up to 9. So, when you subtract 5, you will always get 4. Instinctively, most people will think of Denmark for the letter *D*.

† This difference in choice could be manufactured by how you pose your question. "Name a color . . ." would encourage blurting out the first thing that came into their mind: "red!" While "think of a color . . ." would encourage them to think a little longer, resulting in a likely "blue" response.

- **Playing card: Queen of hearts if said immediately. Ace of spades otherwise. (Feels special, bold, and is often emphasized in games and pop culture.)**
- **Shape: Square. Unless you give them time; then it's triangle (I guess because it stands out as more dynamic compared with squares and circles).**
- **Animal: Lion (especially if you specify a jungle animal) or elephant. (Both are powerful and commonly referenced in stories.)**
- **Tool: Hammer (basic, common, and easy to visualize).**
- **A piece of furniture: A chair, or, with the younger crowd, a bed, for shock value.**
- **A pretty flower: Rose.**

THE MAGIC OF PREPARATION AND CONFIDENCE

I have to share something Chris once told me about magic:

"Magic is just someone going through insane lengths to get the silliest piece of information. That's all it is."

I love that. Because it's true. And it applies beyond magic.

When you commit to preparing in advance, whether for a trick, a speech, or even just a casual social interaction, you create an illusion of effortlessness. People aren't amazed that you planned ahead, they're amazed because they assume you didn't. And *that* can make you seem like a genius.

Magic also has everything to do with confidence. A trick, no matter how brilliant, falls apart if the performer hesitates, second-guesses, or looks uncertain. The secret to pulling off anything—whether it's a sleight-of-hand trick, a high-stakes negotiation, or a bold social move—is acting with conviction. If you carry yourself like someone who knows exactly what they're doing, people will believe you, even if they shouldn't.

One of Chris's favorite tricks before a night out is pure psychological misdirection. Earlier in the evening, he'll visit the bar he plans to go to later, get inside, and secure a hand stamp. Fast-forward to later that evening—he and his friends arrive, and there's a long line. Without hesitation, Chris

GENIUS PROFILE: FRANK ABAGNALE JR.

Frank Abagnale, whose life inspired the film *Catch Me If You Can*, claims to be one of the greatest con men in history. According to him, by age twenty-one, he had impersonated a Pan Am pilot, a doctor, a lawyer, and a sociology professor—all without credentials. In his most brilliant alleged scheme, he forged Pan Am payroll checks while posing as a pilot, studying airline procedures, and flying more than a million miles for free by deadheading in the jump seat.

While journalists have found limited documentation supporting these claims, what's undeniable is Abagnale's genius at *selling his story*. He convinced Hollywood, the FBI, and millions worldwide that he pulled off these cons—itself a master class in reading people, understanding what they want to believe, and exploiting it with total confidence.

walks straight up to the bouncer, waves his stamped hand in front of their face, and confidently says, "You will let us in."

And what does the bouncer do? He lets them in, of course.*

To onlookers, it looks like some *Jedi mind trick*, a sheer force of persuasion. But the real magic is just *preparation*. Chris set up the illusion hours

* Well, maybe only him, since his friends don't have hand stamps—ha! But, hey, with that confidence, maybe the bouncer *will* let them in.

before, creating a situation so seamless that no one would ever think to question it. No one would *ever* think he went to the bar hours early, only to get a hand stamp so that he could later pretend, like he is a living, breathing Jedi. That would be *crazy*!

With that principle in mind, here are a few similar "silly" little tricks that, when executed well, will make people believe you're on another level.

FEELING THE YEAR OF A COIN

People would rather believe that you're some genius with an incredible ability, rather than imagine that you went out of your way well in advance to set up the entire trick to fool them.

Here's one of Chris's tricks that I love. It works best with a quarter. First, keep a quarter in your pocket (I'd even go so far as to say, keep a quarter in your pocket at *all times* so you can do this trick on a whim, at a moment's notice) and make sure you've memorized the year on it.

Off the cuff, ask someone if they have a quarter on them and tell them that you have an incredible sense of touch; that you can rub a quarter and know the year of the coin, just by *feeling* its surface. The more you can build up the story behind the act, the more believable it will be.

Make sure you have *your* quarter hidden in one of your hands, and then have them hand you *their* quarter into your other hand and do a false transfer over to the hand already concealing a quarter (so it looks as if you put their quarter in your other hand, but it's actually yours). There are many ways to do a transfer here, but an easy one is called the Bobo switch:

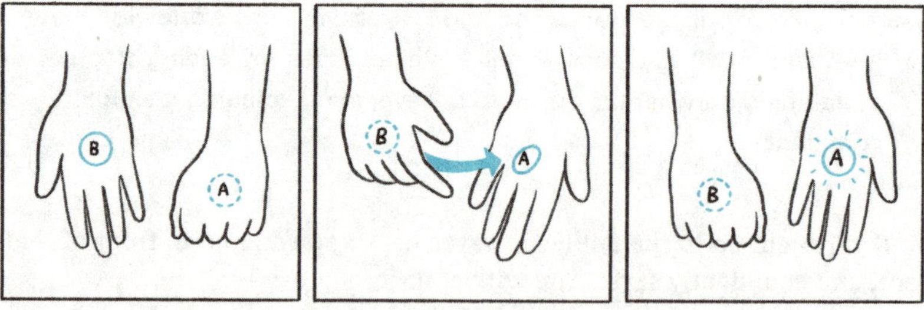

Fake the transfer of coin B while secretly palming it, then flip the other hand to reveal coin A, all in one seamless motion.

Close your eyes and pretend to feel the coin. Hand it back to the person and finish up your act by saying the year. Proceed to watch them look completely bewildered.

MIND-READING ON A NAPKIN

In this mind-reading illusion, start by asking someone to think of any word—literally anything. It could be a random object, a place, even a loved one's name. Once they have it, you ask them to write it down on a paper napkin. No gimmicks, no sleight of hand—yet somehow, you'll be able to guess exactly what they wrote just by "feeling" the napkin.

Sounds impossible, right? The secret is deceptively simple.

This trick is based on an old technique used by card cheats in poker: using a shiner. Back in the day, a dealer might have left a reflective object on the table, like a butter knife, a glass, or even a watch. While dealing, they'd subtly tilt a card just enough to catch its reflection and see its value.

Same concept here. Instead of a knife, spoon, or table surface, your shiner is something you always have on you: the turned-off, reflective screen of your phone.

So, have them write their word on a napkin. Keep everything casual—no rush, no pressure. Your phone should be face up on the table, positioned naturally in front of you. As they finish writing, ask them to turn the napkin face down and hand it to you. While doing this, make a small, natural downward glance at your phone screen. The reflection will show you the word.

To reinforce fairness, you can even say something like, "See? The napkin is totally opaque. There's no way I can see through this." This moment doubles as another chance to check the reflection if you need it. Once you know the word, the reveal is yours to create. You could crumple up the napkin, hand it back, and slowly revealing letters until you get the full word.

Done smoothly, it will truly leave people wondering if you're a mind reader.

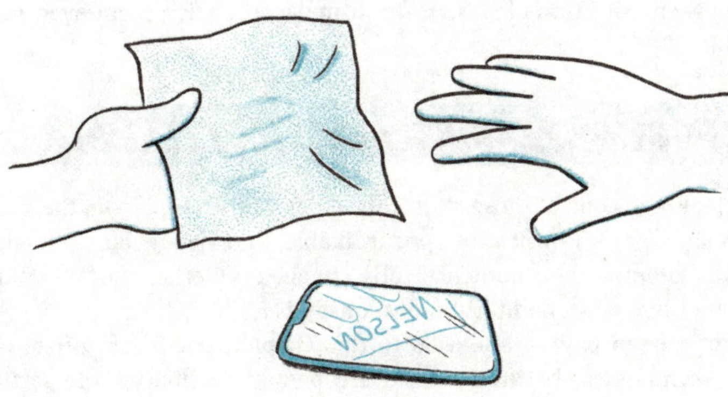

THE CREDIT CARD MENTALIST TRICK

This is a fun, hands-on trick that makes it look as if you have an unbelievable memory. For this to work, you'll need a credit card with raised, embossed numbers (not all cards have them anymore, but plenty still do). You set it up by claiming that you can memorize the last four digits of a credit card just by feeling it, as if the numbers are being transmitted into your mind.

Have them hand you their credit card face down. Hold it lightly at first, then gradually apply pressure as if you're "absorbing" the number. Make sure your thumb is pressed flat against the last four digits and push hard enough that the imprint will temporarily stay on your skin after you return the card. Hand the card back naturally. Now, with a quick, subtle peek at your thumb, you can read the numbers (note that they'll be reversed, so remember to mentally flip them). Reveal the numbers in any dramatic way you like. You can draw it out as if you're reading their mind or go for instant shock value.

For an extra layer of showmanship, you can do this with multiple cards at once, pretending to memorize several four-digit numbers and then revealing them all in rapid succession. It makes the trick seem even more impossible.

PUBLIC SPEAKING AND STORYTELLING

Public speaking is one of those skills that separate the good from the great. The best speakers know how to appear likable, knowledgeable, and confident while keeping their audience fully engaged, whether they're talking to a room of five or an auditorium of thousands.

If you've been paying attention to this chapter, you'll recognize a lot of these techniques—because people are people, no matter the setting.

Whether one-on-one or onstage, the key to being memorable is the same: Know your material, engage with your audience, and deliver with presence.

But before any of that, you need to know how to say what you want to say in the most effective way possible. Let's talk first about being articulate.

THE ART OF ARTICULATE SPEECH

You ever meet someone who just *sounds* smart? Not because they're using a bunch of ten-dollar words, but because the way they speak pulls you in. They pause in all the right places, choose words that hit just right, and sound like they actually *thought* before opening their mouth? That's articulation. And it's one of the most overlooked social skills out there.

Being articulate doesn't necessarily mean you need to have a massive vocabulary or speak like a TED Talk robot. It's about being able to say what you mean with clarity, rhythm, and presence. It makes people want to listen to you, and it makes you sound smarter without trying too hard.

Here are five quick levers you can pull to instantly boost how articulate you sound:

1. EXPAND YOUR "SURFACE LEXICON:

You know way more words than you use. Most of us stick to a comfy batch of approximately 1,500–3,000 words in daily conversation (your "surface lexicon"). These are the words we don't even think about. They're so easy to use (mostly because we use them so much), and they convey everything we need, to get things across in the simplest way. But our brains can recognize up to tens of thousands more! Those words are in your "deep lexicon."

To expand your surface lexicon, you need to pull some of those deeper words up to the surface. And the way to do that is by using them. Saying them in conversation out loud. Repeatedly. Research says you need to use a new word around thirty-eight times before it becomes part of your active vocabulary. (So, yeah, "sagacious"* isn't going to stick unless you actually use it a few dozen times.)

Now, maybe your deep lexicon isn't that deep; maybe it's lacking some breadth in the "smart" word department. That might be the case. No worries! With our memory tools from chapter 1, you have the tools to memorize a

* Genius fact: "Sagacious" means super wise, sharp, perceptive, good at reading situations and making smart calls. A quick way to remember it: Picture a bearded old sage sitting cross-legged, stroking his chin. That's your sagacious dude. Sage = wise. Sagacious = full of sage-ness.

whole bunch of new smart words and add them to your deep lexicon.* Once you do that, use them, and they'll start to rise up into your surface lexicon.

Don't overlook the fact that you probably know more words than you give yourself credit for. So, when speaking, slow down. Give yourself space to find the right word instead of defaulting to "stuff" or "thing." That moment of pause is power. For example, instead of blurting out, "The hike was, uh . . . hard," take a beat and say, "The hike was . . . [pause] strenuous on the ascent, but absolutely breathtaking once we reached the ridgeline."

That pause gave you just enough space to swap a bland, catch-all word for something vivid and specific. Now you sound more thoughtful and precise.

2. COMMAND THE PAUSE

Watch any great speaker: Obama, Jobs, Brené Brown. They pause. Often. And not because they forgot what to say. Pausing creates gravity. It makes your next word land with weight. You don't need to rush to fill silence. In fact, silence is your secret weapon. Use it. Be comfortable in it.

3. CUT THE FILLER FAT

"Um," "like," "you know," "I feel like . . ."—all these common filler words are not helping you express yourself more clearly. Sure, they help speech flow, but when overused, they dilute your message.

I'm not perfect, but I've found a way to train myself to limit them and, in some cases, eliminate them. Here are two ways to stop yourself from overusing these filler words and phrases:

- Slow down at the *end* of each sentence. Be more mindful of how you're talking when your sentence is ending. You'll be much more in tune with the filler words you're saying, and you'll be more active in cutting them out.
- Keep your mouth closed until you actually know what you're about to say. Seriously—actually close it. If your mouth is hanging open while you search for your next word, you're way more likely to toss in a filler to kill the silence. Silence is fine. Own it.
- Practice with feedback. Record yourself talking. Watch it back. Notice the fluff you didn't realize you were saying. Most people are shocked (or mildly horrified) when they hear themselves on playback. That little cringe might just be the fuel you need to make adjustments.

---

* At the end of the chapter (page 265), I'll share a link to some great "smart" words to memorize (and how to memorize them).

4. FEED YOUR BRAIN BETTER LANGUAGE

You speak the way you think. And you think in the language you consume. So, if your daily inputs are TikToks and text threads, guess what your output's going to sound like? Probably more like that! If you want to sound sharper, read sharper stuff. Listen to people who speak well. Surround your mind with better inputs, and your vocabulary (and rhythm) will level up without you even noticing.

5. TUNE YOUR VOCAL INSTRUMENT

Speaking isn't just about words. It's about how they *sound*. Your voice has pitch, volume, cadence, emotion. Be aware of that.

One of the ways I work on this is by reading poetry out loud (bonus points if you can do it from memory). If you've got kids, read their books to them with full-on dramatic flair—big voice, big expression, lots of variation. You've got permission to go over the top, and that makes it perfect practice.

Anything that gets you to notice how your voice rises, falls, stretches, and punches is fair game. The more musical your speech becomes, the more memorable and charismatic you'll sound.

Being articulate doesn't mean being fancy and annoyingly verbose. It means being clear and saying the best words at the right time in the most effective way. It's being intentional and more thoughtful with your words. It's about being heard.

HOW TO MEMORIZE YOUR SPEECH WITHOUT SOUNDING ROBOTIC

Now that you're more aware of how you're saying things, you need to know what you're going to say, right?

Normally, you'd begin by memorizing your speech (or at least locking in your main talking points). But before you do that, there are two crucial parts of public speaking to keep in mind:

1. **Knowing (memorizing) your material well enough to deliver it naturally.**
2. **Performing it in a way that captures attention and leaves a mark.**

Let's break down both.

You can memorize a speech in two ways: word-for-word (WFW), which is best if exact phrasing is crucial, but harder to memorize and can feel rigid; or topic-for-topic (TFT), which is easier to memorize, allows flexibility, and makes you sound more natural.

Either way, you need to internalize the speech so that it flows effortlessly.

The best way to lock in your speech, no matter your method, is by using a Memory Palace.

If you're using TFT:

1. **Break your speech into a sequence of key topics.**
2. **Assign a memorable image to represent each topic (use the techniques from chapter 1).**
3. **Place each image along a familiar route (your Memory Palace).**
4. **Review mentally to strengthen your recall.**
5. **Practice out loud—this is crucial! Don't only rehearse it in your head.**
6. **Simulate performance conditions—stand if you'll be standing, hold a mic if you'll be using one, etc.**
7. **For any specific phrasing or key lines to memorize, create specific images and place them in your Memory Palace too.**

If you're using WFW, do everything above, but instead of storing just the topics, break your whole script into short phrases and memorize them in order. Don't waste effort encoding every filler word—your brain will naturally fill those in as you rehearse.

For tricky passages that just don't seem to stick, there's another technique I and many others frequently use. I call it the First-Letter Method:

1. **Read the passage a few times to get the gist of it.**
2. **On a piece of paper, write down the first letter of every word as it's written on the page (including any punctuation and capitalizations, and honoring line breaks and skips).**
3. **Read the passage from just the first letter version (you'll be surprised at how easy it is). Do this a few times.**
4. **Now the magic: try to recall the passage from memory.**
5. **If there are small slipups, repeat step 3 a few more times.**

Don't forget that no matter which method you choose, rehearsal is *everything.* A smooth delivery will come only from repetition and refinement.

STORYTELLING HACKS FOR ENGAGING SPEAKING AND CONVERSATIONS

Humans are wired for story. From gossip with a friend to a full-length film, nothing captures our attention like a good narrative. It's no surprise, then, that the core of memory techniques is pure, imaginative storytelling. Stories connect us to each other and make ideas stick. But what makes a story good?

A STORY NEEDS CHANGE

Donald Miller, author of the phenomenal book *A Million Miles in a Thousand Years*, says that "a story is a character that wants something and overcomes conflict to get it."

I've always loved that.

A story *needs* to have change. If nothing changes for the protagonist, then you don't have a story, you just have a series of remarkable events. I could tell a story about how I climbed Mt. Everest, but what would be more interesting is how I started the expedition overly confident and how, by the end of the climb, I was humbled. That change in me *is* the story, not my stepping foot on the summit.

START WITH A "FIVE-SECOND MOMENT"

Matthew Dicks, author of another incredible book, *Storyworthy*, says that every great story revolves around a transformational moment—a realization, an emotional shift, or a change in perspective. Typically, this transformation is no more than a five-second moment in a person's life. Start your story right in the middle of this moment. Pull people in with transformation, and build toward resolution.

BEGIN IN THE ACTION

Don't waste time setting up backstory. Drop the audience right into the scene so they're immediately engaged. You have just a few seconds to hook your audience—capitalize on this!

USE SENSORY DETAILS TO BRING IT TO LIFE

As a memory expert, you know that we remember sensory details incredibly well. If you can incorporate them into your story, you will lure your audience with a feeling of firsthandedness. So instead of just telling them what happened, show it with concrete details. Let the audience hear the conversation or see the scene unfold in their mind with lasting, memorable sensory descriptions.

FOLLOW THE "SETUP, CONFLICT, RESOLUTION" FORMULA

Setup: *Give context.* ("Last year, I set out to run my first ultramarathon . . .")

Conflict: *What went wrong?* ("At mile thirty-three, I barely made the aid station cutoff with twenty seconds to spare.")

Resolution: *How did it end?* ("I had to drop out, but it fueled my hunger to come back stronger.")

MAKE IT RELATABLE

The best stories make an audience feel something they've felt before. If you're telling a success story, highlight the struggles so people connect. Going back to my one of my previous examples about Mt. Everest, not many people have or ever will climb Everest. It's not relatable. But if we reframe that story so it's about a father in his late thirties, coming to grips with the reality that his adventuring days are dwindling and questioning whether he's still got any days left of his own, or if his identity is being lost—*that's* a relatable story.

USE THE POWER OF LANGUAGE AND THE PAUSE

As we talked about earlier, the way you say something can be just as powerful as what you're saying. Pauses, tone shifts, and word choice can all help you land key moments.

A well-placed pause before a punch line or reveal can add tension or emphasis. Take the time to discover those moments in your story or speech and then find the best way to deliver them. Whether it's a clever turn of phrase, a sharp metaphor, a quirky word, or a well-timed joke, those little touches make your message more memorable and more impactful. Oh, and remember to cut the filler words. Remove excessive *ums*, *uhs*, and *likes*—they weaken your message.

TRUST YOUR AUDIENCE

Avoid overexplaining, and trust your audience. People aren't stupid. An audience loves figuring something out on their own. It feels good. Allow them the opportunity to do that! They will love your story even more because of it.

END ON A STRONG NOTE

You started strong, in the middle of action, and you should end strongly, too. Make the last thing you say memorable. A great story leaves the audience with something to think about.

MAKE IT PERSONAL AND VULNERABLE

The best stories aren't about what happened to you; they're about what affected you. Share your thoughts, emotions, and flaws to build connection. The more vulnerable you make yourself, the more people will invest themselves into your story and feel connected to it.

CUT THE BORING STUFF

This should be obvious, but be ruthless with what you include in your story. Ask yourself if removing certain details would kill the story. If the answer is no, then take them out. Every sentence should serve the story. If a detail doesn't add to the tension, transformation, or humor, get rid of it.

At the end of the day, social skills aren't about tricking people into liking you; they're about understanding human nature and using that understanding to build real connections. Whether it's reading body language, telling a killer story, or owning the stage with confidence, these techniques help you show up as your best self in any situation.

No one is born with a perfect handshake, an effortless way with presenting words onstage, or the ability to read a room like a magician. But with practice, the skills you learned in this chapter will start to become automatic.

Play around with the techniques, make them your own, and watch what happens. You'll notice how quickly people start to gravitate toward you and open up. You'll realize it's not about being the most interesting person in the room, but rather about making everyone else feel like they are—that's the true genius skill.

EXERCISES AND RESOURCES

- **There are so many social tips in this chapter, the important thing is to go out and try them! Observe how others respond to your actions. Not everything will work equally, but it's all about finding what works for you and what you're comfortable adjusting and/or playing around with. People are all around us; it's the perfect playground to test things out!**
- **Earlier in the chapter, I mention sharing some of my favorite fun facts/curiosities that I keep in my back pocket, pre-memorized, to use in conversation. You can find them here: www.everydaygenius.com/book/curiosities.**

- Try memorizing the Mnemonica Stack I mentioned from Chris's trick (and from numerous other magic tricks). Use the card memorization techniques from chapter 7. Here is the sequence:
  - 4C, 2H, 7D, 3C, 4H, 6D, AS, 5H, 9S, 2S, QH, 3D, QC, 8H, 6S, 5S, 9H, KC, 2D, JH, 3S, 8S, 6H, 10C, 5D, KD, 2C, 3H, 8D, 5C, KS, JD, 8C, 10S, KH, JC, 7S, 10H, AD, 4S, 7H, 4D, AC, 9C, JS, QD, 7C, QS, 10D, 6C, AH, 9D.
- Here's something to keep in mind about social interactions: People don't remember everything equally. Research shows we judge experiences based on two key moments—the peak (the most intense part) and the end (how it concluded). This is called the peak-end rule. What this means for you: Create at least one standout moment in your interactions—something meaningful, funny, or emotionally resonant—and finish strong. Whether it's a one-on-one conversation, a performance, a speech, or a romantic date, the principle holds: you can't rescue a forgettable interaction with just an enthusiastic goodbye. But a genuine moment of connection plus a warm ending? That's the combination people remember.

I reference a lot of resources throughout this chapter, so here they are to help you explore them further:

BOOKS:

- *How to Win Friends and Influence People* by Dale Carnegie—Timeless social skills advice.
- *The Cube: Keep the Secret* by Annie Gottlieb and Slobodan D. Pešić—A powerful personality visualization game.
- *Kokology: The Game of Self-Discovery* by Tadahiko Nagao and Isamu Saito—Fun and revealing psychosocial quizzes.
- *Please Understand Me* by David Keirsey—A deep dive into personality types.
- *What Every BODY Is Saying* by Joe Navarro—Expert insights on reading body language.
- *Handwriting Analysis: Putting It to Work for You* by Andrea McNichol—How to interpret personality through handwriting.
- *Tricks of the Mind* by Derren Brown—Psychological illusion meets practical mind hacks.
- *Psychological Subtleties* by Banachek—Advanced mentalist techniques rooted in subtle cues.
- *13 Steps to Mentalism* by Tony Corinda—The foundational text for mental magic.

- *Talk Like TED* by Carmine Gallo—Techniques to speak with clarity, confidence, and impact.
- *Storyworthy* by Matthew Dicks—How to tell powerful stories that captivate any audience.

WEBSITES/VIDEOS:

- Magic trick tutorials on Chris Ramsay's YouTube channel: www.youtube.com/@ChrisRamsay52
- The Behavioral Arts YouTube channel (taught by the award-winning mentalist Spidey): www.youtube.com/@TheBehavioralArts
- SCAM SCHOOL—Easy magic tricks and bar bets to learn: www.youtube.com/@scamschool.
- My list of recommended smart words to memorize (and how to memorize them): www.everydaygeniusacademy.com/book/words

CHAPTER 9

BEYOND GENIUS

"THE QUIETER YOU BECOME,
THE MORE YOU CAN HEAR."
— RAM DASS

I WAS ON DAD DUTY, JUGGLING SCREAMING KIDS, WHEN THE PHONE RANG.

AFTER A FEW PLEASANTRIES, THE MYSTERIOUS MAN ON THE OTHER END ASKED A QUESTION THAT WOULD FOREVER CHANGE MY LIFE. "HAVE YOU EVER HEARD OF REMOTE VIEWING?"

I HAD NO IDEA WHAT THIS CALL WAS ABOUT, AND EVEN LESS WHAT HE MEANT.

"NO. IS IT SOME KIND OF STREAMING APP TO WATCH VIDEOS REMOTELY?" I REPLIED, SLIGHTLY IN JEST.

HE CHUCKLED, FORCED. "NO. HAVE YOU EVER HEARD OF PROJECT STAR GATE?"

STILL NOTHING.

"THE PSYCHIC GOVERNMENT PROGRAM DECLASSIFIED IN THE LATE NINETIES?" HE SAID, PRESSING ON.

Now I was listening. Something deep in my memory stirred—I might have heard of this before but never really paid attention.

He explained that during the Cold War, the US government trained a select group of individuals—some with alleged psychic abilities, some without—to "see" distant locations without any direct sensory input. He claimed these remote viewers were able to locate nuclear submarines hidden in Russian silos (among many other things) while sitting in a US-based locked room, thousands of miles away.

I half rolled my eyes. But I was intrigued; there's always been a part of me that has been excited by these kinds of stories, even if just for the novelty.

And then he dropped the bombshell.

"We want to train you how to do this."

I blinked. "Me? Why me?"

"We've seen research suggesting that individuals with strong visual memory skills, such as yourself, perform better at remote viewing. We want to train you for a month and then put your skills to use."

"For what, exactly?" I asked.

"We'll get to that . . . but in short, I'm contacting you on behalf of a trading firm. We're going to use your skills to predict the stock market."

Okay, *now* I was really intrigued. Albeit also absurdly skeptical. I let him finish his pitch, then—against all reason—I told him I was in.

At the very least, it'd make one hell of a story: *I was once paid to learn a psychic ability and used those skills to try to beat the market.*

I couldn't deny it—I was buzzing. "So, what's next?" I asked.

"For the next month, you'll meet with a remote viewing expert for an hour a day, five days a week. Once you complete the training, you'll be assigned daily tasks related to the market. We'll pay you two thousand dollars a week for training, plus 1.5 percent of the winnings on our portfolio."

"How big is the portfolio?" I asked.

"About 1.2 million dollars."

Silence. I gulped.

My kids screamed in the background, *Is this real? A scam? This is too good to be true.* But then I reminded myself—most scams ask for money. He hadn't (at least not yet). He was offering to pay *me*.

I steeled myself. "Let's do this."

Little did I know, he was about to change the way I saw the world forever.

What followed in the years after that phone call is even crazier. But that, unfortunately, is a story for another book.

For now, I'm here to teach you exactly what I was taught during that program—along with a few things I picked up at the Monroe Institute (which I first mentioned back in chapter 3).

Before we get into it, let me clarify a few things about my spiritual background (or lack thereof). I grew up in a nonreligious household. My mother had always been an atheist, while my father was a nonpracticing Christian. The only time I ever saw any religious inclination from him was when he teared up after Pope John Paul II died in 2005. Other than that? No church, no prayers—nothing. Yet, somehow, I still got baptized. Go figure.

As a teenager, I decided I was an atheist, like my mother and sister, and set off on my own quest to answer the big questions about the universe. That journey led me to study physics at university, a field I knew, without a doubt, would become my career. To me, physics was the key to unlocking the mysteries of existence. Everything could be explained through mathematics and fundamental laws. I was certain of it. It felt right to me.

And I held that belief right up until early 2021. Until *that* phone call.

What followed was a month of intense, head-down training in a so-called psychic ability that I was told I had (that *everyone* has, to some extent). At first, I resisted. I scrutinized every result, trying to debunk what I was seeing. I searched for logical explanations, desperate to prove to myself that none of this was real.

But some things you just can't ignore.

I kept having experiences that were impossible to explain away. There *was* something to this remote viewing stuff after all. It wasn't bogus.

I'm not here to convince you to go on the same journey or believe what I believe. That's not the point. I'm simply sharing something that worked for me and inviting you to try it for yourself, just to see what happens. Since this book explores every corner of what it means to be a genius, and since these seemingly inexplicable psychic experiences played a part in my own exploration, I think it's only fair to include them. Especially if something here ends up helping you.

I get it—a chapter like this might be very controversial. That's actually why I left it for last. Everything up until now has been tangible, verifiable, grounded in techniques you can test immediately. If you've made it this far and you're thinking, *Nope, not for me. I'll pass on the woo-woo stuff,* that's totally fine. Close the book here and (hopefully) walk away satisfied with everything else you've learned.

However, if even a small part of you is curious—if you feel that itch of intrigue—I'm asking you, sincerely, to stick around. Suspend disbelief for a moment. Assume, for the sake of argument, that what I'm about to share is real. That it exists, even if science can't yet explain it. When the chapter's over, you can dismiss it, pretend it never happened, or even laugh at my expense.

Something compelled me to include this, such that I'm willing to risk skepticism, raised eyebrows, and maybe even ridicule. That should say something . . .

So let's dive into some of the history and set the stage.

The first time I looked into the history of remote viewing, it sounded like something straight out of a sci-fi thriller. Governments funding top-secret psychic programs, spies trained to see distant locations with their minds, classified experiments pushing the limits of human perception—straight-up X-files.

I didn't buy any of it.

But it *actually* happened. And you don't have to take my word for it. You can go straight to the CIA's website and read through the declassified documents yourself.*

Long before remote viewing had a government budget, scientists and researchers were already poking at the idea that the human mind might be capable of perceiving things beyond the five senses.

In the 1930s, J. B. Rhine, a psychologist at Duke University, tested subjects for ESP (extrasensory perception) using Zener cards—you know, those simple black-and-white symbols you've probably seen in old movies where someone guesses the hidden shape on a card? (Think of Venkman's opening scene in *Ghostbusters*.) Rhine's research suggested that some people were scoring higher than chance, hinting that *something* was going on.

Around the same time, the author Upton Sinclair conducted his own experiments in what he called "mental radio." He had his wife sit in another room and visualize an image, then attempted to sketch it without seeing it. The results were shockingly accurate, adding yet another brick to the growing wall of curiosity surrounding the mind's untapped abilities.

In the 1970s, the Cold War was in full swing, and the United States was terrified that the Soviets were developing psychic superspies. (Declassified documents later confirmed that the Soviets *were* investing heavily in psychic research.) Naturally, the United States couldn't let them have the upper hand.

---

* Seriously, here's one of the many links available: https://www.cia.gov/readingroom/docs/CIA-RDP96-00789R002800180001-2.pdf. Or just go to the official CIA government website and search for "remote viewing."

Enter *Project Star Gate*—a secret government-funded program aimed at training and testing psychic spies, better known as "remote viewers."

The program was led by scientists at the Stanford Research Institute (SRI), including physicist Russell Targ and laser scientist Hal Puthoff. They worked with some of the most skilled remote viewers in history—people like Ingo Swann, Pat Price, and Joe McMoneagle. I had the privilege of spending time with Joe McMoneagle, both privately at his home in Virginia and at the Monroe Institute. Let me tell you, he's one of the most impressive minds I've ever met.

What they were doing went far beyond little psychic games. These guys were working on classified missions: viewing hidden military installations, tracking down hostages, and even attempting to *see across time, into the future and past*. Some of the results were eerily accurate.

For example, Pat Price once described a secret Soviet facility with such accuracy that US intelligence was floored when they later confirmed the details. Angela Ford, working with the US military's remote viewing program, accurately pinpointed the location of a fugitive more than a thousand miles away, naming the exact city he was later found in. And Joe McMoneagle, a former army officer, located a downed aircraft and missing people using only his mind.

Of course, as with anything involving the word "psychic," the Star Gate Project had its skeptics. Some critics dismissed the results as coincidence or cherry-picked successes, while others argued that remote viewing lacked consistent, repeatable evidence under strict scientific conditions.

In the mid-1990s, the project was declassified, and an official CIA-funded study concluded that, while some of the results were interesting, the program wasn't *reliable enough* for military or intelligence use.

So, in 1995, the government officially pulled the plug. Or so they say . . .

If you have doubts about whether remote viewing or other psychic programs have *any* legitimacy, ask yourself this: Why would the CIA (and several other three-letter agencies) continue pouring government dollars into a program that "doesn't work" for more than two decades?

Even after Star Gate was *supposedly* shut down, many of the original remote viewers continued their work in the private sector. Some wrote books, gave lectures, and even trained civilians in remote viewing techniques (me!). Others claimed that intelligence agencies never actually abandoned remote viewing—it just went deeper underground.

Regardless of whether you believe in psychic spies or not, the history of remote viewing proves one thing: Humans have always been fascinated by the possibility that the mind is capable of far more than we give it credit for.

GENIUS PROFILE:
INGO SWANN

Ingo Swann was a remarkably intuitive thinker and is widely regarded as the father of remote viewing—the psychic mental technique developed into formal protocols for use in secret US government programs. Working with scientists at the Stanford Research Institute in the 1970s, Swann participated in classified experiments funded by agencies like the CIA. In controlled sessions, researchers would give him only latitude and longitude coordinates with no other information. In one experiment, he accurately described specific features of a moon crater he'd never seen photos of—details researchers later verified against NASA images.

In another now-famous 1973 session, he claimed to perceive details about Jupiter about seven months before NASA's *Pioneer 10* flyby—including the presence of a ring around the planet, something scientists at the time had no evidence for. When *Voyager 1* confirmed the existence of Jupiter's faint ring system in 1979, Swann's account gained an uncanny layer of credibility.

You've seen that theme play out time and time again in this book. So why should this be any more absurd than anything else I've shared?

This ability might not be for *everyone*, but it's available to *anyone* willing to explore it. The door is open. You just have to decide if you want to step through it.

INTUITION: YOUR INNER KNOWING

Intuition is one of the most underrated human abilities. It's that gut feeling that tells you something is off before you can logically explain why. It's that instant knowing that guides split-second decisions.

Whenever I bring up remote viewing, I usually get one of two reactions: an eye roll or a glazed-over look. People often hear the word "psychic" and immediately turn away. But if I ask: "Have you ever had a gut feeling about something and been right? Have you ever felt someone staring at you? Or thought of someone, and then they happened to be calling your phone at that same moment?" most people light up and say, "Yes! Oh my god! That's happened to me."

That's because psi abilities—however small—are a fundamental part of human cognition. We've all had experiences that defy logic, even if we brush them off. Ancient humans relied on intuition for survival, using it to detect danger and make rapid decisions when there was no time to think. It's built into us.

Here's the problem, though: modern life drowns it out. We've been conditioned to overanalyze, rationalize, and trust cold, hard logic over instinct (which has its benefits, of course—if you remember, back in chapter 6, we talked about it in relation to making better decisions). To sharpen intuition, we have to do the opposite. We need to quiet the thinking mind, lower the volume of intellect, and *listen* to the subtle nudges of our subconscious.

HOW TO TAP INTO YOUR INTUITION

This is simple in theory, but as with everything else in this chapter, it takes focus and practice. Here are some of my tips to do just that:

1. SILENCE THE NOISE

Your intuition can't get a word in when your mind is constantly buzzing with thoughts. Practices like meditation, breathwork, or even just sitting in silence help create space for intuitive signals to come through. Some of the techniques you've learned in this book—like visualization and focus training—can also strengthen this skill. The more you can quiet your mind, the louder your intuition gets.

2. PAY ATTENTION TO SENSATIONS AND SIGNALS

Intuition often speaks through sensations, imagery, or sudden *knowing*. But most people are too distracted to notice. Start by paying attention

to how your body reacts in different situations. A tightening in your stomach? A sudden sense of unease? These subtle signals often carry more meaning than we realize. When you notice them, observe what's happening around you or what unfolds shortly after. You may begin to spot patterns. If something feels off, take note. Even if you don't yet understand why. The more you practice tuning in, the more clearly these signals will speak.

3. TRUST YOUR FIRST IMPRESSIONS

That first gut reaction you have before logic sets in is often intuition at work. And usually, it's right (in fact, your intuition probably just instinctively agreed with me there). Is it infallible? No. But a lot of that comes down to how well you interpret the signals. Instead of dismissing those first instincts, listen to them and look for patterns—like suddenly avoiding a street you always take, only to hear later there was an accident there . . . sensing something is wrong with a loved one before getting any news . . . dreaming about a place you've never been, then seeing it in perfect detail days later . . . or knowing the answer to something you technically shouldn't know but somehow just *do*. Track those moments. The more you pay attention, the more connections you'll start to notice.

4. LET YOUR MIND RELAX

Intuition thrives when you're not *trying* to use it. Think about when you get your best ideas—usually when you're falling asleep, in the shower, or doing something mindless; on autopilot. That's because your thinking mind takes a back seat, allowing deeper insights to rise. Keeping a dream journal, meditating, doing breathing exercises, or practicing visualization exercises and walking through a Memory Palace can help train this state of mind.

5. EXTREME SITUATIONS ACTIVATE INTUITION

There's something about near-death experiences, extreme exhaustion, hunger, or sleep deprivation (even those deep-focus flow states) that makes intuition kick into overdrive. When your body enters fight-or-flight mode, all distractions disappear, and suddenly, you *know* what to do. I'm not saying you should put yourself in danger to sharpen your intuition, but think back to times you've had close calls. High-functioning intuitive moments often go hand in hand with those experiences. It's important to be aware that intuition can largely be correct in these situations, so make sure to listen.

LOWER LOGIC. RAISE RECEPTIVITY

The more you analyze, the more you block intuition. Sometimes, the best way to get an answer is to *stop searching* and let it come to you. This is hard for most people (me included). The second we face a problem, we start breaking it down, trying to rationalize our way to a solution. And sure, logic is useful. But it's also limited by what we already know.

Intuition, on the other hand, operates on a different level—one that isn't bound by immediate data. It's wider reaching. And when it works, it can pull in answers from *beyond* what's available in the here and now.

I'm *not* telling you to throw logic out the window, though. Intuition is powerful, but it's slippery.

On the flip side, logic is sound; it works. And most of what we experience in the day-to-day follows logical rules. So don't abandon it completely, but rather add some more intuitive-based decision-making as a complement.

Start small. Use intuition in your daily life; try predicting who's calling before you look at your phone. Guess which checkout line will move fastest. Sense someone's mood before they speak. Keep track of synchronicities.* These little moments may seem insignificant, but they build awareness.

Over time, you can even raise the stakes.

Intuition isn't some mystical gift reserved for a few. It's a natural ability we *all* have. The key is in *tuning in* rather than tuning out.

HOW TO REMOTE VIEW

Let's get to the juicy stuff. Remote viewing is a structured protocol designed to extract information from a target without using normal sensory data.

Think of your attention as a radar. Most of the time, it scans for what we can perceive through our five senses. If we see something, our brain checks it against our internal model of the world. Does it fit? Does it make sense? If yes, we register it as real. Same goes for the other senses. If a scent aligns with what our brain expects to be possible in the environment, we accept it. "I smell something. It must be X. That means it's close." Even when some sensory data is missing, the brain fills in the gaps using context clues.

* Over the past year or so, I've started noticing these moments more intensely—and I've even kept a spreadsheet to track them. Most are small, uncanny coincidences: like reading a specific word in a book at the exact moment a commercial on TV says the same word out loud, or finding dimes everywhere I go. But some are downright mind-bending. Like the time I predicted the winner of the Belmont Stakes days in advance—just had a gut feeling I couldn't shake. I went with it, and I was right. Made a nice chunk of change, too.

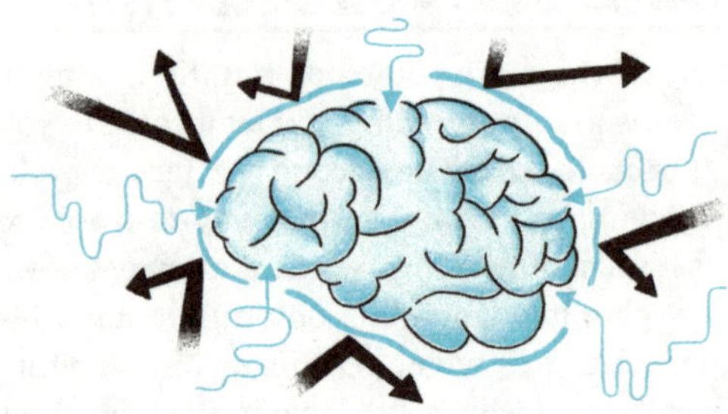

Maybe I can't *see* the lion behind the rock, but if I *hear* it roar, my brain fills in the rest—and that's all I need to start running.

But our senses can also be easily fooled. Magicians exploit this all the time with sleights of hand, misdirections, and psychological trickery (remember the great Internet war over whether that dress was blue and black or white and gold?). And then there are substances, like psychedelics, or states of mind that can make people see and feel things that aren't physically there. Our perception is imperfect.

Remote viewing flips the script entirely. Instead of relying on traditional senses, it taps into *something else*. We still use our internal visualization skills to process the information, except this data isn't coming from our eyes, ears, or touch.

Where is it coming from, then? Who knows. And I'm not here to explain *why* it works. I asked you to assume it does, just for this chapter. My job is to show you *how* to do it.

What I do know is that remote viewing relies heavily on intuition. As I said before, reducing intellect *increases* intuition. The more you can quiet the noise of your left brain—the analytical, logical part—the better your results will be.

Don't think. Just receive; intuit.

HOW THE REMOTE VIEWING PROTOCOL WORKS

Unfortunately, remote viewing isn't as simple as just guessing something out of thin air (even though it kind of is that on a fundamental level). If you *try* to guess, you'll likely use your logical brain. And that's exactly what we *don't* want. We also don't want to just allow our conscious thought stream to flood our mind unguided. Instead, we need a structured, step-by-step process—something repeatable that anyone can follow and get results with; something that provides a kind of guardrail to whatever it is we are trying to remote view.

I mean, sure, it would be nice to just close your eyes and predict the winning lottery numbers, right? But it doesn't quite work that way.

Here's how I think about it: Psychic abilities are a *small* effect. Some people might be naturally gifted and more capable of a larger effect, but for most of us, it's small. That doesn't mean we should dismiss it—just that we need the most refined way possible to access it and extract it. That's where the following remote viewing method comes in.

THE VIEWER AND THE TASKER

In every remote viewing session, there need to be two roles:

1. **The Tasker—the person setting up the task (i.e., choosing what the viewer will try to perceive).**
2. **The Viewer—the person attempting to "see" the target without any prior knowledge of what it is: the remote viewer (the target being the thing the tasker is setting up for the viewer to "see").**

Here's where it gets weird: The Tasker doesn't *tell* the Viewer what to remote view. They don't give them any hints, photos, or descriptions—nothing. The Viewer should not know *anything* about the target; they should be *completely* blind to the target.

The Tasker assigns a random number to the target (called the "target number")—one that has no inherent meaning whatsoever.

The Viewer is then given the target number and from that, on a blank sheet of paper with a pen, will get to work.

THE POWER OF INTENTION

Intention is an integral part of what makes remote viewing function from the Tasker's end. It's what connects the task to the target number.

When the Tasker selects a random number and assigns it to a specific target (an image, a location, an object—anything), they are metaphysically creating a link between that number and the target itself.

Think of intention as a tether—an invisible thread binding all things. The target number is meaningless on its own, but through the Tasker's *intention*, it becomes connected to the target. While intuition will get us information, intention is the thing that connects us to the place where the information can stream in. And as the Viewer, by focusing on that number, they can tap into that connection—like tuning a radio to the right frequency.

You with me? Trust me, at first, I was like *What on earth is this load of crap*? If you're feeling the same way, I get it. But stick with me.

THE REMOTE VIEWING PROTOCOL

There are a few different schools of thought on the correct protocol for remote viewing. The following is the process I was taught, once you've received your target number.*

Grab a pen and paper—no screens, no distractions. Follow these steps exactly:

1. **Write the target number in square brackets at the top of the page.**
2. **Write your full name, the date, and the time in the top-right corner.**
3. **Below the target number, on the left side of the page, write this sentence:**
   "This session is about to begin."
4. **Rewrite the target number immediately beneath the sentence, without brackets.**
5. ***Immediately*, without thinking, place your pen or pencil on the page and draw a quick, spontaneous mark or scribble next to the number. Do not hesitate!**
   - **This is called an ideogram—your first unconscious connection to the target.**
   - **Don't *try* to draw something. Just put your pen down and let your hand move. Whatever comes out, comes out.**
   - **It should be short and quick.**
   - **Once drawn, describe in short sentences, the features you drew, in the order you drew them. For example, in the sample opposite: bar across, big loop around, diagonal down, curve down, down.**

Now here's where it gets interesting.

6. **Hover your finger over the ideogram you've just drawn.**
   - **Imagine you're scanning it like an antenna, picking up on whatever it might represent.**
   - **What *impression* do you get?**
   - **This is called a gestalt—a vague, broad category like *landscape*, *structure*, *life-form*, or *energy*.**
   - **Write down two things. A feeling *you get from the ideogram and that gestalt* you sensed.**
   - **Remember, your psi antenna is attempting to connect with the very broad strokes of the target.**

---

* I will provide some helpful online resources to help you generate some targets for practice at the end of the chapter (page 293).

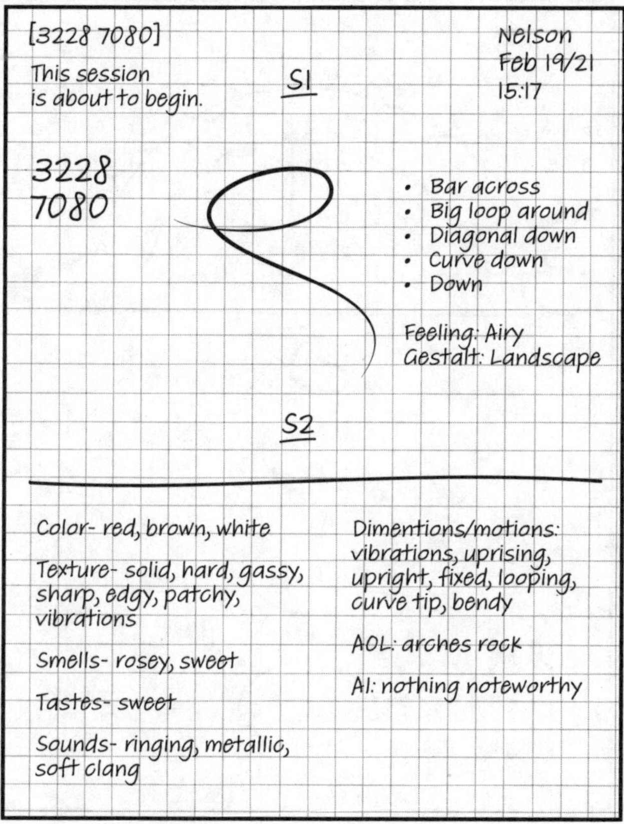

7. **Draw a dividing line horizontally across the page.**
8. **Beneath this line start writing down descriptor words.**
   - **Colors, textures, smells, tastes, sounds, dimensions, shapes, motions, emotions.**
   - **Don't think—just write whatever comes up. Let it flow.***
9. **Be careful not to name things.**

If you suddenly think, *I know what this is!* or *This is kind of like a . . .* STOP! Your logical brain is taking over. We call this an AOL (analytical

* When starting out, I think it's best to go down this list of categories and see what comes out. Colors. What colors are coming to you? Then, textures. What textures are there? Etc.

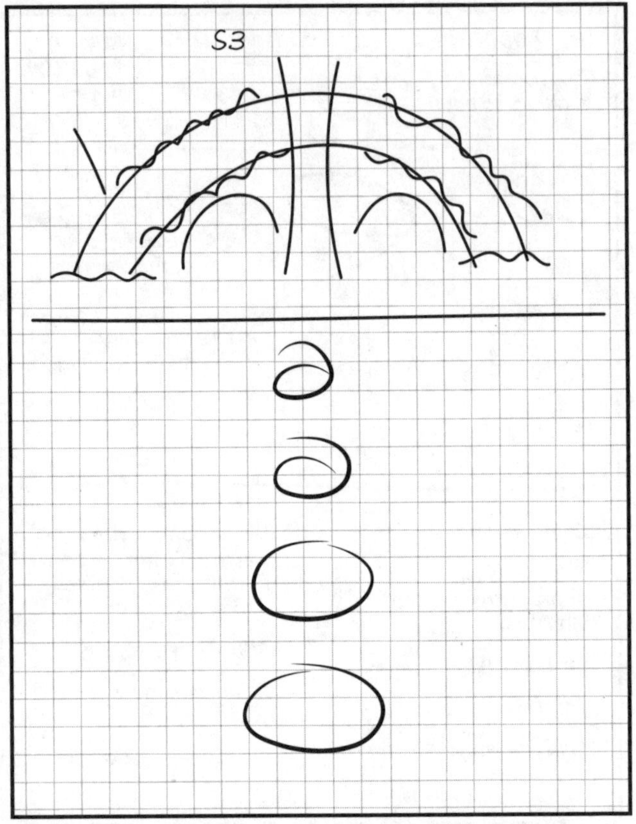

overlay)—your logical brain's attempt to make sense of the unknown. We want to avoid that at all costs, because the moment your logical brain kicks in, you're no longer tapping into intuition.

Instead of indulging it (because that would be us allowing our intellect to shine through and squash our intuition), write "AOL" in the margin, note what you thought, put your pen down for a moment, take a deep breath, and then keep going with your descriptors. Different remote viewers deal with AOLs in different ways; this is my way. I like to address them, rather than ignore them. Let them have their moment to shine in your brain and then let them go and move on.

It's so tempting to name things, but you must train yourself *not* to do that. We are *describing* what we are seeing; we're not saying what it is. Later, once we have enough data, *then* we can start looking at it all from a third-person perspective to see if we can glean any specifics.

10. **Once you're done with descriptors (and you will know when you're done, because it will feel as if the consciousness stream is slowing or ending), *sketch* what you feel, below them.**
    - **Don't try to *draw* the target—just draw shapes and lines and structures that are coming to you; shadings, curves, whatever you feel is coming through. And if you feel like nothing is coming through, you're probably thinking too hard. Put your pen down, take a deep breath, and try again.**
11. **When you feel like the flow of information has stopped, write "END" in big letters at the bottom of the page.**
12. **Your remote viewing session is over.**

There's so much more to remote viewing than what I just outlined. But this is a solid starting point. (The example session on the previous pages was real, by the way—the target was a rose garden with a metal archway. Not bad, right?) Even with only this, you can uncover some surprisingly accurate results. If you choose to go deeper, you'll find this is the tip of the iceberg. The full protocol includes additional layers and steps that can sharpen your connection to the target and unlock incredibly detailed information. I'll provide some resources at the end of the chapter (page 292) for those who'd like to explore further.

YOUR FIRST TASK

Now it's time to try it for real.

Use this target number: **801698**

Follow the steps above, document your session, then check your results here: www.everydaygeniusacademy.com/remoteviewing/801698.

But don't cheat—if you peek ahead, you're defeating the whole purpose.

Once you're done, compare your results with the image. How close were you? On a scale of 1 to 10 (10 being a perfect match), how would you rate your accuracy?

For some, this will be a *holy crap* moment. You'll have described and drawn something eerily like the target image, and your brain will scramble for an explanation. *How could this be? I had zero information about the target!*

For some, it won't feel that convincing—maybe a few details will match, but you'll chalk it up to coincidence. The rest might seem like total nonsense. And that's fine. It's not supposed to be perfect. Your brain is picking up a ton of noise, and some of it will just be that: noise. But with time and practice, you'll get better at tuning that out. Like every skill in this book, remote viewing takes repetition and patience. You might miss the mark at first. That's

GENIUS PROFILE: ROBERT MONROE

Robert Monroe wasn't trying to become some mystic or spiritual guru. He was a successful businessman—head of a radio production company—who just happened to be experimenting with sleep-learning techniques in the 1950s. One night, while lying in bed, he felt a strange vibration run through his body, followed by a powerful sensation of motion. Suddenly, he was floating . . . above his bed. Not metaphorically. Literally hovering in the air, looking down at his physical body as if it were someone else. He panicked, naturally. He thought he might be dying. But just as quickly as it began, he snapped back in. Over the next few weeks, it kept happening. Same vibrations. Same liftoff. He began to explore it, test it, and document it. What started as a bizarre sleep disturbance became the beginning of a lifelong quest to map the edges of human consciousness. He ended up writing three influential books on the topic of out-of-body experiences, as well as founding the Monroe Institute.

okay. Keep at it. The more you train, the clearer things get. Believe in the process, keep showing up, and eventually, the results will follow.

Belief in remote viewing doesn't come from reading about it; it comes from experience. I was skeptical until I had this *one* session where I sketched a whale breaching in the ocean.* When the image was revealed to me, my heart pretty much skipped a few beats. It was nearly identical. That was the moment everything changed.

A few things to note before we move on. Beginners often have a hot streak at first, followed by a period of total misses. Even the best remote viewers (such as Lyn Buchanan, who inspired George Clooney's character in *Men Who Stare at Goats*) hit dry spells at the beginning.

Also, viewing your feedback after a session is over is crucial. Some believe remote viewing is just precognition, meaning what you're seeing in your session is actually the *future* moment when you reviewed the target after the session. Whatever the case, skipping feedback seems to weaken the effect.

I've provided more task numbers at the end of this chapter. Try them, but space out your sessions. Accuracy tends to drop if you do too many tasks back-to-back.

Let's see what you're capable of!

HOW TO HAVE AN OUT-OF-BODY EXPERIENCE

When I was at the Monroe Institute, part of my mission was to have an out-of-body experience (OBE). I had *almost* felt it before—moments where my consciousness seemed to split from my body—but I wanted to be able to do it on command, or to at least have more control.

* Check out my actual session notes and the photo I remote viewed here: www.everydaygeniusacademy.com/remoteviewing/whale.

One of those moments happened while descending from a brutal mountain climb. I had just spent fourteen hours pushing my body to its limits, reaching one of the highest points of Mt. Everest. Exhausted, my body moved back to base camp on autopilot, step after endless step. And then, suddenly, I wasn't in my body anymore. I was *above* it, watching myself from outside myself, as if I were a drone hovering overhead.

The realization hit me—WHOOSH! And in an instant I was *back* in my body, suddenly more alert, more aware, as if my brain had been rebooted. It was the oddest sensation. Being yourself but disassociated from yourself—the body of your self—at the same time.

This isn't uncommon. OBEs are known to happen in moments of extreme exhaustion, sleep deprivation, or near-death experience (though not *only* in those cases). But I didn't want to rely on total physical depletion to make it happen in the future. I wanted to train for it, refine it, and make it *intentional*, so that I could explore it more. That's why I was at the Monroe Institute.

Before moving forward, though, we should define an OBE as when you experience yourself as existing *outside* your physical body—often described as floating above yourself or traveling to distant places. It's a real phenomenon that has been reported across cultures, religions, and throughout history.

There are multiple theories on what causes OBEs. Some scientists believe they're purely neurological, a glitch in the brain's perception system. Others believe OBEs involve *nonphysical* consciousness, allowing the mind to temporarily separate from the body.

Since we're going all in for this chapter, the latter is the explanation I'm rolling with.

HOW TO INDUCE AN OBE

Some people have OBEs spontaneously. Yogis and monks spend decades mastering having them purposefully through meditation alone. The Monroe Institute, however, developed a shortcut—a proprietary sound technology called Hemi-Sync, which uses specific frequencies to shift brain waves into states of higher consciousness where OBEs are more likely to occur.

But you don't need these sound frequencies to get there. If you want to experiment with stepping outside yourself, here are some methods you can try:

1. THE VIBRATIONAL STATE

Many people who experience OBEs describe a *buzzing* or *vibrating sensation* just before separation occurs. Learning to recognize this state—and staying calm when it happens—is key.

- Relax and meditate.
- Let your thoughts drift while staying aware of bodily sensations.
- If you start to feel a tingling or buzzing, *don't panic*. It means you're on the right track.
- Focus on this feeling; lean into it. Sometimes that's all it takes and suddenly . . . WHOOSH, you'll find yourself out of body.

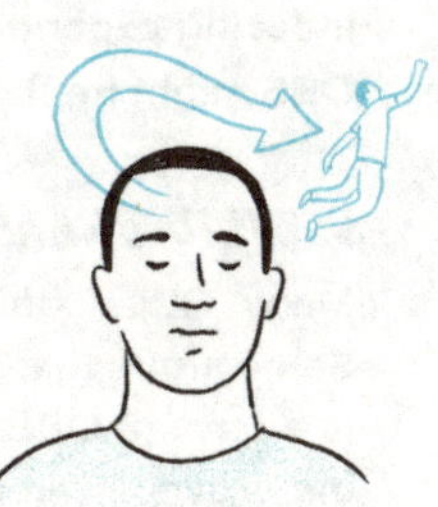

2. THE ROPE TECHNIQUE

- While lying in bed, relax completely.
- Imagine a rope hanging above you.
- Now mentally reach for it and imagine *pulling* yourself up, but without physically moving.
- Focus on the sensation of lifting. If successful, you'll feel your consciousness shift outside your body.

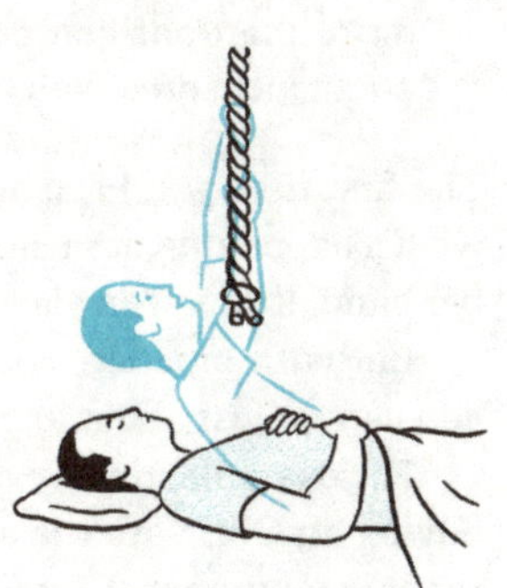

3. THE ROLLING-OUT METHOD

- Similarly to the rope technique, start by relaxing deeply.
- As you sink into a meditative state, imagine yourself rolling sideways, as if you're gently rocking a small boat.
- Increase the movement gradually. Remember, this isn't physical movement; it's in your mind.
- If it's done correctly, you might suddenly find yourself *floating* outside your physical body.

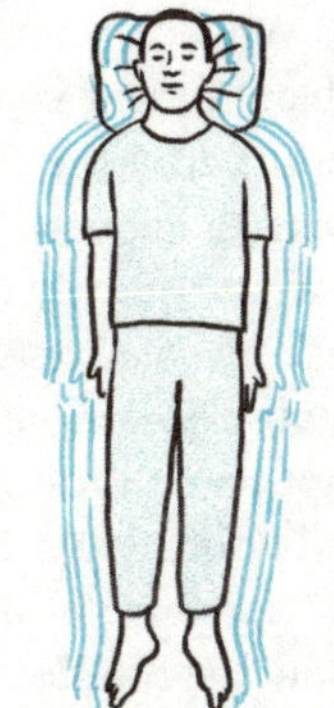

4. DEEP RELAXATION AND MEDITATION

OBEs thrive in deeply relaxed states. Progressive muscle relaxation, breathwork, and guided visualization can help. The Gateway Experience tapes from the Monroe Institute are excellent tools for

inducing expanded states of consciousness.* If you go deep enough, an OBE might be the *least* weird thing that happens.

5. LUCID DREAMING AS A GATEWAY

Many OBEs start as lucid dreams. Some argue that *lucid dreaming itself* is a form of OBE. Either way, practicing dream awareness and setting the intention to leave your body can help make the transition easier. We'll talk about lucid dreaming in a few pages.

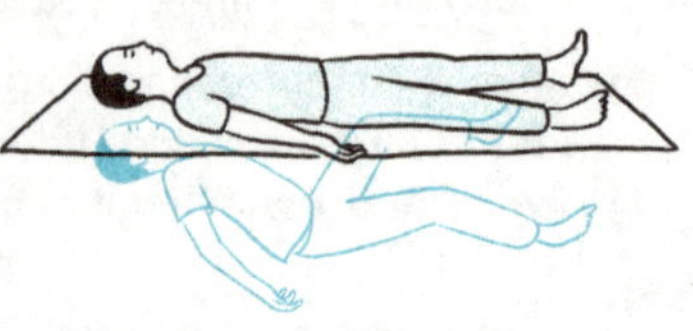

The first time you have an OBE, it won't last long. The moment you *realize* what's happening, it's usually over—you snap back into your body like a rubber band. It's such an alarming realization that it destabilizes the experience.

But with practice, you can stay out longer. And once you gain control, you can do just about anything. Literally, *anything*.

For example, during one of our sessions at the Monroe Institute, I tried having an OBE with the aim of "floating" into another attendee's room and reading a number she had written down and left on her desk. It was a wild idea, but I wanted to see what was actually possible.

While in our next deep meditation session, I focused on the paper on her table. Nothing came. I tried and I tried to "pop" out of my body, but nothing happened. I then decided to just let the experience wash over me if it was going to happen. Surprisingly, as soon as I let go, I started getting glimpses of what I quickly realized was this other person's room. And then slowly, her desk revealed itself to me. I was in her room. And sure enough, there was a small piece of paper, with a number clear as day: *1, 7, 3,* and then the last digit was a bit fuzzy. When I came to, I immediately grabbed my notebook and wrote down *1736*. When she revealed her number, it was 1734.

Not perfect—but pretty darn close. I had told her before the reveal that I saw the number at an angle, making the last digit fuzzy. There were also other details of the room that I asked her about, which I had seen, and she verified them. So I was definitely in her room. Not sure how else to explain it.

Another time, I encountered an *entity* that guided me and answered some deep questions about my life. Answers that led to some wild synchronicities just a few weeks later in my life. In yet another experience, I met with a recently deceased family member who shared information I had never known—information that was later confirmed by other family members.

---

* You can check out the Monroe Institute here (their programs, as well as their tapes): https://www.monroeinstitute.org.

None of this I can explain with normal means of understanding. The fact is that OBEs remain a mystery. Are they purely neurological, or are they proof that consciousness can exist outside the body? From my personal experience, I have a knowing that we are more than our physical body. It's hard to force that knowing on others without their having had the same or similar experiences.

Either way, OBEs offer a fascinating glimpse into human perception and the nature of reality. And it's a powerful tool, for those willing, to explore the possibility of stepping beyond the physical self.

All you have to do is step through.

LUCID DREAMING

Lucid dreaming is the ability to become *aware* that you are dreaming while still inside the dream. In this state, you don't just *experience* the dream; you can control it. You can fly, explore distant worlds, speak with people (real or imagined), relive past experiences, and even access what feels like a deeper intelligence beyond your waking self.

Lucid dreaming isn't a new phenomenon; it's been documented for centuries. Ancient Hindu and Buddhist traditions practiced dream yoga, using dreams as a means of spiritual growth. Aristotle wrote about self-awareness in dreams, and Tibetan monks have trained for thousands of years to wake up *within* their dreams.

In the modern era, Dutch psychiatrist Frederik van Eeden coined the term "lucid dreaming" in 1913 after meticulously studying his own dreams. In the 1970s and '80s, Stanford researcher Dr. Stephen LaBerge conducted groundbreaking studies proving lucid dreaming was real. He trained dreamers to make specific eye movements while dreaming, which were recorded in a sleep lab.

Since then, lucid dreaming has been studied extensively, with applications ranging from overcoming nightmares and trauma to enhancing creativity and problem-solving.

HOW TO LUCID DREAM

Lucid dreaming takes practice, but anyone can learn to do it. Here's how to start:

1. KEEP A DREAM JOURNAL

Get yourself a dedicated notebook for dream journaling. Write down your dreams every morning, immediately after waking. Even better, every time you wake up in the night, write them down if you can. The more data you have, the more insights will come. Over time, you'll start recognizing recurring themes, symbols, and patterns. This is key to realizing when you're dreaming. Once you can notice them in waking life, picking up on them *while* dreaming becomes more of a possibility. Dreams have a way of forgetting themselves *really* quick, so the sooner you jot down the details of your dream, the better.

2. PERFORM REALITY CHECKS

Several times a day, ask yourself: *Am I dreaming?* It may be an obvious *no*, but ask the question anyway and really try to look around you and discern reality. Try one of these tests:

- Pinch your nose and try to breathe through it. If you *can* breathe, you're dreaming.
- Look at your hands. In dreams, they often appear distorted.
- Read text, look away, then read it again. Dream text tends to change upon second glance.

If you've seen the movie *Inception*, you may remember that the characters all had what they called a "totem"—a physical object that they could carry around and fiddle with to test if they were in a dream or awake. This is the same concept. The goal is to build the habit of questioning reality. Eventually, if you do this enough, you'll also start doing it in dreams. And when you do and one of these reality checks fails, you'll instantly know you're awake inside of a dream.

3. USE THE MILD TECHNIQUE (MNEMONIC-INDUCED LUCID DREAMING)

I personally haven't had success with this, but I have friends who have. When you get in bed and before you've fallen asleep, repeat to yourself the following mantra: "Next time I'm dreaming, I will realize I'm dreaming" (or something similar).

Repeat it, over and over again.

Sometimes subvocalized intention-setting is all you need to plant the idea in your subconscious.

4. TRY WAKE-BACK-TO-BED (WBTB)

Set an alarm for four to six hours after bedtime. Wake up, stay awake for fifteen to thirty minutes, and focus on the idea of lucid dreaming. Then go back to sleep with this intention in mind. This technique increases the chances of entering a lucid state directly from REM sleep.

5. PRACTICE VISUALIZATION BEFORE SLEEP

As you're drifting off, *imagine* yourself inside a dream. Picture a scene, make it vivid, and tell yourself that you *know* you're dreaming. Put the visualization skills you've learned in this book to use. This can sometimes lead to wake-induced lucid dreams (WILD), where you consciously enter the dream state without losing awareness. This is where the lines get blurred between dreaming and OBEs and where one could argue that potentially they are the same thing. Or perhaps at least tapping into some external realm of the self.

Once you're lucid, the possibilities are endless.

If you enter a dream with a question in mind, you might gain some insight into how to better problem-solve a solution. Sometimes, insight strikes not in the lab or onstage but in your sleep. Dmitri Mendeleev, the father of the periodic table, struggled for days to organize the chemical elements, until he nodded off and dreamed of them falling perfectly into place. He woke up and scribbled it down, and the modern periodic table was born. Paul McCartney had a similar experience. He woke from a dream with a full melody in his head. He played it on the piano and asked around for weeks, convinced he had accidentally copied it from somewhere. He hadn't. It was "Yesterday." Proof that sometimes your brain solves problems—or writes hit songs—when you're not even awake. So, if you paint, write, compose music, or like to experiment with ideas, exploring your dreams might help open new possibilities without limits. The dream world is the ultimate creative sandbox.

If you could control your dreams, you'd have the ultimate training ground, one where you could practice real-world skills while you sleep. Studies suggest that mental rehearsal in lucid dreams can actually improve performance in waking life.* I've even used this myself to train for the USA Memory Championship finals. I'd enter a dream, and upon realizing I was in one, I'd construct a full championship scenario. In the dream, I'd be presented with a deck of cards, memorize them, and then *win the competition*.

The craziest part was that I often woke up remembering the entire deck in order.

What *really* blew my mind, though, was that these dream decks were high-fidelity constructs—they were *complete*, with every card, suit, and value intact. Somehow, my subconscious knew exactly what a standard deck of cards should look like, constructing it with *perfect* fidelity.

Weird. And kind of amazing.

---

* Daniel Erlacher and Michael Schredl, "Practicing a Motor Task in a Lucid Dream Enhances Subsequent Performance: A Pilot Study." *Sport Psychologist* 24, no. 2 (2010): 157–67.

Other times I would enter a dream and find myself in one of my Memory Palaces complete with weird imagery—the same kinds of bizarre things I'd be imagining mid-memorization in the waking world. And upon awakening from such a dream, oftentimes a burst of creativity would follow.

Lucid dreaming connects to genius in a fundamental way. It gives you access to parts of your mind that are usually hidden in waking life. When you dream, your conscious mind takes a back seat, allowing your subconscious to process, create, and explore freely while tapping into hidden knowledge, unfiltered creativity, and endless sources of inspiration.

GENIUS PROFILE:
SALVADOR DALÍ

Dalí believed his best ideas came from the moments just before sleep—what neuroscientists now call the hypnagogic state. To capture these fleeting visions, he developed a technique he called "slumber with a key."

Here's how it worked: He would sit in a chair, holding a heavy key in his hand. Beneath it, he placed a metal plate on the floor. As he drifted off, his muscles would relax, causing the key to drop onto the plate with a loud clang, jerking him awake at the exact moment dream imagery began to form. He would then immediately sketch whatever surreal visions had appeared.

This method allowed him to dip into his subconscious, steal dreamlike imagery, and incorporate it into his art before it vanished. His entire artistic approach was built on not thinking logically but rather allowing his subconscious and intuition to take over.

By mastering lucid dreaming, you're expanding the very boundaries of what your mind is capable of.

BEYOND GENIUS AND THE HIGHER SELF

Throughout this book, we've explored the extraordinary—memory techniques, speed-reading, problem-solving, social intelligence, mental math, and even the unconventional realms of intuition, remote viewing, and out-of-body experiences. But beneath all these abilities—beneath *all* human skills—lies something deeper: the Higher Self.

Your Higher Self is the unfiltered version of *you*—the part that exists beyond logic, fear, and the distractions of daily life. It's the source of your wisdom, your creativity, and your most profound insights. It's the part of you that *already knows*. It's the part of you where you find clarity when everything else feels noisy.

Tapping into this is the through line to your inner genius. It's there, waiting for you. And it's what separates knowledge from true understanding; it's what allows you to not just exist but *expand*.

Talking about the Higher Self is one thing, but *actually* connecting with it, and experiencing it as a real part of you (not just some fluffy, quasi-inspirational, woo-woo concept), is something else entirely. So how do you actually *tune into* this part of yourself? Here are a few suggestions:

QUIET THE MIND

Just as with intuition, reducing mental noise is key. Meditation, deep breathing, and solitude help make space for the Higher Self.

ALWAYS ASK FOR GUIDANCE

The Higher Self doesn't speak in loud commands, it communicates in subtle nudges, gut feelings, and insights. This doesn't mean praying to a god (though it *can* if that resonates with you). It means *asking yourself*—the genius that you already are—for guidance. Journaling, meditation, and deep reflection are all ways to tune in.

LOOK FOR SIGNS AND TRUST THE SIGNALS

Synchronicities, gut feelings, repeating patterns, or recurring thoughts are often signs from the Higher Self nudging you in the right direction. They are everywhere, providing us information about the world. The more you notice them, the more they'll appear. Keep an eye out and look for signs.

EXPAND YOUR CONSCIOUSNESS

Use some of the things discussed in this chapter. Practices such as lucid dreaming, OBEs, meditation, the use of psychedelics, and deep visualization can create direct experiences of the Higher Self, making its presence undeniable.

LIVE WITH AWARENESS

The more you acknowledge and listen, the more the Higher Self becomes an active force in your life. And when it does, your path becomes clearer, your purpose sharper.

EXERCISES AND RESOURCES

- Here are a few more remote viewing task numbers to try. You can find the images associated with each on my website for reference after: www.everydaygeniusacademy.com/remoteviewing.
    - Task 1: 384192
    - Task 2: 705836
    - Task 3: 129457
    - Task 4: 648203
    - Task 5: 217964
- ARV (or associative remote viewing) is a method for applying remote viewing to situations where you would like to predict the outcome of a binary situation (stock price going up or down, a team winning or losing a game, etc.). Effectively, you are given a task number, you do your session, and then you judge how closely your results match either of two very distinct images that were preassociated beforehand to one of the binary outcomes. If you'd like to play around with this, head to my website for some examples and resources to try it yourself: www.everydaygeniusacademy.com/book/arv.

BOOKS:

- *Journeys Out of the Body* by Robert Monroe—The original modern classic on OBEs. Written like a personal logbook but layered with insights.
- *Entangled Minds: Extrasensory Experiences in a Quantum Reality* by Dean Radin—A scientist's deep dive into how ESP and consciousness might work.
- *The ESP Enigma: The Scientific Case for Psychic Phenomena* by Diane Powell—A balanced, research-heavy look into real-life cases of telepathy, remote viewing, and precognition, written by a neuroscientist and medical doctor.
- *Phenomena: The Secret History of the US Government's Investigations into Extrasensory Perception and Psychokinesis* by Annie Jacobsen—A gripping investigative account of the US government's psychic spying programs.
- *The Essential Guide to Remote Viewing: The Secret Military Remote Perception Skill Anyone Can Learn* by Paul H. Smith, PhD—This guide breaks down the skill from both the practical and the philosophical angle.
- *Associative Remote Viewing: The Art and Science of Predicting Outcomes for Sports, Politics, Finances & the Lottery* by Debra Lynne Katz and Jon Knowles—A more advanced, targeted method of remote viewing designed for prediction and applied outcomes, such as financial forecasting or decision-making.

APPS/WEBSITES:

- ESP trainer: https://apps.apple.com/us/app/esp-trainer/id336882103—A simple, fun way to test and sharpen your extrasensory perception through pattern recognition and rapid feedback.
- Hemi-Sync audio technology: https://hemi-sync.com/—Monroe Institute's signature sound tech for expanded states of consciousness.
- Gateway Experience: https://www.monroeinstitute.org/products/gateway-voyage—The Monroe Institute's full training audio series program. Life-changing!
- More remote viewing practice targets—Visit remoteviewed.com or hrvg.org, or just ask a friend to choose a random photo and assign you a target number.

WHERE TO GO FROM HERE

"A GENIUS IS THE ONE MOST LIKE HIMSELF."
—THELONIOUS MONK

This book has been a tool kit, a collection of strategies designed to push the boundaries of what you thought was possible. But reading it isn't enough. The real transformation happens when you put these ideas into practice.

If you want to be a memory champion, train every day with mnemonics. If you want to master public speaking, start practicing storytelling and persuasion. If you want to read faster, apply speed-reading techniques in every book you pick up. If you want to sharpen your intuition and remote viewing, practice quieting your mind and testing what you perceive. Do the thing!

As technology increasingly promises to think for us, remember: Your greatest power lies in thinking with your *own* brain power.

Genius doesn't have a finish line; it's a lifelong process of exploration. So stay curious.

You now have the tools to think, learn, and experience the world in a completely new way. Whether you use these skills for your career, your relationships, the joy of pushing your limits, or simply to reclaim your own brain capital, you've already taken the first step.

To some, genius may be seen as a gift, given only to a select lucky few. But I see it as a practice, something anyone can nurture and hone.

The mind is limitless. And so are you.

Keep exploring, keep questioning, and you'll keep unlocking more of what's already inside you—the *everyday genius*.

ACKNOWLEDGMENTS

This book wouldn't exist without the support, insight, and encouragement of some truly remarkable (genius) people.

To my family—my wife, Leah—thank you for your endless patience, love, and belief in me through every late night and rewrite. I know I disappeared into this book for a while, so thank you for putting up with me. I love you. Axel, Lincoln, Wyatt, Sofia—I hope you guys read this book one day and master every single skill I put in here. Mom, Dad—thank you for raising me to be curious and for encouraging me to pursue whatever my heart desired. Jen, Spence—thanks for being ugly, but awesome. Love you all.

To my friends and early readers who offered feedback, inspiration, and the occasional reality check—thank you. You helped shape this into something far better than I could've done alone. A special shout-out to Chris Ramsay for inspiring me all these years. If you hadn't reached out to me way back when, this book might never have existed. I've learned so much from you, and I'll always treasure our shared curiosity, spiritual journey, and deep dives into the paranormal. Wes, Trevor, Spidey, Brad, Yusnier, Javen, Brian—thank you for letting me name-drop you in the book and for letting me bounce ideas off you. To Ben Pridmore—years ago, you shared a book with me that you never published. Believe it or not, that one small act planted the seed for this book.

To my editors, Laura Dozier and Zack Knoll (and the Abrams team)—thank you for your clarity, care, and ability to make sense of my mess. To Jim Levine, for once again believing I had another book in me and something worth sharing beyond memory techniques. To Adam Hayes, for yet again delivering some rocking illustrations. And to every mentor, teacher, and genius—whatever the field—whose work helped light the path for me: this book is for you. Also, to whoever placed all those synchronistic dimes I found in the years spanning the creation of this book, thank you. Your presence guided me and let me know I was on the right path.

And finally, to you—the reader—thank you for showing up. I hope this book helps you unlock something powerful within yourself.

INDEX

INDEX

INDEX

INDEX

Illustrations by Adam Hayes
Charts and graphics by Jenice Kim and Samantha Negroni

A Library of Congress Control Number has been applied for.

ISBN: 978-1-4197-8481-1
eISBN: 979-8-88707-893-9

Printed and bound in the United States
10 9 8 7 6 5 4 3

ABRAMS is represented in the UK and Europe by Abrams & Chronicle Books, 22-24 Ely Place, London EC1N 6TE and Média-Participations, 57 rue Gaston Tessier, 75166 Paris, France.
abramsandchronicle.co.uk and media-participations.com
info@abramsandchronicle.co.uk